FOYT

FOYT

BILL LIBBY

HAWTHORN BOOKS, INC.
PUBLISHERS / *New York*

*For Laurie, my daughter, whom
I love dearly*

FOYT

Library of Congress Catalog Card Number: 73-21314
ISBN: 0-8015-2810-0

First Printing: August 1974
Second Printing: October 1974
Third Printing: February 1975

ACKNOWLEDGMENTS

This is a book I have wanted to do for many years. I love auto racing above all sports. And admire the men in it. I truly believe A. J. Foyt to be the greatest athlete I have seen in any sport. It seemed to me he was the outstanding performer in sports who had not had a major biography done on him. And writing biographies is my business. I do not believe in writing "puff pieces" about "cardboard cutouts." Foyt is a very real person. He is imperfect, as all of us are. He has his weaknesses, as we all do. He also has strengths beyond the usual. No doubt my admiration for him shows through. The portrait of him I have presented on these pages is as accurate as I can draw it.

I wish to express my gratitude to A. J. Foyt and those close to him, including Chuck Barnes, for all past interviews. Thanks are also extended to all the drivers, mechanics, sponsors, and writers who have granted interviews, written informatively about events included in this book or otherwise provided helpful information. I also wish to thank Al Bloemker and Charlene Ellis, of the Indianapolis Motor Speedway, Jim Cook and Sue Ovitt, of the Ontario Motor Speedway, the staff at Daytona International Speedway, Jack Mathews of Riverside Raceway, Jep Cadou, formerly of the United States Auto Club, as well as Dick Jordan, Don Davidson, and all others at USAC and NASCAR, Bob Thomas of Bob Thomas Associates Public Relations, Ray Marquette, Rich Roberts, Jim Fulton, Bob Shafer, Dusty Brandel, and all other racing officials and racing people who whenever asked provided help without question.

I am especially grateful to Bob Tronolone and John Posey, who contributed the bulk of the photographs, and all other photographers, including George Rose, Peter J. West, and Dr. Bob Berman, who filled my many requests for photographs.

I wish to thank Matt Merola and Paul Goetz of Mattgo Enterprises, New York City, for participating in the venture. Finally, I wish to thank Charles N. Heckelmann of Hawthorn Books for permitting me to do a book I so much wished to do.

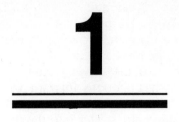

1

Was he mellowing, he was asked, and he said, "Mellowing? Like hell I am," and he sort of smiled as if to say, "What garbage, that day will never come." Then he shook his head, brushing the smile away, and his features took on a serious expression that said he did not want to be asked any more foolish questions, and he pulled on his white fireproof coveralls, snapped them up around his neck, and walked out of the garage and down the track to where his crew and his car waited for him.

It was May, so it was Indianapolis. More than sixty years old, the Indianapolis Motor Speedway is a vast, sprawling place of steel and concrete stands, dirt and grass and trees surrounding a 2½-mile oval asphalt track on which, around Memorial Day every year, a 500-mile race is held, the richest and most dangerous single annual sporting event in the world. Now it was early in the month, so only a few thousand fans were scattered in the seats and in the infield as the drivers and mechanics prepared and practiced their cars.

All the cars are wide, flat, low, and long. The chassis are painted in bright, metallic colors with large numerals and names on them and the decals of commercial sponsors pasted on. The wheels are exposed and carry fat, treadless tires. The engine of each car is largely exposed and mounted to the rear, with a wide wing rigged above and behind it. The cockpit is a single-seater, open and located amidships, between concealed fuel tanks. The chassis is fragile, the engine powerful. The car is an intricate assemblage of functional, lightweight parts, designed to be driven at speeds of more than 200 miles per hour.

The driver goes to his car and looks at it. He walks around it, studying it, talking quietly to his crew. Then he stands by it and looks down the track on which other cars are practicing, speeding through the stretch, proceeding into the corners, turning nimbly through them. They sparkle gaudily in the bright hot spring sun. They give off enormous noise, their engines roaring as they speed past. Their thunderous roar, the stench of spent fuel, the smell of worn rubber, fill the air.

I

The driver takes off his cap and is handed a hard shiny white helmet with a visored front. He puts it on, then pulls fireproof gloves over his hands. He is a big man, and as he climbs into the cockpit and lowers himself into it, he must squeeze into the cramped confines. An aide leans in and fastens the driver's safety harness, his seat and shoulder belts. The driver motions forward with one arm and puts his hands on the steering wheel as a member of the crew inserts the narrow nose of the automatic starter into the rear of the car. It winds up with a whine and roars loudly to life. The crew pushes it away, the driver shoves it into gear and passes through the pits and eases onto the track, heading toward the first turn.

The crew moves to the wall separating the pits and the track and wait, as other cars rush by. Their red-and-white number 14 car rolls by cautiously, its engine warming up. A little more than a minute later it comes by again, less cautiously now as its engine begins to warm up. In less than sixty seconds it hurtles past once more, being pressed toward its best speed. And again, the crew members clocking it on their stop-watches tell one another what its time means. Then the car comes out of the fourth turn slowing, and turns at the head of the stretch off the track into the pit area and glides toward its particular pit as the crew moves from the wall back toward it.

The driver puts his gloved hands on the side of the car and pushes himself up and out of the cockpit and steps outside it. He takes off his gloves and throws them into the seat. He removes his helmet and is handed his cap and puts it on. He stands away from the car and looks at it unhappily. It is not working right. It is not what he had thought it would be when he built it. He did the job himself, so he has no one to blame except himself and his crew, who helped him. He speaks to his crew, telling them how it is working, how it isn't working. It is not what he had thought it would be when he practiced it early in the year at record speeds or when he won a short race with it only a month previously.

Why?

"How the hell would I know?" he growls. "It's only a bunch of goddam metal. It doesn't talk. It doesn't tell me anything. If I knew what was wrong, I'd fix it. That's what I'm trying to do now —find out what the hell is wrong so I can take care of it. If you'll just leave me the hell alone, I'll find out what's wrong and I'll fix it."

He leans on the wing as if to straighten it. He leans on the rear end, bouncing it as if to test the springs. The rear end is not right, it seems. But why isn't it right? What is wrong? He crouches by it, looking as though he could kill it. If he doesn't get it right, it could kill him. Or, at least, beat him.

He doesn't want to be beat. No one does, but he wants it less than others. He has won more than they have. He is accustomed to winning. He is not used to losing. But he is getting used to it. He has been losing a lot lately.

"Maybe I'm getting old," he growls.

"Tex, you'll never get old. You're ageless," a friend says.

"We all get old," he growls, knowing it but not wanting to give in to it.

"Not, you, A. J."

"Yeh, A. J. too," he says, studying the car that is making him feel old. The car, this latest car, any racing car is almost a part of him, an extension of his personality. He cannot separate himself from it; he is stuck with it. He must make the most of it, whatever it is, however it performs. It is a new car, costly, ingeniously put together, imaginatively prepared, but imperfect. It is a new car and he feels himself aging in the grim process of trying to get new cars to work as well as he wants. Sweat is streaming down his face now as he shoves aside a crewman to lean over the car and poke into its guts.

"We all get old," he growls to himself.

Anthony Joseph Foyt, Jr., from Houston, Texas—A. J. Foyt . . . A. J. . . . Tony . . . Tough Tony . . . Tex . . . Super Tex. A professional racing car driver. The greatest auto racer who ever lived. Even those who think others are, or were, would not put him too far from it. He has dominated his circuit as no others have been able to dominate theirs. He has won more different kinds of races on more different kinds of tracks in more different kinds of cars than any other driver in history.

He is the Babe Ruth of auto racing. He has been called a modern American folk hero, a living legend, an immortal in his time. When this is mentioned to him, he grimaces and growls, "I don't know anything about that. I'm good. I know that. I don't know anything about that other stuff."

He says it, but he doesn't mean it. More than good, he is great, and he knows it. He doesn't have to admit it. He doesn't have to put it into words. He is not a graceful man, but he has the grace of greatness about him.

He stands a little under six feet in height and weighs just under 200 pounds. He has a thick, blocky build. You could draw a straight line from his shoulders past his hips. He is a bit broad of beam. He has thick, powerful legs, arms, and hands. He is handsome. His face has strong, good features. His tanned, leathery skin is spider-webbed with pale, faint traces of scars from burns and injuries suffered in racing accidents.

He has dark eyes and dark hair. His eyes glitter, giving off sparks. A hard glint burns through from the base of them. Staring, he seems to see through you. When he smiles, his face relaxes. He has a warm smile that wrinkles his skin and softens the hardness in his eyes. But he is a businessman and his business is racing, and when he is about his business he is serious and his lips draw thin and he does not smile and his eyes glint hard and his jaw juts out and he speaks in taut, profane ways.

No gray shows in his dark hair. Does he dye it? Probably. You are afraid to ask. But he has his vanities. He is tough, but not beyond vanity. He had his hair woven into a rug to fill out the front where it is thinning out. He bought a hairpiece, but wearing it bothered him, so he threw it away. He wears a cap most of the time now. When he takes it off to put on his racing helmet, he removes it quickly and just as quickly slips on his helmet.

Wearing his cap, his arms folded across his chest, he stands now in his white flameproof coveralls by the pit wall studying his car.

A reporter asks, "A. J., you got a couple of minutes?"

Foyt fixes him with a hard look. "No, I don't have a couple of minutes. I don't have one blanking minute. I don't have anything to say," he says. "Can't you see I'm working to fix something that's not working? Why don't you go away and leave me work?"

"Or I'll grab you by the butt and heave you the hell out of here," his manner says. So he is left alone. When Foyt wants to be left alone, he is left alone. Everyone is afraid of Foyt—writers, promoters, sponsors, other drivers, even his own sponsors and mechanics. There are drivers who are not afraid to race him, who feel in their guts that, all other things being equal, they can beat him; and there are some who feel they can beat him because he beats himself now, because they feel he may be washed up. And there are those who would not be afraid to fight him—even those who feel they could not whip him—but everyone is awed by him and afraid of him, just the same.

"He's like a live bomb," someone says. "You don't want to fool around with it for fear it will blow up in your face."

"He has a trigger temper. It's always cocked," someone else says. "He's always going off half-cocked."

"They respect him," Bobby Unser says. Bobby Unser is one of the top racing drivers. He laughs and says of Foyt, "Respect, hell, they're scared of him. He's the man. He's the boss driver."

"He's all right. Hell, he's better than all right. He's the best. He's the best man among them," Bud Poorman says. Bud Poorman was the Indianapolis chief for Goodyear tires, which competes with Firestone for car racing rewards and which sponsors Foyt, among others.

Bud Poorman adds, "If you're his friend, he'll do anything for you. If you're not his friend, he doesn't want anything to do with you. If you're his friend, you know better than to bother him when he's getting ready to race. If you bother him, he'll want to beat on you. He doesn't want to be bothered. He wants to be ready to race."

"I'm a race driver," Foyt has said. "It's what I do. I do other things, but they don't matter much. Racing is all that matters to me. I build cars and I drive them. Racing is all I've wanted to do for as long as I can remember. I've been doing it a long time, but I don't want to stop doing it. The day I stop will be a very sad day.

"A lot of people think I should stop. But I don't want to stop. It's very hard to stop doing what you do, what you like best to do. I may be getting old to be doing this thing I do, but it wouldn't be old if I was doing most things people do, the things most people will never have to stop doing. And as long as I'm doing what I do, I want to do it right.

"I don't ask anything of anyone else I don't ask of myself. I don't want anyone to make any mistakes because this is not a business that forgives mistakes. When mistakes are made, I lose or I get hurt. So I don't want to be bothered into making mistakes. I'll talk to you. I'll fun with you. When it's time to talk. When it's time to have fun.

"I laugh as much as the next guy. But when it's time to go racing, it's not time for fun, it's not time to laugh, it's not time to talk. I'll tell you if I don't like you. I'll tell you right to your face. I'm not going to bullshit you. And if you bother me, I'm not gonna like you. I don't like being bothered when I'm getting ready to go racing."

A member of Foyt's crew says, "Foyt is always right and everyone else is always wrong. Once you figure that out, you're all right, you've got a chance to live with him."

Another one says, "He's the original fish or cut bait man. You figure out what you can do, or rather what he wants you to do, and you do it, and you do it his way or you get the hell out."

Foyt stood there in the Hoosier sunshine watching his crew working on his car, in the fragile, finely sprung chassis, in the temperamental, finely tuned engine. He shoved some of them aside to work on it himself, with a wrench and a screwdriver, loosening this bolt and tightening that. He kicked at a tire, leaned on a wing, bent over to poke inside the engine, dropped on his back to stick an arm under the chassis. He got up and looked at it. It was ready for another test.

He quickly took off his cap and put his helmet back on, then lowered himself into the cockpit until he was almost lying on his back—which is the way a driver fits into it—and a crewman tightened his harness about him and they started the engine up and pushed the car away. He slid onto the track, slowly at first, then faster as he circled the oval, gaining speed, while his crew watched and clocked him.

After a couple of laps, he came back in and got out, growling, his jaw jutting out, and he quickly took off his helmet and just as quickly donned his cap, and talked to his crewmen, to his father who heads up his crewmen, and they looked here and poked there and tightened this and loosened that and then he crawled back into the cockpit and was pushed off again.

It was growing cooler now, the wind whipping up and blasting between the stands in gusts that shoved the lightweight racers around on the track. Foyt returned, grease and sweat smearing his face, sticking to his uniform, and he unhooked himself and climbed out, cursing under his breath. Swapping his helmet for his cap, he muttered something to his father and another crewman and then they pushed the car away, down the line, toward Gasoline Alley and their garage, where they would work on it in the private shadows of the shielded sanctuary. He followed after it, looking thick and solid and strong from the rear, limping a little from injuries of the past that linger in his bones. He walked alone, a maverick, a member of the establishment, but a man set against it, a man who marches to his own distant drummer, a man who dances only to his own tunes. He is a soloist in a team sport.

Car racing is more of a team sport than any other. Even in football, the coaches do not control the outcome of a game as much as the crews do in auto racing. The sponsors who decide how much money is to be spent on the cars, the men who build the chassis and components and engines, the men who develop the tires, the mechanics who ready the cars for races, and the drivers who drive them—all share in the responsibility for the success or failure of a racing project.

Dame Fortune has her role to play, too. Properly prepared operations are at the mercy of parts costing pennies that may break or come apart from the pounding pressures and stresses exerted on them. One wonders why cars costing so much, supposedly prepared properly, fail so often. The reason is they are so high strung, tuned to such a pitch, pushed so near their limits and often past their limits, that these driven, pressured men and machines frequently fail.

The cars are more important than the drivers. Bad drivers cannot win often, even in good cars. But good drivers cannot often win in bad cars. The greatest of drivers sometimes can win in an ordinary car, as Foyt often has, but Foyt has been beaten by cars that came apart under him in countless races, often when he was leading or within a few miles of winning. He could not carry his car across the finish line first. He is not even permitted to push it home.

When Foyt was young, a great rival, Rodger Ward, accused Foyt of abusing his cars by pushing them past their limits. Ward was one who was willing to wait to win, who carried on conservatively while the chargers wore out themselves and their cars. Foyt, of course, was a charger, who forged as far in front as he could from the start.

Foyt snapped, "I don't ask a car to do anything it wasn't meant to do. If it isn't together to run farther and faster than the rest, it isn't worth driving." But, as he has gotten older, Foyt has learned to make the most of his machines, to push them to their limits but not past their limits. He has learned to practice patience.

His three Indianapolis 500 triumphs each were achieved when he did not have the fastest car, when the leaders fell out in front of him.

"I have found out that to finish first you first have to finish. I have learned that you have to find out what a car can and cannot do. I have learned to do what you can do and not try to do what you can't do," he says. Then he smiles and adds, "Maybe I can just do things others cannot do."

Ward did not like Foyt, but he came to admit, "Foyt can do more with cars than others can." Another great rival, Parnelli Jones, has stated, "There are some cars no one could win in. But Foyt can win in cars no one else could win in."

Eddie Sachs once said, "You have to respect Foyt because he is the best. Everyone always believes he is the best, that given the best cars he will be the best driver, but down deep we all know that Foyt really is the best. He has had the best cars a lot of the time, but he has beaten us a lot of the time when he did not have the best."

In a given year, a great driver in a great car prepared by great mechanics may dominate all rivals but usually the next year another crew comes up with another car that is better and another driver dominates.

There was a time when front-engine heavyweight cars built by A. J. Watson were prepared for races by him and by others and driven by Rodger Ward, Jim Rathmann, Parnelli Jones, Jimmy Bryan, and Tony Bettenhausen and dominated the circuit through the 1950s. But then Colin Chapman came along in the 1960s with the rear-engine lightweight "Lotus," which became the model that was most copied and most successful. Watson went over to these models, but they have not worked well for him. Bignotti's cars, first reshaped "Watsons," then reshaped Lotuses, carried Foyt to domination of the circuit, which endured six years before Bignotti broke up with Foyt.

When the new cars came in, Bignotti was one of the old guard who was able to make the switch successfully. Into the 1970s he continued to be the dominant mechanic on the circuit. First he built or reshaped "Parnellis" or "Colts" for the Parnelli Jones team. Then he turned to reshaping "Eagles" or "McLarens" for the Andy Granatelli–Pat Patrick team.

The Eagles were developed by Dan Gurney and they were the fastest but not the most durable racers on the trail. They and the McLarens, developed by Bruce McLaren and improved by the Roger Penske team, became lower and wider than the original Lotuses, and they added wider treadless tires and airfoil "wings" to increase traction. With improved power-plants becoming available when Ford developed a racing engine to compete with the Offenhauser engine, which had dominated racing, speeds increased drastically.

Foyt grew up in the old cars and was not comfortable in the new models. They were frail and he feared them. But when they came in, he had to switch over to them. He was the last driver to win the Indianapolis 500 in one of the old heavyweights and the first American to win it in one of the new lightweights. In one five-year stretch—before he was thirty—he won more championship circuit races—27—than any other driver ever had won in an entire career.

In his first ten years on the title trail, he won 37 races. But his victories on the trail have come infrequently since that time. He made his father his chief mechanic and began to supervise the building, preparation, and racing of his own "Coyotes" himself. Eventually he took over the Ford racing engines, which were renamed "Foyts," and the road became rougher for him. For a while a wave of foreign drivers led by Jimmy Clark assaulted American shores and stole away with many laurels. After the European enthusiasm for American racing declined, first Mario Andretti, then Al and Bobby Unser, Mark Donohue, and Joe Leonard became dominant drivers of their circuit and won most of the major titles. Foyt no longer was king.

There are several racing bodies sanctioning numerous racing

circuits in this country and around the world. The richest is the U.S. championship trail, sanctioned by the United States Auto Club. The races on this tour alter from year to year but usually have consisted of from 10 to 20 races of 100 miles or more contested in Indianapolis-styled cars on oval tracks.

Points are awarded based on the length of each race and the finish of each car and determine the driving champion annually. The centerpiece of this circuit has always been the Indianapolis 500, which draws the largest crowd and pays the largest purse of any single annual sporting event in the world. In recent years the California 500 at Ontario and the Pennsylvania 500 at Pocono have sprung up at fancy new facilities patterned after the Indianapolis Motor Speedway. Foyt has won more of these races—45—and more driving titles —5—than any other driver.

USAC also sanctions stock car, sprint car, and midget car circuits. Foyt has taken some of these titles and won more of these varied races than any other driver.

To protect promoters of lesser races within each circuit, each sanctioning body prohibits racers from competing in races on other circuits whenever the events are scheduled competitively. Thus, Foyt has not been free to pick his spots, entering the major races of each circuit.

When Foyt has been free to race elsewhere, he has won elsewhere. He has won more National Association of Sports Car Racing (NASCAR) Grand National races on the southern stock car circuit, including the cornerstone of that circuit—the Daytona 500—than any driver who was not a regular on that trail. He has triumphed in sports car classics at Daytona and at Nassau in the Bahamas. He is the only Indianapolis 500 winner to have also won the most important race in sports car racing—the 24 Hours of Le Mans in France—and both triumphs were racked up within two weeks.

He has taken top honors in more major races on more major circuits than any driver who ever lived, but he has never sacrificed the time and money necessary to attempt to win a Grand Prix race. He owed it to his immortality to try, but it remains the lone gap in his incredible record.

A friend says, "He has a big ego and would have loved to have won one, but he can make more money sticking to what he knows best and money has meant more to him than fame. He's the smartest, shrewdest guy in racing, but he prefers to pretend he's just a simple country boy."

We have called the championship circuit Heartbreak Highway. Many have left their high hopes along the way. Some have left their lives. The trail has bent machinery, broken bodies, and dashed dreams all along its tortuous length.

The survivors wear their battle scars as if they were medals. There are people in car racing who would prefer to pass over the unpleasant aspects of their sport, but these are integral components of this dangerous profession. Foyt somehow has survived dreadful smashups that have broken his bones, scarred his skin, and left him limping, yet he goes on.

Thirteen of the 33 starters in his first 500 were killed racing. Foyt is the only one of the survivors who has not retired. Many more have been killed since. Men who started racing long after he did have had successful careers and retired while he goes on.

He celebrated his twentieth anniversary in racing in 1972. He did not bother with a party. He blew out no candles. He made no mention of the historic moment. He has admitted he was driven by a desire to become the first man to win Indy a fourth time. Now he denies it. He made an unprecedented sixteenth consecutive start in the Indianapolis 500 in 1973. He did it without calling attention to it. He just went on toward a 17th start in 1974, which would be the most times any man has dared this classic contest.

The great racing driver develops with experience. Few reach the heights at a young age. If they do, they often are tempted to take chances the older drivers will not take. Some drivers get by in racing without taking many chances. However, the truly great driver knows when to take a chance and when not to. He is thoroughly aware of his own capabilities and makes it his business to know his cars, his rivals and their cars, the races, and the tracks. He must control powerful but delicate cars in tight traffic over tricky courses at top speed. He executes passes when he can do so cleanly. He leads when it is time to lead. He drives just fast enough to win. He does not waste time, himself, or his equipment.

The great racing driver is the greatest of athletes because, beyond all the physical skills and mental discipline any athlete must possess to succeed, he must be imbued with an incomparable courage that enables him to function flawlessly against such threats of severe injury or even death as no other athlete has to endure. The great racing driver is a special breed of athletic animal.

Rodger Ward once admitted, "I will put myself in places on a race track most drivers will not go. Foyt is the greatest of drivers because he will put himself in places no one else will go."

Parnelli Jones said, "I succeeded in racing because I had more determination than most drivers. But Foyt had more determination than anyone. I would do *almost* anything to win a race. But Foyt would do anything."

Ward added, "They like to talk about sportsmanship in racing, but it is not a profession for sportsmen. There are guys who will run over you to win, and if they try it you have to run the sons of bitches right off the track before they run you off."

Al Unser has said, "Foyt will cheat to win. Maybe I shouldn't say cheat, but he will bend the rules as far as he can get away with and if there's a loophole he'll sneak through it. So will I. So will any driver worth his salt. Foyt showed us how. He wrote the book. The guys in racing are very tough. Foyt is tougher than the next guy. He will not hurt you to win, but he will risk hurting himself. We just practice what he preaches."

Foyt himself has said, "I could never settle for being anything but the best. I've always loved racing more than anything in my life and if I couldn't be the best at it my life wouldn't mean much to me. Everyone wants to win, but not everyone is willing to make the sacrifices it takes. There have been a lot of guys as good as I am, but not many willing to do what you have to do to win. I want to win as much now as when I first started. Maybe more.

"Nothing that has happened in my career has changed that. I have been depressed when good friends died racing. I have learned how to handle that. I try not to make close friends in racing. I try not to let anyone get too close to me. I am friends with a lot of guys in racing. I also am a bit of a loner. I don't want anything to stop me from doing what I have to do. I know it's a dangerous sport. Nothing can change that, so I try not to think about it. Men die doing a lot of things. I figure when your number comes up, it's up, no matter what you're doing, and there's nothing you can do about it."

In the early days of his career, he drove 40 to 50 races a year. He participated in big and small races. He drove for big purses and small purses. Many times when he didn't get his own cars into races, he bought someone else's starting position just so he could drive. In numerous instances, he started far back yet finished far in front. He often took tremendous chances.

Asked once what Foyt might say if his sponsors dared to order him to stop risking their fortunes in minor races by competing like a madman in minor events, Parnelli Jones laughed and replied, "I reckon ol' A. J. would just tell 'em to go to hell."

Told this, A. J. laughed and allowed as how that was just what he would do. He said, "If there's a race anywhere, I want in it. If I'm in it, I want to win it. This wasn't meant to be a safe and easy business."

He rode so high for so long a period that few people felt he ever would fall. But he fell. He has been losing and looking bad in recent years, like a boxer pushing himself past his prime, getting hurt a little more each year. Many fear for him. Possibly he fears for himself.

"Foyt shouldn't allow himself to look bad," an old friend says. "He is the best driver who ever lived. But he wants to be the best builder and the best mechanic, too. And he is a good builder and a good mechanic. But he is a better driver than he is a builder and a mechanic. He is too much of a perfectionist, who can't quit tinkering with his cars. He gets a good one going good and he tries to make it more and he makes it less. No one can do it all and win it all. He is too proud now to drive for someone else and too stubborn to see he is going at it all wrong."

He won the 1967 Indianapolis 500, but he has not won one since. Of course, most men never win it. But Foyt is not most men. The differences dividing winners from losers in racing often are so small as to be maddening. The difference between the honored winner of the pole position and the disgraced loser who does not even make the starting field at Indianapolis, for example, is often less than *one second per mile*. A man cannot count it off. A part costing ten cents can break a car and beat a man. Foyt has come close many times in recent years. He has lost many races he might have won. His cars have just been a tick of time too slow. At other times he still seems to be on top of things. In 1973 he won the 500 at Pocono, for example. In 1972 he won the Daytona 500. He often has had the best car on the southern stock car circuit. When he has the best car, he still can win.

He is nearing 40 now. He has passed through many changes in his profession. Old rivals have retired or died. Old masters have lost their touch and new marvels have taken over. The cars have changed completely. It took a speed of approximately 145 miles per hour to make the starting field at Indianapolis his first year there. In 1973 it took close to 200 miles per hour.

The cars cost twice as much as they did. Independent men used to be able to scrape up $100,000 and go to Indy and make their mark. Now it costs that much to get a single car together, and it takes a million dollars worth of equipment to succeed there. Wherever Foyt races, whether in a stock car at Trenton or a sports car at Riverside, the cars cost more and go so fast, so close to the hairy edge of disaster that he says it is like shooting yourself from a cannon. He doesn't race sprint cars or midget cars much anymore. He doesn't drive 50 races a year anymore. He doesn't drive half that many. But he goes on.

His body has thickened, his hair has thinned. In the beginning he was marked for success and now he has been marked by it.

He has lived and loved and brawled his way through life, somehow larger than life, fighting with fellow drivers and officials, feuding with fans and writers, being frequently fined and suspended, but too big to be banned. Ol' A. J., that two-fisted, tough-talking, steely eyed son of a gun—what is he doing still here, you wonder, as he works on his car now at the end of a long day, the sun sinking, the wind rising, the cold chilling him to the bone through his sweat-soaked, fireproof coveralls, grease staining his scarred face.

Crash-helmeted, strapped in, he steered his frail, roaring, winged creation over the old course at speeds past good sense, seeking the elusive seconds he needed. They remained out of reach and he brought the car in and climbed out of it and cursed it under his breath and told his crew to tow it back to the garage. It wasn't right, he said. But they would get it right, he swore. If they had to work all night, they would get it right.

2

A. J. Foyt, Sr., was saying of A. J. Foyt, Jr., one year at Indianapolis, "Naw, I didn't figure he'd be here until he started driving back home. He said he'd come here and he did. I was back here in the forties, just foolin' around. My daddy, he used to run motorcycles. He had a garage. I raced a lot around Houston in the thirties before I got my garage. A '25 Hudson was my first car. I was about fifteen or sixteen. No, I never won none of my races. We run for nothin'. We more or less were just having a bunch of fun.

"I bought my boy a toy racer just for fun, but he really took to it. Then I built him a midget car. He was only five. But it would go 50 miles an hour and he would go 50 in it. Was he a natural? Not for a while. He just liked to drive. But he was driving a stock car before he was seventeen and a real midget car at seventeen. They were all our own cars at the time. And he did real well.

"That's all he had interest in—cars. He worked right on 'em—the engines, the chassis, everything. Naw, I ain't had no trouble with him. Nothing but car trouble. I'll tell you, he's pretty dang hard to beat. If the stuff stays together, he'll get it up there. Anything he puts his mind to he makes a go of."

The father, who is known as Tony, is a plain person who puts on no pretenses. He looks a lot like his son, except he is older, of course, although you would not know right off looking at them together that they are father and son. Tony has his son's solid, stocky build, though he is not as heavy. He limps a little when he walks, from an old injury.

He was never a great racer, though maybe he could have been if he had had a real, early opportunity. He has worked hard for a living all his life.

If you ask him a question, he will give you a straight, honest answer. But he doesn't like to be asked questions. He doesn't have a whole lot to say. He's a lot like his son in this respect. He's a no-nonsense guy. Like his son, he's very tough. He's very proud of his son, who is very protective of him. Tony doesn't ask any of the spotlight. He's satisfied to see A. J. get it. He wants A. J. to win. He helps him to win. If A. J. wins, Tony wins.

A. J. has said, "Dad always wanted to win. I guess that's the only way to be. What's the use of competing if not to win?"

A. J. was born on January 16, 1935. When he was just three, his father presented him with a blood-red miniature racing car. It hooked him on the narcotic of racing.

"I thought that little ol' car was the most beautiful thing there ever was," A. J. recalls.

When Foyt was five, his father built him the midget, and the boy took to it like he was born in it. Soon he was driving it in exhibitions between races at a Houston track. It had a three horsepower engine and could travel 50 miles an hour, and he drove it to the limit. He was a cocky kid, and one night he challenged a local driver—an adult named Doc Cossey—to a race and beat him. Foyt's father served as a crew chief for this debut in competition. Years later, Foyt laughed and said, "That was the biggest kick of my life. I guess it was then and there I knew I wanted to be a race driver."

He hung around his father's garage all the time, listening to race drivers talk, asking them about racing, watching work on race cars, doing whatever he could to help. He used to sneak his own car out onto neighborhood streets and speed it up and down until the neighbors called the cops.

"Oh, we had that little ol' car, all right, but a lot of kids have little race cars and don't grow up to be A. J. Foyts," his father says. "I'll tell you when it really started. It was in 1946, right after the war, when A. J. was eleven. I owned two midget cars in those days, and Mrs. Foyt and I took one of them to Dallas for a race. We left one of them home, and we left A. J. home, too.

"When we got back—it was about 5:30 in the morning, I guess— we found the whole yard torn up. I mean everything was gone. The grass was chewed to pieces and there were tire gouges all around. The swings we had in the yard had been knocked down. I knew right away that A. J. had got some of his buddies to push him and they had got that midget started up. It didn't have a self-starter, of course.

"And then, when I went into the garage and saw the midget, I knew why A. J. had quit. He had caught the thing on fire and burned up the engine. It was sitting there with the paint all scorched.

"I went into the house and right into his bedroom. He played like he was asleep, but he wasn't, I could tell. But my wife said, 'Don't say anything to him right now when you're so mad.' So I didn't get him up. But I know right then, standing there in that kid's bedroom, that he would have to race, there just wasn't going to be any other way. The next day, I told him, 'If you want to race, all right, race, but promise to always drive something good.' "

He bawled out the boy and A. J. apologized, but he was pleased his father recognized his desire to race which had not been extinguished by racing a car in his backyard until it was ablaze. He further promised to drive only good equipment, which is something that has stayed with him. Many drivers who might be good never get into the cockpit of a good car. If Foyt couldn't get a good car, he didn't race. He wasn't going to be branded a loser because he was in a car that wouldn't win. Even today, a race official says, "If the price is right, most drivers will race. The price has to be right and the car has to be right before Foyt will race. Oh, he'll take a car that isn't running right and run it in a race to get the most out of it. No car runs right all the time. But he won't campaign a car that can't be made right, sooner or later, If you put the right amount of money up front, Bobby Unser will go. But if you don't put it on the nose of a car that's right, Foyt will forget it."

As a teen-ager, Foyt raced motorcycles and practiced driving his father's midget cars. For a while it was his father's responsibility to see that his son had something good to run. Foyt was a pretty good football player and probably could have been outstanding. He was a good running back. But he did not stay with it because he did not remain in school. He wasn't interested in studying. He was interested in racing. So he quit Lamar High in the eleventh grade at the age of seventeen to start racing full time.

His mother, Evelyn, was not happy about it. What mother ever is when her son quits school? She has said she wanted him to go on with his education. But she had a husband who had been in racing or around racers all his life and she knew how he felt about it, so she was not surprised when he passed on his passion to his son. It was all they talked about. When they went out, they went to a race.

She was a good, decent woman who worried when her son started to race because she knew it was not safe, but as the wife of a man in racing she had lived that life so long she had learned to accept it. She had a daughter, A. J.'s sister, Marlene, who was more interested in school. But Marlene too, was swept up in the family feeling for racing. She loved her brother and rooted for him and worried about him, as she still does.

A. J. has explained, "I couldn't study anymore. I was racing for my dad and working in his garage and taking home $75 a week and you know how it is—I just couldn't wait any longer."

He really was racing before he legally was of age, but his first official race of record was at Houston's Playland Park in 1953 when he was eighteen. He says he was so scared he didn't know which way to go, but he set a track record in qualifying for his first night as a real racer and he won the feature event his third night of competition.

He raced midgets and modified stock cars around Houston and throughout Texas and the Southwest and was successful from the start. At first he fancied himself something of a dude. Strikingly handsome, he wore brightly colored silk shirts and freshly laundered white trousers in every race and was nicknamed Fancypants.

No one would dare hang such a moniker on him now. Nor did they do so often then, for his fists were as fast as his temper and he got into many fights and won most of them. In any event, this fascination for fancy duds was a passing phase. He outgrew it rapidly. Racing was what really mattered, and he swiftly switched to coveralls, neat but not gaudy.

He shifted into sprint cars, too, and extended his territory to the Midwest and East, beating his way up through the bushes on dusty, dangerous, rutty dirt tracks in small stadiums with small crowds scattered through splintery wooden stands. A lot of drivers die in these races and many more get hurt. One was killed crashing over Foyt's car in one race on the International Motor Car Association circuit, but A. J. went on, nearing graduation from IMCA—the minors—to the majors.

"He was too goddam good for those guys," a racer remembers. "He knew it and they knew it. He'd boil over when he got beat by any of them and they'd boil over when he beat them. He was somewhat reckless in those days. Behind the wheel, he was a wild man. It was a while before he became a wise man, too. But he was learning. He was fighting his way up. And I mean fighting. Often with his fists. He was scrappin' his way up to the big time."

"In some ways, the early days are the most dangerous," Foyt once observed. "You run races that aren't real fast, but you run 'em as hard as you can; the tracks aren't real good, the cars aren't real good, and a lot of the drivers aren't real good. You get a bad guy in a bad car and you got a rough situation for the rest of the guys. And if you get in trouble there aren't many safety features built into the track.

"Sprint car racing probably is the most dangerous form of racing. They're the most high-powered cars you run on short tracks. They're not powered as much as championship cars, but championship cars run on tracks that have room for running. I always liked sprint racing because I was always good at it. Sprint cars race on dirt tracks and I was always good on dirt tracks. Racing dirt, on a short track, it's more the driver than the car, and I like that."

The chunky cars careen around cramped quarter-mile and half-mile dirt tracks in short dashes, usually 4-lap or 10-lap heat races and 30-lap features, which wind up with the driver being bussed by some bikinied beauty queen and handed a piece of tin that serves as a trophy and a check for a couple of hundred dollars.

Seeking the shortest way around, the drivers broadside their erect machines sideways through the tight turns so they will be pointed straight ahead when they conclude the corners, then accelerate them straight through the short chutes, throwing up rooster-tails of dirt and clouds of dust that coat their cars and windshields and visors, their uniforms and goggles and skin, and shower spectators in the lower rows of the stands with hunks of earth.

The drivers wear bandannas around their mouths to keep from choking on the dust and they frequently are cut by rocks and stray pieces of metal sucked up from the track into their faces. They sit exposed in the open cockpit cars and steer their clumsy mounts around in close quarters with the competition, sometimes touching, more often just missing, bouncing along over the oily, rutty track, trying to keep off the flimsy fences but flying within inches of them.

When Foyt was driving sprinters, the cockpits were not enclosed by cages made of roll-bars and the drivers did not all wear fireproof coveralls as is now the case. It was more dangerous then than it is now. Indianapolis drivers apprenticed in sprinters on dirt tracks and in midget cars on small paved ovals. Today drivers are more likely to emerge from sports car ranks, having developed their skills in the cockpits of sophisticated cars on smooth courses among a moneyed crowd.

Foyt's was a different day of development, just before racing became big business. The good drivers who emerged from his era were less educated, hungrier, and tougher than the well-schooled, well-financed stylists who come along in these times. Foyt was typical of his type. He never finished school. He worked his way up without much money. He drove physically. Fortunately, he was shrewd. That set him apart from the rest. At first, his strength was his weakness. But he learned to harness his strength, to drive intelligently as well as hard.

In a day when dirt track races were an important part of the championship circuit as well as the sprint circuit, Foyt felt at home. In a day when the cars were big and bulky and heavy, Foyt fit comfortably. He could bull those beasts around. He could broadslide through turns with the best of them. He could cut corners. He could take a bouncing around. There have been many drivers who were especially adept in big cars on dirt courses, but Foyt has topped them all. Because the driver is more important than the car on short dirt tracks, Foyt was bound to be the best.

He moved up to the majors in 1956, joining the United States Auto Club. He drove only one USAC race that year, but he drove 35 midget car races, five championship car races, and four sprint car races in 1957. His first USAC victory came on May 12 of that year in a 100-lap midget event on the quarter-mile dirt track at Kansas City, Missouri. Later, in mid-September, he won another midget race, a 50-lap event on a paved quarter-mile race in Xenia, Ohio.

He did not win another USAC race of any sort or his first sprint car race in USAC ranks until 1960, when he took a 100-lap midget car race at Ascot Park near Los Angeles in February and a 30-lap sprint car race in Reading, Pennsylvania, in April. For years after that he won frequently. But midget and sprint car races do not pay much.

In 1962 he began to drive USAC stock car races. Then a few years later he began to drive the bigger NASCAR southern stock car races that were open to him, and he passed up the dangerous sprint car and midget car races, which he rarely drives now. For five years he entered 40 to 50 races a year, but since 1965 he has reduced his schedule to 25 to 30 races a year.

He says, "Stock car racing is the safest form of racing and only championship car racing pays more. You can bump in stock cars and get away with it. You can't in champ cars, but they pay you well to take the chance."

Entering 1973, his record in USAC competition showed 45 victories in championship cars, 28 in stock cars, 26 in sprint cars, and 20 in midget cars. He is the only driver in USAC history who has won 20 or more races in each of its circuits. He has won 118 races in more than 500 starts. This is an unsurpassed .200 plus batting average, equal to .400 in baseball terms.

The drivers who win the season championships on these circuits usually are the ones who concentrate on one or the other, but Foyt won one stock car crown, in 1968, to go with his five championship car crowns, and often he has been second or third in the standings of the various divisions. In 1971 USAC introduced a dirt car division and the next year Foyt won that title.

He hit the trail hungry. When he was driving for others and keeping only about 40 percent of his winnings, he went without many things. He had married and begun to have children long before he reached Indianapolis and gotten into the big money. In 1957, his first full year on the USAC circuit, his earnings were less than $10,000 and he kept less than half of that. But he more than doubled that amount the next year. And he doubled that figure the following year, and again the year after that.

He has won from $50,000 to $100,000 a year most years since and close to $200,000 some years. He also has commanded approximately $200,000 a year in guarantees and side monies for some years now. He has won a record sum in racing of between $2 to 3 million.

He has long since passed the point when he could retire without ever wanting for anything. He does not want to spoil his children, but he comes close to it. His wife gets whatever she wants. He is generous to a fault with his family, but he is conservative with himself. He now is able to live a life of luxury, owns some expensive toys, and travels first class, but he seldom spoils himself.

The memory of hard times and empty stomachs sticks to him like some stain. His money has not come easy and he will remind you of it. Once he stuck out hands, scarred from having been scalded by hot engines and cut and twisted while working in the guts of cars.

"Looky here," he said. "I got these scars from working on engines. I got them the hard way, when there wasn't money for mechanics."

A. J. Foyt (*Photo by John W. Posey*)

A young A. J. Foyt in his first year at the Indianapolis Motor Speedway sits in Dean Van Lines golf cart with Al Dean, who was to become his sponsor, and talks to Clint Brawner, who was to become his mechanic. (*Indianapolis Motor Speedway photo*)

Fifteen-car first-lap pileup in Foyt's first Indy 500 race in 1958 in which Pat O'Connor was killed in car number 4, the nose of which is shown at extreme left of picture, pointed sideways. His skid marks can be seen on track. (*Indianapolis Motor Speedway photo*)

Tony Bettenhausen (*Photo by John W. Posey*)

Jimmy Bryan signing autographs (*Photo by John W. Posey*)

Rodger Ward (*Photo by John W. Posey*)   Eddie Sachs (*Photo by John W. Posey*)

Dan Gurney (*Photo by John W. Posey*)   Parnelli Jones (*Photo by David G. Knox*)

Foyt in number 1 Bowes Seal Fast Special trails Eddie Sachs in number 12 Dean Van Lines Special during Indy 500. (*Indianapolis Motor Speedway photo*)

Foyt speeds to victory after refueling in 1961 at Indianapolis. (*Photo by Bob Tronolone*)

Foyt surrounded by his family after victory. Left to right: sister Marlene, wife Lucy, father Tony, Foyt, and mother Evelyn. (*Photo by John W. Posey*)

A. J. Foyt in number 35 Scarab moves outside of Dan Gurney in number 21 Cobra in Daytona Continental Sports Car Classic. (*Photo by Flip Schulke, "Black Star"*)

A. J. Foyt, a sweaty, soiled, weary winner in the 1961 Hoosier 100 (*Photo by John W. Posey*)

The embattled mechanic and his driver—George Bignotti and A. J. Foyt—in a calm moment during USAC 100-miler at Sacramento, California, in 1964 (*Photo by Bob Tronolone*)

A concerned Foyt studies car he hopes will outlast new turbocars in 1967 Indianapolis 500. (*Photo by Bob Tronolone*)

A hot July afternoon calls for a cup of cold water and a canful poured all over Foyt during pit stop en route to victory in 1964 Firecracker 400 in Daytona, Florida. (*NASCAR photo*)

This is the skid that triggered a blazing seven-car pileup that took two lives in the 1964 Indy 500. Dave MacDonald, from El Monte, California, slides sideways (foreground). Eddie Sachs, a veteran Detroit driver (not shown), crashed into MacDonald and was burned to death. MacDonald died in a hospital two hours later. (*Photo by Wide World*)

This dramatic picture shows racers weaving through the flaming wreckage of the seven-car pileup that occurred during the second lap of the race. (*Photo by Wide World*)

Foyt flashes by Parnelli Jones (in bottom car) en route to his triumph in
the 1964 Indy 500. (*Photo by J. M. Stitt*)

Foyt, the 1964 Indy 500 winner, and his wife, Lucy, respond to the
photographers' pleas for smiles as Foyt holds an Indianapolis *News* in his
lap (printed within minutes at the track) telling not only of his triumph
but of the deaths of Eddie Sachs and Dave MacDonald in the race.
(*Indianapolis Motor Speedway photo*)

3

The Indianapolis 500 is a human comedy, a drama of danger, a circus of speed.

The Indianapolis Motor Speedway was built in 1909, less than twenty-five years after the automobile as we know it was first developed and not long after men began to race cars. The first driver was killed there before the first 500 was staged in 1911. The original dirt track proved so rutty and dangerous that it was replaced with a surface built with bricks.

In the 1960s "The Brickyards" was paved over with concrete. But it had very slight banking in the beginning which has never been increased so as to make meaningful the improvements in men and machines as their speeds have increased over the years.

The course was constructed for cars that raced at close to 90 miles per hour while today they travel more than twice as fast. Yet it is no more dangerous now than it was then. The first cars were flimsy and clumsy and easily overturned. The drivers had little protection. They go faster today, but the cars are sturdier and more agile and more stable, and safety features have been built into them and safety equipment has been provided for the drivers. The danger remains, of course. The two drivers who died at Indianapolis in 1973 were the 35th and 36th to lose their lives there.

In the early years European cars and drivers dominated the event. But after World War I Americans made this classic contest their own, except for a brief period in the 1960s when European interest reawakened for a while. Barney Oldfield may be the most memorable name from the early years, but he never won the race. Many of our greatest drivers tried many times and failed at Indy, including Ted Horn, Rex Mays, and Tony Bettenhausen.

The points from winning the 500 propelled many men to the national title, but many national champions never won here. It has been an unforgiving place that has frustrated many fine racing men. Ralph DePalma was the greatest of the early winners, but his cars broke down within reach of winning several 500s and he triumphed only once. Years later Parnelli Jones came close to winning several times but actually succeeded only once. Mario Andretti broke down many times and also won only one. Some of the sport's most generous sponsors, such as Al Dean and Lindsey Hopkins, have poured millions of dollars into this race without ever gaining a victory. Seventy or 80 cars are entered annually and only 33 even get to start it.

Lou Meyer became the first three-time winner of the event in 1936. Wilbur Shaw became the second three-time winner in 1940 and later was appointed president of the track, popularizing the ceremonial command, "Gentlemen, start your engines."

Mauri Rose finished first for the third time in 1948, but his first victory had come as a relief driver for the starter, so he cannot truly claim this "triple crown." Bill Vukovich led near the finish four straight years in the 1950s, but he crashed the first and fourth years and was killed the fourth year. Fourteen of the winners later died racing, two of them at Indy. It was not until Foyt won his third 500 in 1967 that the race really had its third three-time winner.

Howdy Wilcox broke through the barrier of 100 miles per hour in qualifying in 1919. Jimmy Snyder sped past the 125 mph mark in 1937. Parnelli Jones burst the 150 mph barrier in 1963. Jimmy Clark sped past 160 two years later, but A. J. Foyt surpased him that same day to capture the pole position. Four years later Foyt won the pole position as the fastest qualifier on the first day of time trials for the second time. Rex Mays captured the pole four times, but never won the race.

Speed alone will not win it. But the cars must keep up with the competition, which was closing in on 200 mph in the early 1970s. This awed the drivers themselves.

Foyt complained, "The track wasn't built for such speeds. No track has been. And humans can't control the cars properly at such speeds."

Some drivers are easier with this life than others are. Some can sleep through the nights before big races and some cannot. A few hold their wives' hands all night and worry away the hours. Some bed the broads who pursue them, partying away the time they should be resting. Others get drunk or pop pills. Most, however, do not. In the mornings most of them can smile and swap small talk, but others shake and slip away to hide in the shadows. A handful seek refuge in their garages or go off somewhere to throw up.

Sooner or later they have to go out onto that track and stand by their metal monsters during those tense final moments. Some go gently into their cockpits and concentrate coolly on the task confronting them, while for others it is as though they have been laid out in their coffins, and they pray. Some want to win, others want only not to lose, while a few think only of surviving.

No one forces them to become race drivers. Parnelli Jones once said, "It's something you do because no one else could or would do."

A. J. Foyt said, "Everyone dreams of doing something different. For us, this is it."

Rodger Ward said, "It's a sort of sickness. Like a narcotic, it hooks you."

Tony Bettenhausen said, "Some guys are dead without knowing it. They don't appreciate life. Risking it makes us feel alive. I've never felt afraid in a race car."

Bettenhausen died in a race car. Now his sons, Gary, Merle, and Tony, Jr., race. Merle lost an arm racing but went on with it.

Bill Vukovich died racing. Now his son, Bill, Jr., races.

Jerry Unser died racing. Now his brothers, Bobby and Al, race. Bobby says, "Racing was what my brother wanted to do. It's what we want to do. He wouldn't have wanted his dying to have caused us to give it up."

Their mother says, "It's been this family's life. We wish it could be safe, but we know it isn't. We love it for what it is."

When you see the sons and brothers of men killed in racing go on in racing, you know it is something to them that it cannot be to its critics, who condemn it. The critics are trying to live other people's lives for them, sparing them risks the drivers are willing to run. Critics blast as bloodthirsty the fans who live with it but do not die from it, whose risks are not real, whose dangers are only dreams. But few of the fans wish to see men die. They want to see drivers risk death but defeat it. They are a part of it, too. Without them, there would not be racing.

The first Indy 500 drew 80,000 fans. Now, more than sixty years later, the renewals draw more than 300,000 fans. Closed during World War II, the Speedway drifted into disrepair and the race was threatened. Tony Hulman purchased the place for $750,000, resumed the race in 1946, and has since presided over enormous improvements year by year.

During the month of May half a million people pay to see the practices, the time trials, and the race itself. The race day crowd is incredible. It pours into the vast arena to make of it a city within a city larger than most cities in this country. The elite chew fried chicken and sip champagne in penthouse pews. Lesser mortals laze on blankets in the infield, which may be muddy from rains, drinking beer, and often making love unashamedly. For some, this is a better show than the one on the track. Many never see a minute of the race. The event is a happening. Just being there is enough for them.

The fans pay from a few dollars to fifty dollars for a ticket. Hulman never reveals exact figures, but with radio receipts and delayed television take the gross probably exceeds $5 million. The first 500 paid out $27,500 in prizes with the winner getting $14,000. Hulman's first 500 in 1946 paid $115,000 with the winner getting $42,000. By 1970 he celebrated his silver anniversary as proprietor by presenting the field with more than a million dollars and the winner with more than a quarter-million.

The race is a carnival of chaos. It has spawned imitations. There now are similar races on newer, faster tracks with finer facilities for racing and viewing the race. From most seats at Indianapolis you can see only a small part of the track. And here, as at most tracks, scorekeeping is so antiquated it is impossible to keep up with the standings. But racing has a hold on the public and the competitors. And you cannot create the history and tradition, which by now are built into the Indianapolis 500 and sets it apart from its rivals. This is the classic contest and it is incomparable. The men who enter it compete in many other races, but this is the one they truly anticipate. They plan and work and wait the year around for May at Indy.

There is no way the history of an American racing driver such as A. J. Foyt can be detailed without dwelling on the Indianapolis 500, for he inherited its history, he came to write much of it, and he became a part of its traditions; he is a part of the track and it is a part of him, and his race has been run harder here than anywhere else.

For all the other races he has run and won, it is at Indianapolis in the 500 that he attained his true immortality. It is here he became an American hero. It is through this cruel contest that he was truly tested by Jimmy Bryan, Tony Bettenhausen, Rodger Ward, Jim Rathmann, Parnelli Jones, Eddie Sachs, Jim Clark, Dan Gurney, Mario Andretti, Mark Donohue, Al and Bobby Unser, and all the other daring rivals who attempted to block him from fulfilling his ambitions.

Jimmy Bryan once said, "If you have never won anything else all the rest of your life, if you have won Indy, you always are someone." Bryan was a burly, fun-loving, cigar-smoking cowboy from Phoenix. He was a physical driver who aggressively wrestled his cars around a track and was especially hard to beat on dirt. The first two years after Foyt joined the USAC circuit, Bryan was its champion. When

Bryan vacated his Indianapolis car for a better car, Foyt got Bryan's old car for his first Indianapolis ride. Foyt's first 500 that year was won by Bryan, who was only one of several standout drivers who were running when Foyt arrived on the scene and whose careers became intertwined with his.

Tony Bettenhausen was born and reared on a farm in Illinois. After his father died, the farm was sold to provide for the family. Years later Tony bought back the farm so he could raise his own family where he had been raised. He loved the farming life and often talked of retiring to it, but he loved racing, too, and could not bring himself to quit it. He was a big, genial outgoing guy who was an enthusiastic spokesman for his sport.

He once said, "I think our maker cuts everyone out for something different. It so happens some of us want to be race drivers."

He was a race driver more than twenty years and took the national driving title in 1951 and again in 1958. But the one he wanted to win most was the Indianapolis 500. He once said, "Maybe if I win it I'll quit."

Rodger Ward came from Kansas, settled in Southern California, started in racing there, and became an even more articulate spokesman for his sport. As a boy he wanted to grow up to be an airplane pilot or a race driver. He learned to fly fighter planes during World War II. After the war he learned to race cars. He was skilled but unwilling to sacrifice for success.

A handsome man with curly hair, a swift smile, and an appealing personality, he loved the ladies, liked high living and drove with the daring of a man who could care less about tomorrow. He went through several marriages, spent most of the money he made, and had to survive countless crashes. Wearying of wasting himself, he got serious about his profession after he got a good ride with A. J. Watson.

"I had to learn some hard lessons before I could take from the sport what it had to give," Ward said. "You can't run risks, make mistakes, and survive forever. I learned that you have to finish to finish first. I know now that patience pays off. I know the only lap you really want to lead is the last one."

Jim Rathmann came to the racing circuit from California with his brother Dick. Dick was the older of the two, but Jim became the better driver. Jim got to the Indianapolis track first—in 1949. Dick got there a year later, driving the first creation of A. J. Watson, put together in a Glendale, California garage. Called "The Pots and Pans Special" and financed by friends, it did well enough to call attention to Watson.

Dick never reached the top in racing, but Watson did and so did Jim. Soft-spoken and shy, Jim disliked the spotlight, but he was a steady, smooth racer. By the middle 1950s he had driven the 500 five times and finished second once.

He said, "Sooner or later, I will win it. If I didn't believe that, I wouldn't drive."

A. J. Foyt arrived at Indianapolis wanting to race there and everywhere else. His first race in USAC competition took place across the street from the Indianapolis track, on the old West Sixteenth Street Speedway, in a midget car on the quarter-mile dirt oval. Here, on the day and night before the big race, races were held for fans who wanted to view some competitive event while waiting for the big one.

On May 29, 1956, afternoon, evening, and late-night programs were scheduled. Foyt failed to qualify fast enough to make the feature field in the afternoon. He failed to qualify for the evening feature. But he got his car going well enough to qualify sixth fastest for the late-night show. He placed fourth in a heat race, finished 13th in the main event, and won $68.

Foyt stayed around to watch the 500. He wanted to see it before he raced it. In the 1955 race an axle had snapped on Ward's car, sending it out of control and triggering the accident that cost the defending champion, Bill Vukovich, his life. In the wake of public criticism, the American Automobile Association had given up as the governing body of the championship circuit and the United States Auto Club had been formed to take over. The 500 in 1956 was the first over which USAC presided. Pat Flaherty had raised the qualifying standard above 145 miles per hour and went on to win the race by 30 seconds over Sam Hanks.

Foyt has recalled, "There's a lot of people honestly believe I've always had it made. That really bugs me. Those people weren't sitting down there in the first-turn bleachers with me the first time I came to Indianapolis. Those people don't know this place scared the devil out of me that day. Somebody blew a tire right in front of where I was sitting and I thought sure a bomb had plopped right in my lap. And I just knew the driver would be killed. But he wasn't. I eventually lost my fear of this place, but not my respect for it."

Paul Russo was in the ninth lap when a tire blew on his car and he was sent into the wall, striking it with enormous impact. The sound of the crash and of rending metal is remembered as especially loud and dreadful. By some miracle Russo was able to walk away from it. Ten of the 33 starters in this race later were killed racing.

One of them, Keith Andrews, was killed in practice for the 1957 race. Young Foyt had managed the money to return for another look at the event. This one was safe, with only a couple of minor mishaps. Pat O'Connor had taken the pole position but his car struggled in the race itself, which was won by Sam Hanks. Jim Rathmann pulled in second for the second time, about 20 seconds back, and Jimmy Bryan took third place. Hanks announced his retirement in Victory Lane immediately after his triumph.

When Hanks stepped out of the Belond Special, built by George Salih, a revolutionary racer with the lowest profile to appear at the track, Bryan asked for and received the ride in the car, departing the Al Dean team and its mechanical boss, Clint Brawner. This in turn created a vacancy that was filled by Foyt.

Foyt had become busy among the best in 1957. He had driven 35 midget races, five sprint races, and five championship races on USAC circuits that year. He scored his first victory in a USAC race in a midget car at Kansas City in May. He made his first championship car start at the Illinois State Fairgrounds in Springfield in August. Rodger Ward won the 100-mile race on the one-mile dirt track and Foyt finished ninth. He was twenty-two years old and impressed observers with his potential on the trail the last half of the season, although he did not have a competitive car and did not finish among the leaders in any of his starts.

A. J. had not wanted to tackle Indy until he had a competitive car with which he could challenge the leaders, show himself off to advantage, and project himself into future opportunities. One day that summer, while strolling around the garage area at Indianapolis, where most top teams headquartered, he stepped into Bryan's car just to try it on for size. He fit it just fine. He was almost as big as Bryan, and sitting there he reminded Brawner of his fellow southwesterner.

Brawner watch A. J. drive the high banks of the sprint circuit that summer and was impressed by him. When Bryan vacated the Dean car at season's end, Foyt asked for the ride. Disappointed by the departure of the veteran Bryan, Brawner decided to break in the rookie, who might be more loyal. He recommended Foyt to Dean, and the latter, who let Brawner decide these things, approved. It was not a new car but it was a good car and had carried Bryan to the national title in 1957. Bryan had wanted a faster car for the 500, which is why he went over to the winner when Hanks retired from it. However, the car Bryan left was a good one for a rookie to get.

Rookies at Indianapolis are required to pass a driver's test, running laps at speed alone on the track under the observation of officials and veterans. After rainy weather wiped out many of the early practice days, Foyt passed his test without problems on the ninth day of the month.

He later observed, "It's a very tricky track. Every turn is different. The wind blows different through the stands in different places, making conditions different all over. You have to follow the groove laid down by the veterans before you can find your own way. You have to get used to running at this sort of speed. You have to go hard, but you can't go too hard or it starts to get away from you. Once you reach a certain speed, more miles per hour come very hard. You try one way and you actually lose speed. You try another way and you lose. You have to keep trying until you find the right ways. It take a lot of practice and the only place you can practice for this place is right here."

Hardboiled Brawner said, "This guy can go. It may take a little time. You don't become a Bryan overnight. But Foyt can become one of the best."

The more optimistic Dean said, "Bryan's boots are big ones to fill, but Foyt may bring me my first 500 victory one of these years soon. This kid can cut it. I really believe he can run with the veterans right off."

On opening day of the time trials Dick Rathmann was the fastest qualifier, capturing the pole position at a new record speed of just under 146 mph. Ed Elisian was second fastest, and Jimmy Reece completed the front row. Foyt qualified 12th fastest at a bit above 143 mph, fitting into the outside starting spot in the fourth row, right behind Bryan. Race day found Foyt feeling fine, although at the age of twenty-three he was the youngest driver in the field. He later admitted his guts were twisting some:

"I wasn't exactly scared. I was nervous. It was a big thing, something I'd been looking ahead to and longing for for a long time and it put your nerves on edge with all the waiting and then being there ready to go and wondering if you'd ever go and wondering what would happen when you did go. Damn it, it's a worry waiting and it's something you've got to get used to."

The bands played and the singers sang the traditional, ceremonial numbers, "On the Banks of the Wabash," "Back Home Again in Indiana," and "The Star-Spangled Banner." A bugler blew taps in memory of men killed in wars and in racing. Fake bombs exploded in the air. Hundreds of balloons were released to float colorfully into the blue skies. The drivers got into their cars and were strapped into their cockpits. Helmeted, a red bandanna around his mouth.

Foyt stared straight ahead, his gloved hands on the steering wheel. Tony Hulman was introduced over the loudspeaker and the murmuring crowd hushed.

"Gentlemen . . . start your en-gines!" he said.

The mechanics shoved their automatic starters into the noses of the cars and the engines roared loudly alive. The enormous mass of humanity packing the place came to its feet hollering and the cars were pushed away and began to glide around the oval, drifting into their positions during the warmup laps.

There is nothing in sports quite like the start of an Indianapolis 500, and it grips some spectators and some drivers and never lets go of them. There is the rising sound of the crowd and the sudden hushes as the ceremonial music spins sentimentally into the spring air. Usually the sun is hot at Indy on Memorial Day. The fans, who have waited a long time, are sweating before the start and will only get hotter as the dizzying day spins on. The drivers may roast in their cramped cockpits, the heat of their engines and the asphalt track assaulting their senses. You watch them before they leave and you cannot help wondering if all will return.

Then there is the last of those sudden hushes and that awesome order to start and finally the great rush of sound as those mighty engines fire up. And the hubbub among the fans swells in volume as the cars, their bright colors sparkling in the sun, slowly begin to circle the track, picking up speed.

At last they enter the homestretch at the finish of the final warmup lap. Then the pace car pulls off the track, the starter waves a green flag, and the 33 racers accelerate into a tight tangle of traffic with a dreadful din of engine sound and the sharp stench of spent fuel and tires, speeding into the first turn and through it with everyone in the stands seemingly screaming at once.

It is always a dangerous time—that first turn of the first lap, when the cars are crowded close together and speeding up at once. This time Rathmann and Elisian began racing before the race actually started. They caused confusion and the field was out of shape as it sped toward the starting line, but the starter sent them on their way anyway. Rathmann accelerated ahead of Elisian and held him off through the second and third turns, but Elisian pulled abreast as they charged toward the third turn. They entered the turn side by side, neither one wishing to give way.

Rathmann finally slowed a little, dropping outside of Elisian. Elisian charged into the corner at top speed. He began his turn before he started to slow. His tires lost traction and his car skidded sideways, taking Rathmann's car with it into the wall.

Reece, running right behind them, braked sharply and was rammed from behind by Bob Veith's car, which was sent into the path of Pat O'Connor's car. O'Connor's car climbed Veith's, sailed through the air, and crashed fifty feet away. Following cars angled in all directions in an effort to avoid the careening, crashing racers.

Foyt spun his car completely around, avoiding cars in front of him but triggering a series of crashes by cars braking behind him. Paul Goldsmith braked his car and Jerry Unser's car climbed over it and cleared an outer wall, landing on its wheels outside the track.

Before the melee ended, 15 cars had been involved in the banging, screeching madness. When the dust settled, seven cars had been so badly wrecked that they had to be withdrawn from the race and eight more required repairs before they could continue. Almost miraculously, Unser survived, but O'Connor was dead. That horrifying fracas on the first lap of his first 500 remains etched on Foyt's memory.

He later admitted, "That really shook me up. If I'd started closer to the front, I'd have been right in the middle of it."

He wasn't far from it as it was, but by the time he got to it, he had time to spin out of it. His car was undamaged and he was able to resume.

The survivors covered 50 slow miles under the yellow caution flag while the track was cleared of debris, and then the race resumed at speed. Foyt couldn't keep up. He ran hard but well back until the 148th lap—130 miles from the finish—when he hit an oil slick, spun around, and slid 1,000 feet backward before ramming the wall in the first turn and coming to a stop. He emerged by himself, unhurt, waving that he was all right to the crowd in the corner where he had once watched the race as a spectator.

The engine in Rodger Ward's car and the steering in Johnny Thomson's car failed. Bryan, driving the car with which Hanks had finished first the year before, pulled away from George Amick, Johnny Boyd, Tony Bettenhausen, and Jim Rathmann in the late stages to win it for the first time. Amick was voted "rookie of the year." He was killed in a crash at Daytona the following year. Rookie Foyt finished in 16th place, 17 drivers having gone out before he did. He collected $2,919 for the Dean team. The winner, Bryan, won $111,327 for his team.

"My crash scared me some, but when I walked away from it I felt better about it. Any time you can walk away from one it wasn't a bad one and you can laugh about it later," Foyt stated afterward. "But that was some experience—that race, that crash right off, then my slide. I could see right off what it was. It sure as hell wasn't easy. It gets a hold of you and won't let go. It's more people and more money than a man could dream of, the fastest cars and the best drivers anywhere, dangerous as it could be and so damned nervy and exciting it sort of sends a shiver through you. Nothing can compare to it. You race wherever you can, whenever you can, but May at Indianapolis is what matters most."

They ran a 500-mile race at Monza in Italy that year, but Dean had hired the great international star, Juan Manual Fangio of Argentina, to drive for him. Sponsors would not pay expenses for Foyt to accompany the team, but Foyt wanted to go and Brawner talked Dean into picking up the tab for A. J., so the youngster went along.

The race was staged in three heats. A cracked piston was discovered in the Dean car shortly before the first heat and it missed the first and second heats before it was repaired. Then it quit in the second lap of the third heat with fuel pump failure. Meanwhile, backers of the Sclavi and Amos car were dissatisfied with the performance of Maurice Trintignant of France in finishing ninth in the first heat and offered Foyt the ride in the second heat.

He accepted, gave the car a hard ride, ran with the leaders for a while, and finished sixth. He was rewarded with the ride in the final heat and ran up high for a while again before breaking down and settling for seventh. The car placed sixth in the overall standings.

Jim Rathmann won by sweeping all three heats. His average was an astonishing 166 miles per hour, but this was a fast, steeply banked track. Bryan, who had won this event in the Dean car the year before, finished second by placing second in two heats and third in the other in his new car. This was the second and last time this race was run, but it served to direct considerable attention to the young Foyt, who had run well with some of the world's best.

Still, it turned out to be a difficult year for him. He placed second and third in a number of events but did not collect top honors in any races of consequence. Bettenhausen finished second or third enough times to take the national title. Bryan had finished first in the big race, but he did not drive many races after that and said he was retiring. However, when it came to making the actual decision, he could not bring himself to do it.

In 1959 the practice runs at Indianapolis turned out tragically. This was the first year roll-bars and fireproof uniforms were made mandatory. But they did not save the lives of Bob Cortner and Jerry Unser, who were killed in crashes. Tony Bettenhausen cracked up, too, blasting through a wooden barrier and flipping upside down, but he escaped with a bloody nose. His car wasn't repaired in time and Bryan's car had engine trouble, so both missed qualifying on the first day of time trials. They got into the race later, far back. Then on race day the engine in Bryan's car wouldn't turn over when the field started. When the car did start and Bryan joined the field, the engine conked out after only one lap.

Foyt also had trouble in practice. His engine blew up. Dean bought him a new one, but A. J. had to wait until the second Saturday of qualifying, the third of the four weekend days set aside for trials, to make the field. He fell short of 143 mph and settled for a spot in the middle of the seventh row. Johnny Thomson set new qualifying records with one lap above 146 mph and a four-lap average just below it. Eddie Sachs and Jim Rathmann filled the front row. Dick Rathmann, Bobby Grim, and Rodger Ward went into the second row.

In the first stages of the race Foyt moved up fast. On one early lap he passed Paul Goldsmith in one corner, then Don Branson in the next stretch. On another lap, he couldn't get by Jimmy Daywalt on the inside, so he ranged up high and roared past him on the outside. He was driving with a lot of daring, moving his powerful car through thick traffic at a pace well above 140 miles per hour. Meanwhile, up front, Ward, Thomson, and Jim Rathmann were dueling for the lead.

Within ten laps Foyt had improved six places, and in the next ten laps he cut down Jack Turner and Bob Veith to barrel into eighth place. It got tougher after that. He had fast cars in front of him. But before the midway mark in the race was reached, he gunned his car past Bettenhausen and Grim to gain sixth place. Then, just past the midway mark, he cut down Bill Cheesbourg to edge into fifth.

Still, it is a long, tricky race. On the 130th lap Duane Carter tried to slip by Foyt and hit him from behind, denting in the rear end of Foyt's car. It wasn't a heavy hit, but it was sufficient to propel Foyt out of shape for a split second. His tires shrieked and his car reeled toward the wall and he later admitted, "It was a bit hairy there for a second. I was all squirrelly."

But he wrestled the wheel and regained control of his car and set out again. The incident seemed to sap something from him or his car, however. When he came in for his last pit stop, he overshot his space a little and, while he stopped just in time, it looked as though he was starting to struggle.

Former winner Pat Flaherty had flashed into the duel for the lead, but he crashed with a little less than 100 miles to go. Johnny Thomson's car slowed and he fell off the pace. That left the issue between Ward and Rathmann, who were running wheel-to-wheel in a bitter battle. Meanwhile, Foyt was falling back. In the late stages Johnny Boyd got by him. Then Eddie Johnson. With five miles left Paul Russo passed him. By that time Ward had pulled away from Rathmann.

At the finish Ward took top honors with Rathman second and Thomson third. Foyt was the fastest and closest tenth-place finisher in history, but tenth still was far from first and not nearly close enough to suit him. Nor did it suit Brawner, who was disappointed when Foyt was passed by those other cars in the late stages. Brawner felt the driver should have done better, while Foyt felt Brawner's car should have done better. It was at this point that their relationship began to come apart.

Brawner admits, "Foyt was not then as temperamental as he became later. He didn't give me any trouble. It's just that these guys always blame the cars and not themselves when they don't do well. You could see he was going to do well. It was just a question of how well. He was just a young guy who wanted to go fast and he wasn't happy when he didn't go fast enough."

Foyt ran the full 500 miles for the first time in a little more than three hours and 45 minutes and finished a little more than four minutes after Ward. Ward won in a car built and prepared by Watson. Ward was in his late thirties and his ninth 500 before he won one, but Foyt, in his middle twenties, already felt frustrated after competing in two 500s. He had watched Bryan win the big one after leaving a Brawner car for a better one, and now A. J. wanted to follow this lead.

Bitterness simmered between Brawner and Foyt through the long summer as Foyt failed to win a race on the title trail, though he came close a couple of times.

"Close isn't enough," he said at the time. "You win or you lose. I can win, but I don't think the car can."

Brawner bristled, "My cars have won plenty."

Sachs smiled and said, "A. J. is an impatient son of a bitch. He won't wait for anyone or anything."

A. J. began to ask around about available rides with top teams. When he got a good offer from the Bowes Seal Fast team, he grabbed it. Bob Bowes, the sponsor, was willing to spend the money for a top operation, and his chief mechanic, George Bignotti, a former driver from San Francisco, was regarded as a gifted guy who might make it big.

Foyt said goodby to Brawner and went over to Bignotti for the 1960 season. Sachs grabbed the ride on the Dean team. A disappointed Dean said, "I'm getting tired of giving guys breaks and having them get away from me. I hope Sachs will be more loyal than Foyt or Bryan were."

Brawner says, "I was surprised when Foyt left. It takes awhile to get together and we were just getting things right. But he was in a hurry."

"You could see Foyt was a comer," Bignotti added. "We had a pretty good operation and pretty good equipment, but we didn't have anyone as fast as Foyt was going to be."

Foyt shrugged and said, "You have to go where the dough is going to be."

Foyt's jump did not pay off at first. In this third qualifying effort at Indianapolis in 1960, his new Bignotti car was so slow in the first trial effort that he was called in. He fidgeted around in frustration while Bignotti worked on it, finally late in the day accepted a slow speed, and settled for 16th starting position just to get into the race. Bettenhausen, Bryan, and Thomson also encountered trouble. But Sachs, in a new car built by Brawner from Watson plans, won the pole position with a run above 146 mph, three miles an hour faster than Foyt. Jim Rathmann and Ward were next fastest. On the fourth and final day of trials Jim Hurtubise, a rookie, drove fastest of all with a record run within a few ticks on the stop watch of the magic 150 figure.

In the race Jim Rathmann, at the wheel of a car sold by Watson, whipped Ward, driving the Watson team car, in an electrifying duel. Rathmann pushed his car hard all the way, but Ward would have won if he had not slowed slightly in the final miles when a tire started to go bad.

Rathmann, who had waited ten years for the coveted triumph at Indy, said, "He had won, and I had not. Maybe I wanted this one more."

Ward shrugged and said, "Sometimes discretion is the better part of valor."

Johnny Thomson fell back in the late stages and finished fifth. Foyt, Sachs, Bettenhausen, and Bryan all broke down. Foyt's car faltered from the first. He struggled around, steaming, as cars charged past him. Finally his clutch caved in at 235 miles and he was through for the day. He finished 25th.

The following month, on his beloved dirt at Langhorne, Pennsylvania, Bryan was cut off in traffic, turned too sharply, and caught his wheel sideways in a rut. His car bucked into the air, nosed up high, then came down heavily, front end first. In the cockpit Bryan's harness snapped and he was flung back and forth and rag-dolled to death. Three months later Thomson crashed and was killed in a sprinter on the dirt at Altoona, Pennsylvania.

Although he had remained the youngest driver in the field in what had been his third 500, Foyt had been so frustrated by his car's failure that he had threatened to quit. He felt Bignotti's car had done no more for him than Brawner's had.

After the race he stormed around his motel room and said to his wife, Lucy, "Damn, that's disgusting. I've been trying so long and so hard to win and what have I got to show for it all?" He growled all evening. He told Lucy, "This is it. I've had it. I'm through."

She knew better. She knew he was young and impatient and reasoned he only needed encouragement. She later said she would have been just as pleased if he had quit, but she sensed he would never have been happy if he had. She said she had no way of knowing how good he would get to be, but she realized he had to find out. Showing wisdom beyond her own years, she pleaded with him not to give it up too soon.

A. J. Foyt had married the former Lucy Zarr, his schooldays sweetheart, a beautiful blonde teen-ager with a puddin' soft Texas voice, in 1955. They had been introduced by mutual high school friends. She was four years younger than he. Her stepfather, Elliott Flowers, was a lawyer in Houston. She and her mother had been provided a comfortable existence. The life of a race driver's wife loomed rough by comparison. But A. J. was a handsome, strong young man with a dynamic personality, and she fell in love with him, as he did with her, and they married.

She played a larger role in his career in its early stages than later on. Although he was always confident, he was not as sure of himself at first as he was later, and he needed more encouragement. She gave it to him. Sometimes she traveled with him and he often stated that no matter how rugged the road, she never complained. She said later she just did what a wife was supposed to do. She was a sort of old-fashioned girl who was willing to sacrifice her own interests to her husband's.

It is not easy being a race driver's wife, and she proved perfect for the role. Some might say it could not be easy to be married to the temperamental Foyt, but of course he does not treat her as he does others. And he has always remembered she was there when he needed her.

Their first child, a son, Tony, was born in 1956, before A. J. even got to Indianapolis. Their second, a daughter, Terry, was born in 1958, the year he first raced there. Later another son, Jerry, would be born in 1962. After the kids started to come, Lucy could not often travel with A. J., though she usually managed to be with him at the big races. He did not get home to Houston most summers and he did not seem to have time for vacations, but she made a constant effort to be with him whenever she could. Thus she was with him after the 1960 Indy 500 when frustration with his racing career came close to curtailing it prematurely. She suggested he give it another try, in the next race, at Milwaukee.

Later he recalled, "I said I'd try it just to please her. But I also said if I didn't do well, I was gonna pack it in."

He did well, finishing second behind Ward, so he did not pack it in. Bignotti had finally got the car right, and Foyt forced it to its limits. On one lap he whipped past Bryan and Bettenhausen as if they were ordinary racers. Ward's car may have been better. Possibly Ward still was more effective on a smooth surface. But on rough dirt it was another story.

Foyt won his first championship trail event at DuQuoin, Illinois. He garnered the prestigious Hoosier Hundred at the Indiana State Fairground in Indianapolis. He was top man in Sacramento and he won in Phoenix. All were 100-mile races on one-mile dirt ovals.

There now was no doubt the strong, tough Texan could bull a big car around dirt, but there remained doubts about his ability to get the most out of the more delicate cars that required a gentler touch and competed on slick pavement.

However, with four victories in the last six starts on the trail, Foyt picked up enough points to win his first national driving title. It was quite an achievement for one as young as he was.

No race so aptly typifies the Texan at this time in his career as the last event of that first title season. Going into the Phoenix race, Foyt had to fail and Ward had to win for Ward to capture his second straight championship. Adopting conservative tactics, Foyt could have coasted to the title. But he was not cut to a conservative style. Worrying Bignotti and Bowes, risking all, Foyt flew from the first, storming into the lead, stretching out, extending his car, lapping his rivals.

The young Foyt was something to see on dirt. He bulled into the corners a little deeper than his rivals, braked a little later, came off the brakes a little earlier, kept his car in its controlled sideways skid a little longer, accelerated a little harder out of the turns and into the straights. He seemed on the verge of losing control at all times as he charged around the course flat out all the way, accelerating, braking briefly, sliding hard, throwing up rooster-tails of dirt, and accelerating again.

Most drivers made their passes low. Foyt executed many of his

high, scooting daringly above the rubbery groove, where the dirt
was thrown and was loose and slippery. He stormed by Sachs entering one turn, riding so high that his wheels spun and he started to
slide and the fans screamed, thinking he was going to slide right into
their laps, but he held it on the track and, as he laughed later, just
"outbraved" his rival.

When Ward dropped out with engine failure, the title was safely
Foyt's. Still, Foyt flew on, hurling showers of dirt into the Arizona
air, running hard for the sheer thrill of it. He lapped the entire field
a second time, passed under the checkered flag, and didn't brake
until he reached the ceremonial victory circle. Grimy and greasy,
he grinned as a relieved Bignotti bent over him to tell the Texan
he thought he was crazy. Foyt clambered from the cockpit smiling,
ready to receive the cheers of the crowd, the backslaps of his crew,
the congratulations of the officials, and the kisses of the race queens.

"Indianapolis, here I come," he confided to a friend, confident to
the point of cockiness.

4

The winds of change swept over the Indianapolis Speedway in 1961. They blew in dark clouds and stormy times that obscured the spring sun. All was madness that month of May. The big cars were closing in on 150 miles per hour. The track was not designed for such speeds. No more than it was for 200 miles per hour a decade or so later. The track stays pretty much the same. The cars improve in speed and power. But how much can men improve? How much faster can their reflexes become, how much more complete their concentration?

In the beginning of the 1960s, 150 miles per hour seemed madness. "We're all a little crazy," laughed Tony Bettenhausen, who came closest to that magic mark all month, pacing all practices in his Lindsey Hopkins car. Never had a Hopkins car won Indy. Nor had Bettenhausen. He was 44 and this was his 15th year at Indy. "It's the first year I've ever had a car which was running faster than the other cars. This year, I'll get that 150, I'll get the pole and I'll get the checkered flag, too," he vowed.

There was one car at Indy that was different from the competition. The others were all high, heavy, front-engined cars. The exception was a low, light, rear-engined car. It was called a Cooper-Climax. It had a Cooper chassis and a Climax engine, both built overseas. It was styled after the Grand Prix cars that competed primarily in Europe. Driven by an Australian Grand Prix champion named Jack Brabham, it was sponsored by an American millionaire sportsman, Jim Kimberly.

An American Grand Prix driver, Dan Gurney, campaigning to bring the greatest of the European Grand Prix racers into this greatest American classic had succeeded in interesting Brabham and Kimberly in a test entry. The car was painted British racing green. American drivers considered the color green unlucky on a race track. They are a superstitious lot, anyway. They did not like this little green car. They laughed at it. It was nimble but underpowered. It could not keep up with the faster cars.

Veterans Rodger Ward, Eddie Sachs, Don Branson, and Jim and Dick Rathmann, youngsters A. J. Foyt and Jim Hurtubise, and rookie Parnelli Jones were running fast through the final days of practice, but Bettenhausen still was the fastest. On the day before the first day of time trials, Tony was sitting in the pits when a pal, Paul Russo, asked him to test-hop his car. He had been having trouble with the car and couldn't figure out what was wrong. He was a friend who had helped Tony on his farm the previous winter. Tony always wanted to help a friend. It was dangerous to drive a car at speed before practicing in it, but Tony wanted to do it.

He went to his sponsor, Lindsey Hopkins, and asked permission: "I'd like to help Paul if I can."

Reluctantly, Lindsey consented. "If you want to, go ahead. Just be careful."

Tony took the car out. He turned several fast laps in it, trying to sort out its actions. He had slowed down and was heading for the pits when he sped up and angled onto the track again. Apparently, he had decided to try one more lap. The car seemed to sway, then swerved into the mainstretch wall. It vaulted onto a concrete ledge, guillotined five iron posts, and tore down 300 feet of steel wire as it flipped along the barrier before it shuddered to a stop in a tangle of wire.

Bettenhausen once said, "I've driven these go-buggies a lot of years. I never worry about my accidents as long as I can count them." He never counted his 29th.

A ten-cent bolt holding a front support had fallen off. When the car swayed and Tony braked, the car swerved into the wall.

Eddie Sachs said, "I saw Tony heading for the wall. I watched it until it was over. Then I sat down and cried like a baby."

A. J. Foyt said, "It is something I'll never forget. Tony was special, a great driver and a great guy. He helped other guys. Which most won't. You got to go on. But when a guy like Tony goes, it gets harder. I threw my helmet against my garage. And after a while I got it and went back to my car."

A friend called Tony's wife. "There's been an accident," he said.

"Tony?" she asked.

"Yes, Tony."

"All the way?" she asked.

"All the way," she was told.

Twenty-three cars went out to practice after Bettenhausen's fatal accident before the track closed for the day. Workmen labored by floodlights much of the night to repair the fence that had been destroyed. The long black streaks of the accident still stained the wall when the track was opened the next morning as more than 150,000 spectators poured into the place for the first day of qualifying runs.

A first-day record number of 36 cars took time trials. Sachs in his Dean Van Lines car number 12 flew fastest and was the only entrant to top 147 miles per hour for his four laps. Dean and Brawner embraced him when he came in smiling, having captured the pole for the second year in a row.

Old Don Branson and young Jim Hurtubise were next fastest, filling the front row. Of "Hercules" Hurtubise, former 500 winner Mauri Rose said, "Every once in a while a fellow comes along with no worries. He doesn't feel like he's strapped in an electric chair. He's relaxed. He enjoys it. He loves it. It's fun for him. He doesn't know it's supposed to be tough."

Herc smiled and said, "It's not so tough," He and Foyt had become fast friends.

Ward, Jones, and Dick Rathmann placed in the second row. Jones was driving J. C. Agajanian's number 98 car, prepared by Johnnie Pouelson. Aggie had inherited a wonderful way to wealth. He had a pig farm and a garbage collection company. The garbage was used to feed the pigs. The pigs were butchered to make food. It was a complete and perfect cycle. "I'm not embarrassed by it. It's honest," he laughed.

An Armenian American, he had a marvelous mustache and always wore a Western hat to hide his balding head. One of the most colorful characters around racing, he had long embraced the sport and sponsored races and racing. He had won at Indianapolis with Troy Ruttman in 1952. Winning was too much for Troy. He partied himself out of shape and his life went sour. Aggie went on without him. He brought in a rookie, Jones, in 1961. He was the most impressive rookie to break in at Indianapolis in years. Even Foyt had not been as impressive his first years there.

Foyt was seventh fastest at just under 146 miles per hour, taking the inside spot in the third row, in Bignotti's Bowes car, a snow-white creation trimmed in red and blue that proudly bore the number one on its nose by virtue of its driver having finished number one in championship points the preceding season. Former winners Ruttman and defending champion Jim Rathmann fit in farther back.

Brabham brought his undersized rear-engine novelty into the fifth row, which surprised observers. But no one considered it a contender and it was not. It was generating an electricity that would transform the race, but few felt it at the time. It takes time for new developments to take hold on this track.

Twenty-two cars qualified on Saturday, five more on Sunday. Practice resumed on Monday. It was interrupted on Tuesday while many of the drivers attended Bettenhausen's funeral, but afterward it was back to business again as those who were safely in the starting field prepared for the race and the stragglers struggled toward the speed needed to make the fastest 33. On Saturday the field was filled as speedier cars bumped out slower ones. On Sunday, the final day, 20 cars tried but only two made it, bumping out two more. One of those bumped out was Paul Russo, who had gotten a ride in another car after his original ride was wrecked.

On Memorial Day, race day, a bomb burst in the dark sky at 4:00 A.M., the gates were opened, and the cars of fans who had been waiting on line for hours rushed through the gloom in quest of the best infield locations. At 7:30 A.M., as the enormous mob was coming in and beginning to crowd the awesome arena, the race cars were pushed by their crews onto the pit apron. Then the bands began to march around the oval, blaring their strident tunes behind the pretty girls in skimpy costumes.

Foyt, who had gone to bed at midnight in his nearby motel room and had gotten up at 8:00 to eat his usual pre-race steak, arrived at the track and went into his garage to take off his civvies and put on his uniform. This is a very hard time for the drivers. The youngest of them looks old in these last hours before a big race. But then, no driver ever really is young.

The Purdue University band played "On the Banks of the Wabash," which sentimentally moves Hoosiers at Indy for the race. The cars were pushed onto the track into their starting rows with the fans cheering. Almost all the fans were assembled by now. The grandstands were full as far as one could see. The infield area was mobbed. Even the track was crowded in those last minutes; the crews and drivers gathered around their cars.

The cars rested there in the sunshine, sparkling, silent, menacing. All that could be done to them had been done. Foyt stood by his car at attention with the rest as "The Star-Spangled Banner" was played. A bugler blew taps, and "Back Home in Indiana" was sung into a sudden, startling stillness. As it ended, fierce sound erupted. The people cheered, bombs burst, and balloons of many colors were released to drift into the blue spring sky.

It was 9:50 A.M. Foyt tied a red bandanna around his mouth, pulled on his hard helmet and his gloves, then stepped into his big car. He was strapped in. The others were in now, too. Eddie Sachs was in. He closed his eyes, crossed himself, then opened his eyes, looked at the people around him, and smiled.

Foyt's star had crossed the star of Sachs. Their fates were inter-twined. There comes a time at last when the driver is alone in his car, but he is never alone on his team and he is never alone on the track. He is only one part of his team—the most important part—but only one part. If the car has not been put together correctly, he cannot run it right. And he does not run alone but in company with the cars driven by drivers of other teams. In the career of any racer, there are certain other racers who play a paramount part. He beats them while they lose or he loses while they win their key races. They die while he lives or he dies while they live. One falls while the other rises. They are the best of friends or the worst of enemies. There were several such for Foyt, none more meaningful than Eddie Sachs.

Edward Julius Sachs was born in Bethlehem, Pennsylvania. His parents divorced when he was five and he went with his father to live in Greensboro, North Carolina. His father was a traveling man. Long before Eddie was old enough to get a driver's license, his father let him sit on his lap and drive the family car. One summer when Eddie was fourteen, his dad took him on the road. Eddie would sleep in a hotel room all day while his dad worked. Then his dad would sleep in the car all night while Eddie drove on to the next town. His dad wanted Eddie to make good time. If he woke up and saw they were going less than 80, he would ask, "What's the matter?" and Eddie would gun it back to speed and his dad would doze off again.

Eddie went back to Pennsylvania to go to school, but what he found of interest to him there were the dirt races all across the state. Studies could not compare to this excitement. He rented a room in Allentown and took lessons at a school for racing drivers located at an amusement park.

He conned owners into rides in their cars, but he cracked up in his first race and kept on crashing. Owners grew afraid to risk their cars with him. He took what he could get and worked on the side to support himself. He was a happy-go-lucky guy who lived high and blew what money he made. Once his own car was repossessed. Another time he got a couple of bucks ahead and opened a bar, but it went bust.

He did not become serious about racing until he saw his first 500. He was hooked. He went back, hoping to beg a ride, but was without any credentials and was thrown out by guards.

"I'll be back," he shouted at them, embarrassed and defiant. "Remember the name, Eddie Sachs!"

He was back the next year with a pass provided by a sponsor, but when he took his test, he failed and was told to get more experience. He worked day and night that month, in the pits as a flunky by day and in a restaurant as a dishwasher by night just so he could stay close to the race. No indignity could keep him from it.

He got experience, battling his way up through the bushes, beginning to get better. He was no natural, but he was willing to work at it. They used to say of him, "He learned to race before he learned to drive."

He admitted as much. "I was *ab-so-lutely* the worst race driver ever to come to Indianapolis, but I'll win the 500 some day, you can be sure of that."

He returned the next year and flunked his test again. He came back the year after and finally passed, but he qualified only 34th fastest and missed making the race by one position. He finally got into the starting field in 1957 but broke down his first four starts.

He was not discouraged. He became known as The Clown Prince of Racing. He once brought a jazz band to play for the fans at a track. He stood up in his car before the race, grinning, and led the band in a rousing Dixieland number. He once followed the marching band at Indy, strutting and grinning broadly while waving an imaginary baton. He married a beautiful woman named Nance and had a son, Edward Julius Sachs II, but dad remained a boy himself.

He was cocky and colorful. He bragged a lot, but it didn't bother anyone—that was just Eddie. No one ever interviewed Eddie—he interviewed them. Traditionally, winners are interviewed over the loudspeaker after races. When you handed Eddie a mike you risked never having it returned. Once he spoke for an hour. When he looked up, the stands were almost empty, the pits were almost deserted, and almost everyone else had gone home.

He was always available to newsmen. If a writer criticized him, Eddie shrugged it off, ordered extra copies of the newspaper, clipped the story, and sent the writer an autographed photo, thanking him for the publicity. Someone once commented, "If you stood on his scrapbooks, you could touch the stars." That's what Eddie was trying to do—reach the stars.

Eddie's answer? "They laugh at me, but that's all right. I'm having more fun than anyone. I'm selling Eddie Sachs, and I sell auto racing while I'm at it."

Almost all drivers love racing or they would not be in this bitter business, but Eddie's love for it seemed somehow purer than that of his pals. He wanted it to be better and said so. He always had a lot to say. He did not always say the right things. He was suspended from racing one year because of a speech he made that was critical of racing officials. His friends disowned him and he was left alone to face the storm. Asked to prepare an apology, he produced a five-page statement taking back what he had said.

Reinstated, he said sadly, "I'm ashamed I didn't stick to my statements. I wasn't a man. But I had to get back into racing."

Racing hospitalized him fifteen times in twenty years, once for six months, another time for five months. He suffered broken arms, legs, and ribs, and five concussions and needed plastic surgery on his face and skin grafts on his body. Once he ripped through a fence and fell from his ruined racer. Standing over him, someone said, "Looks like he's a goner, doc." Eddie jumped up, hollering, "I'm okay, I'm okay."

Another time he was hospitalized after a flip. In bed, he pushed himself up painfully on bruised arms, cracked a grin on his scorched face, and said about soaring through the air in a car, "I'll tell you, you get a helluva view of the race from up there."

Of death in racing, he said, "You don't have to be afraid of it, but you have to be sorry for it. In the long run, death is the odds-on favorite. I don't want to die, but I don't want to stop racing. Racing is life. I've said I'll quit when I win Indianapolis. Sometimes I think I don't want to win Indy because I don't want to quit. Quitting will be like dying. But I do want to win Indy. I want it more than anything in life."

Eddie then added, "I think of Indianapolis every day of the year, every hour of the day, and when I sleep, too. I dream of the 500. Winning it would be a dream come true. Everything I ever wanted in my life, I found inside the walls of the Indianapolis Motor Speedway. I love it all, from the first to the last day in May. On the morning of the race, if you told me my house had burned down, I'd say, 'So what?' The moment that race starts is always the greatest moment of my life, and the day I win that race it will be as if my life has ended. There is nothing more I could want out of life."

In 1961 he got up a 4 A.M. on the first day of May so he could be the first man on the track when practice started hours later. He waited in his car but when it was time his car would not start and another driver, Shorty Templeman, drove on past him, laughing at him. They all laughed at him, but they couldn't hate him. Eddie laughed, too. He didn't hate anyone. He got his car going and glided onto the track. And on the first day of time trials he got going faster than anyone else and captured the first starting position for the second straight year.

And on race day he was ready. Oh, he was late getting to the track. But he was always late. Once they were frantically searching for a substitute driver for him when he rushed up while the national anthem was being played and jumped into the cockpit. Maybe he didn't want too much time to think about what lay ahead of him.

After the 1961 race he said, "You never want to think about it too much. It just screws you up. You just want to do it. But this year as I sat there just before the start I was thinking I was going to win. I had said other years I would win, but this was the first year I really felt I would. You can't imagine how much I wanted it."

They all wanted it. Foyt wanted it. But if anyone wanted it more than Foyt, it was Sachs. You never know for sure, but Foyt was sure he would win some year if not that year. Sachs thought he would, but he was never sure. He was good, but he wasn't as good as Foyt, he wasn't as good as the best of them. He was good enough to win, but that didn't mean he would win. There are those who are good enough to win but never win. Maybe there is one year they can win and it gets away from them.

Sachs didn't know too much about race cars. He just drove them. He drove them hard, but he wasn't really daring. Foyt knew cars and he was a smart and daring driver. Foyt wasn't favored in 1961, but his car was right and he was ready. Sachs was one of the favorites and he had the fastest car.

"Gentlemen, start your engines!"

Tony Hulman spoke the traditional command in his flat midwestern tones and the mechanics thrust the starters into the noses of the cars and the 33 metal monsters reared to life. The drama had begun.

Jim Hurtubise hurtled from the outside of the front row to the front of the pack as Sachs and the rest settled in behind him. Branson, the second fastest qualifier, was finished on the second lap as his engine fouled up. Lap by lap, cars cracked. Before the race was half over, ten more dropped out, including Jim Rathmann's car.

Then there was a major mishap along the mainstretch. Don Davis spun his car. It hit a wall and lost a wheel before sliding 100 yards down the middle of the track. Following racers steered around him safely until the stunned driver emerged and staggered toward the pits. Bearing down on him, A. J. Shepherd braked and his car skidded into Bill Cheesbourg's car. Trying to avoid both of them, Jack Turner scraped a wall with his car and spun like a top down the track, colliding with cars driven by Roger McCluskey and

Lloyd Ruby before skidding to a halt. By that time, five cars were wrecked and the remainder had to dart through the debris.

Hurtubise had held the lead for the first 35 laps before fading and after a while he was finished when his engine conked out. Jones and Sachs swapped the lead back and forth for another 40 laps. Jones led during the long slowdown period following the accident. When hard running resumed and he accelerated, a loose piece of metal left on the track was sucked up and struck him just above his right eye and goggles. He was jolted by it and almost blinded by the rush of blood into his goggles. Raising his goggles, he emptied them, but as soon as he dropped them back over his eyes, they filled up again. He had to keep emptying them of blood while he drove in the lead. Somehow he hung onto the lead until a cylinder went out, robbing his engine of much of its power. He had led for 75 miles when he began to drop back, still running, but with the also-runs. Foyt forged to the front.

For 50 miles, Foyt and Ruttman alternated in the lead. Just past the midway point, Ruttman's clutch gave way and his car collapsed. Foyt held the lead for 75 miles then, but Sachs caught him with a little less than 200 miles remaining. Sachs surged past. It was as if Foyt was caught off guard.

He went after Sachs furiously. Diving underneath him, almost off the track and onto the grass, Foyt's snow-white number one car recaptured the lead as they sped into the third turn. Foyt tried to accelerate away, but Sachs stuck to Foyt's tail-pipe. He hung there for three laps. Then, thundering down the mainstretch, he sped past on the inside.

This time Foyt would not let him pull away. He chased him for four laps, then rode daringly up high through the short chute between the third and fourth turns to get past him again. Sachs seemed to have the faster car so he was superior through the straightaways, but Foyt outdrove him in the corners. Over a stretch of 100 miles, they traded the lead between them ten times. Ward stayed with them for a while and even got in front for a short time, but then he fell back and ceased to be a factor.

Finally, it was between Foyt and Sachs, tightly contested and enormously exciting. The fans were screaming as the leaders raced side by side, passing and repassing. Lucy Foyt was standing and screaming sometimes, too. She and Foyt's mother and sister stood and looked down the track anxiously for the cars each time they came around, straining to see which would be in front, touching each other for reassurance, hugging briefly in moments of triumph.

Lucy said later, "It was the most breathtaking thing. It like to took my breath away. It was like it was hard to breathe."

A. J., too, later said, "It was the most breathtaking race I was ever in."

"There was no margin for error, no room for a mistake," Sachs added. "It was a matter of which one of us would break first."

Foyt's father, sweating it out in the pits, seemed transfixed as he peered into the fourth turn, waiting for the cars to come by, waiting to help out.

With 75 miles—30 laps—remaining, both had made the last of their three planned pit stops for fuel and tires. The Brawner and Bignotti crews figured to be finished for the day. The rest was up to the drivers dueling alone on that track. After many years of losing here, Foyt's former team—the Dean team—had its best shot ever at victory, and the crowd rooted sentimentally for Dean, Brawner, and Sachs.

Foyt had no sentiment for them. He ran flat out, slowly and inexorably increasing his lead, over Sachs by one second, two seconds, then three. He began to pull away from his rival. He led by six seconds, seven, eight. But in the Bignotti crew there was concern. Frank Catania, a member of the pit crew, had been unable to attach the hose to the tank during the last fueling operation. The nozzle wouldn't screw down and the rushed crew had sent the driver on his way without additional fuel. Now Foyt was running out of fuel. His crewmen knew it and they realized they had to tell their driver.

Bignotti hurried to the wall. A sign was held aloft for Foyt. It read, "FUEL LOW." When Foyt saw it, he was furious.

"I couldn't believe that sign," he stated later. "I couldn't believe I was running out of fuel that close to the finish. There was no reason for it."

Many in the crowd saw the sign. The announcer noticed it and passed the word on to the rest of the crowd. Sound swept through the stands as the spectators stood up, startled. Foyt had appeared to be well on his way to winning but now, suddenly, there was reason to wonder and worry. Racing crowds and crews are used to abrupt, startling shifts of fortune. It was what gifted the most one-sided of events with suspense. Now suspense had begun to build.

The Brawner crew surged to the pit wall and urged Sachs on. For several laps, the Bignotti crew kept flashing Foyt a sign saying, "KEEP GOING."

But Bignotti could not let him go on. There was no way Foyt could finish with what was left in his tank. A new nozzle was readied. Finally, resignedly, Foyt was signaled, "COME IN." Lucy saw it and sat down and bit her lip, lowering her head.

Amid gasps, an angry Foyt came cursing into the pits with

less than 50 miles left to the finish. Swiftly he was fed fuel and sent on his way again. Even then they were not sure he had been fed enough to finish. But they had taken all the time they could spare, and there was real danger that it would prove to be too much.

They had used up 10 seconds and, with the time it took Foyt to slow to a stop in his pit and the time it took him to accelerate back to top speed after coming out of the pits, Sachs had gained a 15-second lead. This is a lifetime in a race of this nature. There was no way Foyt could catch Sachs in the remaining laps of the race. Under the circumstances his crew should have taken more time to feed Foyt more fuel. It would have been fool's work if he had run dry before the finish.

Before Foyt could return to the track, a surprised and happy Sachs had sped into the lead. Foyt poured it on in pursuit, but it was hopeless. Bignotti and his aides stood at the pit wall expressionless, despairing. Brawner and the Dean crew stood there smiling, hoping, waving their driver on. Sachs sped on, showing the fans white teeth in a joyous grin, even waving at the crowd in the corners as he came around. He should have eased off, conserving his equipment. His lead was long. But he was swept up by the triumph of it and he could not contain himself. He hurtled around on his way to his destiny, the crowd cheering him toward triumph.

In the stands, Nance Sachs was crying happily and counting off the two-and-a-half-mile laps that were left—nine, eight, seven. An attendant came to escort her to Victory Lane. Superstitiously, she refused to leave until Eddie had won. Tears were streaming down her face as she watched intently for her husband's car to come by each time—six, five. . . .

At that moment, Eddie Sachs felt his car wobble. Shocked sick, he looked back and saw rubber peeling off his right rear tire, uncovering the warning layer of white. His crew saw it, too, and there was a sudden commotion in the pits.

The announcer screamed, "Something's going on in Sachs' pit. Something may be wrong with Sachs." The spectators surged to their feet again in shock, bringing Nance Sachs up with them as she pleaded with her eyes, frantically searching for her husband's car.

There was pandemonium at the Speedway then. No one could believe the race could turn upside down again so suddenly, but it could. As Foyt's crew jumped up and down, waving him on, Foyt sensed some unknown factor had entered the race and relentlessly pressed on. Meanwhile, Sachs had to make a swift and critical choice. If he went on, he might win, or the tire might blow, sending him out of control, possibly to his death. If he stopped for a new tire, he would not win but he would live to finish second and try again another year.

He had little more than a minute to make his decision. His life and his reason for living hung in the balance. He looked back at his tire, agonizing over his decision. Suddenly, with three laps left, as he was speeding out of the fourth turn and into the mainstretch, he swerved into the pits. In the stands, a tear-stained Nance Sachs let out a strangled sigh, "Oh, no, Eddie. No, no, no."

Sachs' crew frantically fell on the car, pulling off the bad tire, slapping on a new one, shoving him away as Foyt sped into the fourth turn, his crew jumping up and down and waving their arms at the heavens. As Sachs pulled away, a member of his crew fell to his knees and in his frustration forlornly hurled a hammer after the departing car.

Sachs had to get out of the pits and into the first turn ahead of Foyt to hold the lead. As Sachs accelerated toward top speed, Foyt's car came thundering through the mainstretch. Sachs sped for the exit while Foyt roared toward the corner. As Sachs came out of the pits and angled onto the track, accelerating as hard as he could, he saw Foyt's car barrel past. Sachs bulled through the turn but all he could see was the number one on the rear flank of Foyt's car as it pulled away from him. Before Sachs reached top speed, Foyt was ten seconds in front of him. Lucy stood smiling, clenching a fist and shaking it in nervous excitement. Foyt's mother and sister stood with her, hollering at A. J. to go. All around them, fans were screaming.

Foyt was safe now, unless he ran out of fuel. Sachs was chasing him without a chance. Jubilantly, Foyt charged through the remaining laps . . . two, one, none. Foyt rolled under the checkered flag. One second, two seconds, three, four, five, six, seven, eight—then Sachs barreled across. Electronically, the margin between the two was timed at 8.28 seconds. Count it off. It is not much time. But it was a lifetime. It was the second closest finish in the history of this classic, the closest since Wilbur Shaw had held off Ralph Hepburn by 2.16 seconds in 1937. This is a house of numbers and those were the mathematics of victory and defeat. The first 500 was in 1911. This was 1961, the Golden Anniversary race. Foyt would prove to be a appropriate winner of such an anniversary event.

As Foyt rolled triumphantly around the track, he ran out of fuel. He coasted into Victory Lane and Sachs pulled into his pit. Ward came home third, a lap late. Shorty Templeman finished fourth, Al Keller fifth, Bobby Marshman seventh. Lucky seven? Four of them would die driving. Brabham in his sporty car settled for ninth and went unnoticed, but he had broken down a door through which revolutionists would follow. Parnelli Jones took 12th, fading at the finish, but he would be back, a rising contender whose star would cross Foyt's.

In Victory Lane, Foyt was embraced in a great crush of crowd. A bottle of milk was handed to him and he drank deeply from it, his smiling face stained with sweat and grease. He kissed the race queen, kissed his wife, and hugged his crew. He was asked how he got there.

He smiled and shrugged. "Racing luck," he said. "My good luck and Eddie's bad luck."

Outside this circle of contentment, on the perimeter of madness, Eddie Sachs stood alone, watching enviously, wistfully scuffing his foot in the dirt. His wife called to him from the stands and he went to her. They touched through the protective screen.

She asked him, "Oh, Eddie, did you have to come in?"

He hunched up a little and said, "Yes, honey, I'm sorry, I did."

Then he went off to his garage and when he thought no one was watching, he sat down for a moment and put his face in his hands and cried.

He'd had his chance and it had gotten away from him. It stuck to him, the thought of it, for the rest of his life. Others debated his decision. Most racing people said they would have gone on, run the risk in quest of the reward. But the decision had not been theirs to make; it was not their risk to be run. Foyt said, in his honest way, "I'd have gone on." Knowing him, you believed him, but would it have been wise? No one will ever know.

A depressed Dean admitted, "I don't know what Eddie should have done. I wanted him to keep going, but then I wasn't in his place. If he had blown the tire and been killed, I would have felt a helluva lot worse than I do now."

Brawner said, "I think if I'd have been him, I'd have kept going. We want this thing so bad and come so close and keep missing. Now I feel like maybe we had our chance and blew it. But I've never lost a driver yet, and I'd a helluva lot rather lose a race, even this race, than a driver."

Sachs was shaken. "I'd rather finish second than finish dead. I had to come in. Y'understand? I had to." He sighed and shook his head. It took time for him to get a grip on himself, for the old Eddie to bubble up to the surface. Later, it did. "I'll tell you something. I found out something today." He grinned, winking conspiratorily, screwing up his old self. "Oh boy, I found something out there today, something about driving the turns. I lost, but what I found out—and I'm not telling anyone what it is—will win me the race next year."

No one believed him. They dismissed it as bravado, but he had seen something all right, something Parnelli Jones had discovered in the race, a way of broadsliding through the turns almost as drivers do on dirt, which you are not supposed to try on pavement, a controlled, brief slide that pops you straight out of the corners, which Jones hit on in this race, which Sachs saw when he was trailing him through a turn, which helped Jones win the race the year after next, but which was not enough help for Sachs to win the race the next year or the year after that.

Sachs seemed to think there was some secret to winning the race, something most drivers overlooked, something he some day would find that would win it for him. But there were no secrets that *won* the race, only secrets that *helped* win the race. Foyt found out fast that the secret to winning really lay simply in taking advantage of the opportunities that present themselves. It is precisely the way he won this race the first time and the second time and the third time—and on each occasion he did not have the fastest car. It was what Sachs did not do, though he had the fastest car this time. He wanted it, but he wasn't tough enough to take it. It is sad, but this usually is a sad business. Brawner is sad every time he looks at that tire which is almost every morning of his life. He took it and put it on a rack on his garage and it sits there even today and every morning when he goes into his garage he looks at it and wonders about it.

So Foyt seized his opportunity and was soaring to success even as Sachs was falling from it. Their paths crossed, Foyt in his new Bignotti car and Sachs in the Brawner car, which would have been Foyt's car, and Sachs went one way and Foyt another. At the Victory Dinner, $400,000 in prizes was split up. Foyt's team collected $117,975, of which A. J. got 40 percent, while Sachs' team took $53,400. That tire cost almost $65,000.

All the Foyts were at the dinner, held in the old Murat Temple. Because of the lack of air conditioning, the place was stifling. Mom and pop and sis and Lucy, of course, were there and full of pride for A. J. Lucy looked lovely and radiant. She was asked when she had stopped worrying.

"Last night sometime," she replied with a smile. "I couldn't quite believe it was real for a long time."

She was asked where she and A. J. were going for a vacation to celebrate.

"What vacation?" queried. "I'm going home and A. J.'s going to Milwaukee to race. Race drivers race, so their wives don't get vacations."

Foyt said, "I don't have time to celebrate. I've another race to run."

He went on his way. The big one had been his first triumph on a paved track along the title trail. He lost to Ward at Milwaukee and to Sachs at Trenton on paved tracks, but when he got back on the dirt he was almost unbeatable. Ward beat him at Syracuse and Sacramento, but Foyt beat him at Langhorne and at DuQuoin.

And in the Hoosier Hundred at the Indianapolis Fairgrounds Foyt flew from behind, swept past Ward and Sachs on the same lap, "skating on marbles" as he barreled through the loose pebbles of dirt up high in a daring maneuver some still speak of. At twenty-six he became the youngest driver ever to win the 500 and the national title in the same season. And he took 15 other races in sprint cars and midgets and collected more money for his team—in excess of $170,000—than any other driver had ever won in any other year.

He had become the dominant driver in racing and he was beginning to exhibit the temperament of a star. When all went well he was gracious, and when it did not, he was not. When he won a race, he would talk to the press courteously, sign autographs for the fans, and smile at the people and exchange small talk. But before a race he drew within himself and hid behind a sort of barrier he seemed to erect.

"I'm busy," he'd mumble when approached.

If others wanted to take the time for small talk that was their business, he explained. He was serious about his business and it took all his time to prepare properly for a race, he said. He didn't want to be rude, but racing came first. And after a loss he was silent and almost sullen and he brushed by reporters and fans. "Let them talk to the winner," he said. "I'm sorting out why I lost so I can win the next one."

Even winning the 500 did not completely please him for all had not gone well with the victory. He conceded later that, when he found out he had not been fueled properly because of the foul-up with the hose connection and had to return to the pits, "I wanted to run right over those guys."

This formed the first breach between Bignotti and Foyt, for Foyt blamed Bignotti whenever anything went wrong in the pits, and this was, of course, Bignotti's area of responsibility, no matter how well he did his work otherwise.

They exchanged sharp words that night and harsh words other nights whenever things went wrong. Their egos ground on one another and their tongues cut into each other. One night, as they worked in their garage, their profanities echoed through dark Gasoline Alley and an associate, pulling nervously on a cigarette outside, said, "You get between them and you get bent out of shape. You got to get away."

Winning pleased them. When they won, they worked well together. Each had a lot to give the other. They were, after all, the best in the business at their specialties. But they were people of deep pride and each felt personally responsible for the team's success and resented it when the other was singled out for credit. They respected each other and resented each other at the same time. They were temperamental stars and they crossed each other often.

5

Foyt sat in a diner with his big hands wrapped around a steaming cup of coffee, sipping from it, stoking himself against the chill of the damp, gray morning outside that fogged the windows. All around him drivers and mechanics were sipping their own steaming cups of coffee, eating eggs and toast, getting rid of the taste of booze from the night before, cutting through the layers of sleep that fuzzed their minds from the moment they forced themselves from their beds in their motel rooms.

They were talking loudly and laughing and making a lot of noise, readying themselves for the day's racing that lay ahead. Some were laughing uproariously about a driver who had been momentarily blinded by oil in an accident and had wound up crawling in the dirt as though looking for something, possibly for himself.

"He was looking for his eyes. He was looking for his goddam eyeballs. He thought they'd fallen out," someone said, and immediately the others laughed. They are hard men who can laugh at such things. The driver had lived, hadn't he?

Foyt said, "If you can drive well, without panic, you've got a chance. It's dangerous if you make mistakes. I try not to make mistakes. But it comes down to luck. When you flip one of those heavy sons of guns on your head at high speed, it's either your time or it isn't. Hell, you keep racing, you're gonna get it. I know that. But I'm not gonna' worry about it. I love it too much. I don't fear death. I don't think about it."

Could he help thinking about it when one of his close friends died in racing?

"I don't make close friends," he replied. "Oh, hell, I have friends in this business. It's my business and the guys in it are the only guys I feel close to. They're the only ones who know what this thing is for me. Outsiders don't know. But I try not to get too close to the guys. When you get too close to a guy, and he goes, it's hard to go on. We pretend we accept what happens when a guy buys it, but you get sick, you want to throw your helmet away and run.

But you stick around. Who knows why? It's your life, that's all."

Bettenhausen and Bryan had bought it, and Sachs would, too, before long. The early 1960s were difficult and deadly for racers. Foyt won his first 500 and his second national title in 1961, but in the last race of the season, as Parnelli Jones won his first race on the title trail, Al Keller was killed at Phoenix. The 1962 season was worse. Several drivers were killed. They were not big winners, but they were partners on the road.

The first championship race of the 1962 season was staged at the Trenton track on the New Jersey State Fairgrounds. It was a dreary day in April, chill and overcast. A crowd of nearly 20,000 turned out, however. Foyt and Jones dueled. Always impatient, Foyt won the drag race at the start into the first turn to take the lead, but Parnelli pressed him hard as they charged through the early laps over the cement course.

Parnelli's car seemed quicker but for a few laps he could not get by A. J. The Texan did not obey the rules of the road. He did not move over to let his fellow driver past. He jockeyed around on the track, high and low, closing off the passing lanes. However, under pressure, he finally angled too high into a turn and lost control a little coming off the corner and, as his car wobbled while he wrestled with it, Jones dove under him and shot past to take charge. Foyt quickly regained control of his car and followed Jones closely for 20 laps, waiting for an opening.

When Parnelli drifted a little high coming out of a turn, Foyt accelerated and shot past on the inside to resume the lead. He ran flat out after that. And he never made another mistake. He never gave Jones another opening.

Foyt fought a flawless fight. He held the groove, which is the shortest way around any track the rest of the 100 laps. He cut the corners to straighten out the turns as much as possible. He let centrifugal force carry him up to the walls along the long straights and shot through them flat out so near the barrier you could not have put your hand alongside the right side of the car without losing it.

He drove deeply into turns, but not too deep. He tapped the brakes, but not too much. He slowed just enough to carry the corner smoothly, then accelerated out at just the right instant to carry him up to the wall, but not into it. Round and round he went, as if he were riding on rails. Running at a record speed of more than 100 miles per hour for the 100 miles, Foyt held off Jones the rest of the way.

He came out of his car in Victory Circle, got banged on the back by Bignotti, shook hands with promoter Sam Nunis, accepted his trophy, and told the public address announcer, the broadcasters, and the writers wedged into Victory Circle that this was one of those days when everything worked, that Parnelli drove a mighty powerful race and worried him all the way, and that he was mighty lucky to have won. Later, Bignotti asked him about his bobble, when he'd almost blown it. Foyt flared up and said something about the way the car handled.

Indianapolis was something else. On the bigger track, Jones' Agajanian Special, number 98, a car built by Watson and prepared by Johnny Pouelson, proved the fastest car. Dan Gurney's Thompson-Harvey Special, a rear-engine lightweight created by speed king Mickey Thompson, was the most interesting car.

So anxious was American Gurney to introduce his European friends from the Grand Prix circuit to the greatest American race that he paid the way for the brilliant Briton, Colin Chapman, mastermind of Grand Prix champions, to come to watch the race. Later, Chapman repaid Gurney. The Thompson car broke down in the race, but Chapman was impressed with the race, the rich rewards, the publicity that accompanied it, and the potential for revolutionizing it with Grand Prix-styled rear-engine lightweights.

Tall, lean, blond-haired, extraordinarily handsome and articulate, Daniel Saxon Gurney was born and reared in Long Island. His father was an opera singer and wanted his son to study voice. But after he retired his family to an orange grove in Southern California, his son discovered car racing and that was what he studied from then on. He became a mechanic while in the Army in Korea. Discharged, he scraped up the money to purchase a sports car, quit college, and went racing.

He worked his way up to the Grand Prix circuit and became one of the few Americans ever to win one of those classics. He won four. However, he was a sort of hard-luck guy who lost a lot of races he might have won.

He once said, "You prepare for a race, work hard, lead, then, bang, it's all over. You stand there by your broken machine wondering why you bother, why the hell can't there at least be another race tomorrow?"

He was aware of the risks. "I watch someone else go all out and I say, 'What a brave bastard,' and it scares hell out of me. But then I catch myself getting too brave. And I get scared Anyone who thinks you can take chances forever and get away with it is a fool. I will not take chances much longer."

However, driven by dreams of conquering Indianapolis, he was still taking chances in 1962.

Rufus Parnel Jones, out of Texarkana, Arkansas, was another

who was settled in Southern California, got hung up on racing, and took chances. Called Parnelli, he has said, "As a kid, I used to flip buggies in the field for kicks. I thought I was the bravest bastard in the whole world. I always figured I had more guts than anyone. I always figured race drivers had the most guts, so I started wanting to be one. It's dangerous, but without that it would be something anyone could do. I never wanted to do just what anyone could do."

Raised in a tough area near Los Angeles, he grew up a tough kid who got into a lot of fights as he worked his way up the rough road, going from jalopies to sprinters to championship cars.

Parnelli would eventually retire to successfully operate his own racing team, as would Gurney. Parnelli did not have Gurney's grace. He was more like Foyt, simple and unsophisticated but tough and smart. Like Foyt, he liked to play the part of the country boy. But he fooled no one, and he himself was nobody's fool. He learned from Foyt. Foyt could be ruthless. He changed sponsors when he felt it would be wise, and he fired Bignotti when he felt he should.

Jones, on the other hand, stayed with his first major sponsor, Agajanian, most of his career and refused to fire his mechanic, Pouelson, even when he and Aggie saw it would be best. It cost Parnelli. He became a driver comparable to Foyt. Some considered him superior to Foyt. But he never won like Foyt. So when he got his own team he grew tougher. He reached out for the richest sponsors, the best mechanics, including Bignotti, and the top drivers. And then he started to win.

Pouelson was a good mechanic, but he couldn't stop tinkering with his cars, even when they were right, and sometimes he spoiled them. Jones led a lot of races, but he didn't finish many, so he didn't win many. Some said he drove his cars too hard. They said the same about Foyt. Ward was one who said that about Foyt. Infuriated, Foyt suggested that Ward should drive his own car and let him drive his. Foyt said he never asked anything of a car it wasn't supposed to do. However, both Foyt and Jones asked more of their cars than they had to give them at that year's 500. Both suffered brake failures. Meanwhile, Ward's Watson car went on to win.

Ward won the only way he had to win, by waiting in hopes the hot cars would break. He could not keep up with Foyt and Jones. Only Foyt could keep up with Jones. Parnelli penetrated the 150 mph barrier in time trials. Foyt got in more than a mile slower. But in the race Parnelli could not pull away from Foyt. They ran far in front, for almost 175 miles. Others made mistakes, but they did not. On the 18th lap, Jack Turner tangled with others and for the second straight classic went cartwheeling down the mainstretch. He was in the hospital, doped up against the pain of broken bones, before the race was over. He never ran this race again, and he retired after cracking up in practice the following year.

When Parnelli pitted on the 59th lap, Foyt forged past him. When Foyt pitted on the 69th lap, Jones regained the lead. In the pits, Foyt shouted that something had snapped in his brakes. It turned out to be a broken bolt. His crewmen stood around as though no one knew what to do. Foyt angrily jumped out of the car, threw open drawers, and searched without finding a replacement. He sent an aide to the garage for one, yelling, "Run, damn it." The guy ran and returned in short order.

A hurried repair was made while Foyt's car was refueled and some tires changed. Back behind the wheel, Foyt charged back onto the track. He had just resumed the chase when his left rear wheel flew off. His car careened out of control. Desperately, he fought it, wrestled it back under control and worked the three-cornered cripple somehow to a safe stop in the infield grass.

Angrily, he emerged from it and stood looking at it, kicking at it as if he could kill it. He took off his helmet and stood helplessly. The race was on the track and he was off it and out of it. His hard eyes turned toward the pits, where he had been betrayed.

Somone was waving at him, signaling him to hurry in. That could only mean he was wanted to drive relief for another driver in another car. Foyt forgot his own misfortune for the moment and broke out in a run. He ran hard for more than a mile, his helmet swinging in his hand, until he got back to the pits. There a troubled car awaited him. Two drivers already had tried it and given up on it. It had swiftly worn out Elmer George and Paul Russo. But the owner wanted it to go on.

Foyt wanted to go on. He squeezed into the cockpit and took off. The cockpit was too small for him. It had been tailored for the smaller starter. The big Texan was so cramped he could not easily get his foot on and off the accelerator. It was terribly risky to run this way. But he pressed on for a while before abandoning the effort. Finally he left it and walked back to his garage, anger rising in him anew.

When Foyt threw his wheel, the car spun past a startled Jimmy Daywalt and the tire bounced past Parnelli's car. Parnelli jammed on his brakes and his foot went to the floorboard. He had lost his brakes and he was beaten. He did not quit, but he could not drive hard and deep into turns after that and he had to scrape along the walls to stop in the pits. Inevitably he lost time. At 300 miles he lost his lead and in the last 200 miles he fell farther and farther back.

The hot cars had cracked and Ward, playing his waiting game, was ready when his opportunity came. He and Len Sutton, in a sister car, pulled in front. Sachs, who had started far back after losing a wheel during time trials, worked his way up to third place, but Brawner and his crewmen were slow servicing him in the pits and he could not catch up. Ward won by 11 seconds over Sutton and 20 seconds over Sachs. Watson had serviced Ward in 62 seconds. Brawner had taken 87 seconds to take care of Sachs. The difference defeated Eddie. He shrugged wistfully and walked away.

In his garage, Foyt had showered and changed. The sweat and oil had been washed from his face. He wore a freshly starched yellow sports shirt, black slacks, and alligator shoes. He looked good, his handsome face was relaxed. He was telling others about his spinout, and he was laughing.

"I was passing Jimmy Daywalt when the wheel went. I went spinning past him, and it looked like his eyes would pop clear out of his head. I thought he'd have a heart attack." The others laughed at it, too.

Then he was asked why the wheel had come off. His face tensed and darkened.

"They didn't tighten it," he said grimly.

Incredibly, while changing the wheel on his last pit stop, a member of the crew had neglected to tighten the bolt. It could have cost the driver his life. It did cost him the race.

"I was up there, wasn't I," he growled. "I was going as fast as any of 'em." The disappointment welled up in him. "The only man in the crew I can trust is my father," he raged. His father was a member of his crew, but Bignotti and the rest were held responsible for the error. Privately, the young Texan was tough on them, telling them off in no uncertain terms. "There is no room for mistakes in this business," he snapped.

Foyt won at 100 miles on the pavement at Milwaukee ten days later and on the dirt at Langhorne in early July, but he had been bickering with Bignotti more than ever since Indianapolis and in late July he broke with him. They argued and he grabbed his gear and stormed out. Lindsey Hopkins wanted him for his team and Foyt joined him and went to work for mechanic Jack Beckley.

Bob Bowes was so disenchanted that a week later he broke with Bignotti and sold his cars and equipment to Indianapolis businessmen Bill Ansted and Shirley Murphy. Bignotti went to work for them and hired Bobby Marshman as his driver to race under the Sheraton-Thompson banner.

Foyt had little luck with Beckley, and Marshman had little luck with Bignotti. Foyt ran six races for the Hopkins team without winning one. He racked up second place twice, including once in a 200-miler at Milwaukee when Ward held him off at the finish by less than a car length, which really infuriated Foyt. He had been stalking Ward in the last laps of the hot race, held on a hot day on the paved oval at the Wisconsin State Fairgrounds before a roaring crowd of more than 30,000.

However, when he went for it, the car didn't have it. He barreled through the last corner sharply, cutting inside of Ward, below the groove, shaving the distance between them until they were almost even. But as they accelerated out of the turn, Ward's car was in better shape coming out of the groove and it picked up a few feet and held that distance as they sped down the stretch. Foyt had his foot jammed to the floorboard, but his car would not go faster than Ward's and the veteran passed across the finish line under the checkered flag just in front of Foyt. The crowd was screaming and Foyt was storming.

As Ward drove into Victory Lane, Foyt parked in the pits, jumped out and jerked away angrily. When he picked up his check he didn't think the money was all that was owed him. He argued with the promoter about it and threatened to punch him. Others had to separate them before Foyt departed in a range. USAC officials reported the incident and Foyt was fined $1,000 and suspended briefly, but he paid his fine and apologized and was reinstated.

Subsequently, Marshman quit the Sheraton-Thompson stable. Foyt quit the Lindsey Hopkins team and mechanic Beckley and jumped back to Bignotti, his old car, and new sponsors.

Bignotti, reluctant at that time to discuss their on-again, off-again, on-again relationship, simply said, "Foyt and I have had some arguments. They're forgotten now. I don't know who was right and who was wrong and I don't think it matters now. We both want to win. We're together again. We'll see what we can do."

Foyt said, "Bignotti wasn't wrong. It's just that he wanted to do some things differently, and we argued so much I thought we should call it quits. But after we cooled off we decided we could still help each other.

"If I didn't work on a car and it doesn't work, it's not my fault. My job is to win races and I've proven I know my job by winning a lot of them. He's won a lot, too. He knows his job, too. We just have to work things out between us to get the job done."

As the season was drawing to a close, Foyt took Bignotti's car to victory at 100 miles on the dirt at Sacramento, which helped him into second place in the final standings to determine the driving title. But with points from other victories, the big bundle of points from his Indianapolis victories, and his consistently high finishes, the steady Ward had already clinched the championship. Foyt, the dethroned two-time king, was dissatisfied with the number 2 on his car, which he was awarded as the result of his final placing.

Ward later said, "I was the champion when Foyt was breaking in and he had his sights set on me. When he won the title from me and then lost it back, it hurt him. Pride is very important to a race driver and Foyt is very proud. He's also young and impetuous. He's hot-tempered and often does things and says things without thinking. But underneath it all he's a real nice kid and I really like him.

"He's also as tremendous a driver as I've faced. He doesn't always use all his ability. He runs too hard too often and takes too much out of his equipment. You have to know when to run hard and when not, when your car can take it and when it can't. As you gain experience, your judgment improves. Foyt is gaining experience. Right now, he doesn't always use good judgment. But he's hard to beat.

"If he seems to want to beat me more than anyone else, I can understand that because that's the way I feel about him. A couple of times last year, I came from behind to beat him, and, believe me, it tickled me. And I can remember him coming from behind to blow me down, too. I didn't like it, but I'm sure he did. It's only natural to want to beat the best."

Foyt said, "We don't hate each other. We're polite to one another. We just don't have much to say to each other. I respect him. Hell, why do we have to be friends? We're out there trying to knock each other off the track and we can't all be friends. He criticizes my driving, but I don't criticize his. He's a more conservative driver than I am. That's all right. That's his style. It works for him. It's not my style. I'm not sure it would work for me. I'm impatient. I'm trying to be more patient. I'll beat him any way I can. He's been on top for quite a few years. Maybe I figure it's my turn."

In 1963 Foyt seemed to feel the pressure of his prominence. "Everyone wants to beat Foyt. It gives the boys a big laugh," he told us in an interview during the season. "Well, we'll just see who'll beat Foyt this time. We'll just see who'll be laughing."

He was the fastest gun from the Southwest and he felt the tough guys were coming from everywhere to take a shot at him. After a sprint car race, he stormed into young Johnny White's pits, charging that White had "chopped him off" in a corner and went at him, with the result that he was suspended again briefly. His conduct was stormy as he set about regaining his precious title.

The season opened at Trenton with a 100-miler. Lloyd Ruby in a rear-engine lightweight Lotus was the fastest in time trials, but Foyt out-dragged him into the first turn to take the lead. Eddie Sachs, like Foyt in a heavyweight, shot up to Ruby's tail and the three pulled away from the field through the first 20 laps on the one-mile track with Ruby trying to get by Foyt and Sachs trying to get by Ruby. Ruby was resisted until the 22nd lap when Foyt drifted too high between the third and fourth turns and the little lightweight sped underneath him. Then it was Foyt's turn to press Ruby. The pressure mounted for ten laps until Ruby got a little high in the third corner and Foyt dove under him to regain the lead.

It was a very intense three-car race with a crowd of nearly 20,000 rooting hard on a cool late-April afternoon. For a while, Ruby kept trying to cut Foyt down, but Foyt, ranging high and low, would not let him past. Ruby pressed his car to its limits. trying to pass on almost every lap, but Foyt just wouldn't give way, until Lloyd's lightweight finally broke, the engine coming apart, and he retired at 41 miles.

Sachs issued the challenges for the next 35 miles, but Foyt made no more mistakes and repelled several attempts at passes until Sachs' engine started to go sour and he dropped back and finally quit at 76 miles.

Parnelli Jones' great car, affectionately called Ol' Calhoun, broke a rear end shaft in practice and he was forced to drive a lesser car and could not keep up. In the last minutes he and Jim Hurtubise had the only cars on the same lap with Foyt, and Foyt was closing in on Hurtubise and about to lap him when A. J. drove under the checkered flag, the winner. He had lapped everyone else, including Ward, and had driven the distance in less than an hour at a record speed of better than 102 miles per hour and it was worth $21,000 to his team. Afterward, Parnelli told Foyt it would be a different story at Indy and Foyt laughed and said they'd see about that.

Well, Parnelli was right. Ol' Calhoun was ready to run at Indy and cut a lap above 143 the very first day of practice, and Parnelli stood in his garage with Foyt and said, "I'm ready to go."

Foyt laughed and replied, "I'll ask 'em to move up the race to tomorrow, buddy boy."

Parnelli had to wait, but he remained the fastest throughout a punishing two weeks of practice in which he pushed his rivals to desperate tactics. There were some awesome spins, slides, and crashes, though no serious injuries resulted.

On the opening day of time trials he took the pole position, although high winds held him to just above 151 miles per hour. The winds were a hindrance all day, and only seven drivers managed to qualify. Foyt wasn't satisfied with his speeds, and he waited until the second day when he accepted a 150.6 to fit into the eighth starting slot.

Foyt's car simply wasn't as fast as Parnelli's, and A. J.'s only hope was that Ol' Calhoun would break down. Jim Hurtubise had a fast car, but it wasn't fast enough. The only cars that seemed competitive were Colin Chapman's little Lotus-Fords, driven by Dan Gurney and Jim Clark.

The rear-engine revolution was for real. Of 66 cars entered in the race, 11 were these Grand Prix-styled lightweights, and Mickey Thompson had entered 5. These were wider than the others, more like sports cars. They really were the shape of the future, but no one realized it then. They weren't right at the time. They weren't ready. But Chapman's cars were ready.

Compared to the 1,400-pound roadsters, these weighed 300 pounds less and were far more frail. Instead of the eight-cylinder Offenhauser engines, which burned methanol-alcohol fuel blends, the new cars were powered by four-cylinder Ford engines, which burned gasoline. Firestone developed smaller tires for them. These cars were not as powerful or fast through the straightaways, but they were more nimble and quicker through the corners. They were easier on fuel and rubber and could run 500 miles on one or two pit stops instead of the three or four required by the others.

The establishment considered the new cars unsafe. They were 12½ feet long, 2½ feet wide, 2½ feet high, and did not have beefy construction. Instead of sitting in them, the drivers almost lay on their backs, surrounded by fuel tanks full of explosive gasoline.

"You run a risk any time you get into a race car," Foyt stated. "But it looks to me like you run a greater risk riding in one of those funny cars."

Meanwhile, the Europeans considered the Indianapolis track unsafe. Unlike their road racing courses, which are surrounded a lot of the way by open fields, this speedway was enclosed by hard barriers and lacked escape routes. And the Europeans were not used to steadily running at such speeds as 150 miles per hour. Nor were they accustomed to spending a month preparing for a race. While other teams were working 20 hours a day all month, the Grand Prix group commuted back and forth to Europe to continue their racing there.

"A month is too long to prepare for a race," Chapman said. "There's simply not that much to do."

Clark called it "an unnecessary bore."

Chapman was tall, handsome, and distinguished looking. He gave the appearance of being an English actor. He was well-educated, soft-spoken, and polite. He did not fit in with the rough racing crowd, except for the fact that he was clever and could compete with them and beat them at their own business.

Likewise, Clark did not fit, except that he was skilled at the profession. He was short and slender—a nice-looking lad, shy, reserved, and introverted. But he became aggressive on a track. He once admitted, "The only time I'm relaxed is when I'm behind the wheel of a racing car."

Chapman was a Royal Air Force fighter pilot who went on to attend a university and become a development engineer. At the time he developed his Lotus cars, they were shorter, lower, lighter, and more frail than the other cars on the Grand Prix circuit and were regarded as dangerous. He drove them himself for a while but did not succeed with them until he signed Clark, the son of a Scottish farmer, to drive them for him. Eventually Clark won 25 Grand Prix events in Chapman's Lotuses and they became the copied cars. Gurney aroused Chapman's interest in Indianapolis, and Chapman reshaped Lotuses for this race and brought cars for Gurney as well as Clark.

Gurney laid a Lotus on the wall in the first day of time trials but qualified for the 12th starting spot on the second day in a reserve car. Clark got in fifth fastest on the first day. Foyt eyed the little cars unhappily and admitted, "I hate to say it and I don't believe it yet, but these funny cars might be the coming things."

They could not keep up with Ol' Calhoun, but they could outrun the rest. The Chapman team wasted time with leisurely pit stops. Clark lost time observing the rules and holding his position during caution slowdowns, while Jones ignored the rules to pass slower cars under the yellow signals. The members of the Chapman team simply had not taken the time to prepare properly. They underestimated the race and how ruthlessly it was run and they did not practice pit stops sufficiently. Parnelli set the pace almost all the way. With a quarter of the race remaining, he led Clark by 48 seconds.

At that point, one of those shifts of fortune that so often turn things topsy-turvy in auto racing intervened. A crack developed in Parnelli's oil tank and oil began to issue from it, creating gusts of black smoke as it dripped onto the hot tail-pipe and creating slippery oil streaks on the track.

Cars leaking oil are supposed to be black-flagged out of the race, but Jones was so far in front and so close to the finish that chief stewart Harlan Fengler hesitated. Chapman rushed up to argue the point with him and Jones' boss, J. C. Agajanian, hurried in to protect his interests. The three debated heatedly near the finish line in full view of the crowd.

As Jones slowed, slipping in his own oil, Clark started to close in on him. Clark closed to within ten seconds before he, too, backed off. Sachs spun twice, the second time right in front of Clark, who was slipping, too, and Jimmy later explained, "I decided it was better to keep it on the island than to chase Parnelli into the ocean. I waited, sure that he'd be stopped, but they didn't stop him and he didn't stop himself, so that was that."

Abruptly, Jones stopped throwing oil. The crack was horizontal, and when the level of oil dropped below it, the liquid stopped coming out of the tank. When this was pointed out to Fengler, he let the car continue and Parnelli started to pull away from Clark again.

Meanwhile, Foyt had been running a race for slower cars. He held sixth place during most of the early going. At 200 miles he made a move against Hurtubise and got around him on the high side to take fifth. At the midway point he challenged Sachs and sped past him on the low side to take fourth. At 350 miles he fought past Gurney's little lightweight, hanging to him through the second turn, and then outpowering him through the backstretch to take third. Sachs got by Gurney, too, and for many miles Sachs and Foyt dueled for third. Sachs caught him high on one lap, but Foyt got him low on the next.

Roger McCluskey got past Gurney and joined the tussle for third for a while. But McCluskey and Sachs couldn't seem to handle the slippery going as well as Foyt. Sachs crashed with 19 laps left and McCluskey spun out with just two laps left. Parnelli finished 33 seconds in front of Clark and another 30 seconds in front of Foyt. Ward wound up in fourth place while Jim Rathmann finished far back and never raced again.

Jones was happy to have triumphed, but others were unhappy at the manner in which the victory had been achieved. Foyt was one of the few who accepted it. He shrugged. "You win any way you can. He had the fastest car and deserved to win."

Ward agreed. "I wouldn't want to lose to the officials when I was running that far in front."

But Clark disagreed. "I thought there were rules here. Now I know better and will act accordingly next time. You can't expect the establishment to make it easy for outsiders."

"It's their race, and they can run it any way they want," was Chapman's curt comment.

McCluskey said the officials were inefficient for permitting Jones to continue in the race. Sachs maintained that it was the first time a man had won the race but didn't deserve it. He repeated this to Jones at an awards luncheon at the track the next day and Parnelli punched him in the face. They wrestled to the floor before being separated.

Following the 500, however, the Agajanian car began to go bad, breaking down in race after race. The team was torn by disappointment. Chief mechanic Pouelson quit three times, but each time Parnelli loyally talked him into remaining.

Meanwhile, Foyt and Bignotti began to pull things together. The Chapman team ran again only in 200-milers at Milwaukee and Trenton.

At Milwaukee, Clark set records as fastest qualifier and first finisher. Jones broke down early. But while Foyt could not catch the Clark car, he could and did catch the Gurney Lotus. Ward challenged Gurney several times but could not get by him. However, Foyt came from 13 seconds back to make a move on Gurney during the 81st lap, and with one bold move coming off a corner he darted beneath and past him, then held him and Ward off the rest of the way to finish second.

Later, at Trenton, he chased Clark and Gurney relentlessly until Clark's car quit at 49 miles and Gurney's car collapsed at 147 miles. Foyt flew in front free after that, winning by 40 seconds.

Still later he sighed and said, "It doesn't look good for our cars. We can only improve them a little each year, while the new cars are just starting and can be improved a lot. I think they're too damned dangerous, but if they turn out to be the fastest cars, I suppose I'll have to get me one."

For the time being, Foyt was fast enough. He had gone to work for Goodyear and at the company's five-mile test track north of San Angelo, Texas, Foyt took his Indianapolis car and became the first driver ever to circle an enclosed course at better than 200 miles per hour. There was room to stretch to such speeds here. He turned two laps at above 190, was dissatisfied, came in, grabbed a metal scissors, sliced two inches off his windshield to reduce wind turbulence, then went back out and got a 200.4 to set a new world's record.

He won again at Trenton at 150 miles as Sachs crashed and fractured his shoulder. At Langhorne A. J. rode to victory again, nursing a sick car skillfully over the rugged dirt grind as other cars cracked up all around him. And he won on the dirt at DuQuoin, whipping by Ward at the midway point and driving with daring and determination the rest of the way. Though Ward managed to beat him in three events, Foyt finished all 12 races on the trail, which was something for a fellow who was supposed to be hard on his cars.

He had learned some difficult lessons that season and had shown considerable character into the bargain. When he couldn't keep up at Indianapolis, he didn't park his car but coaxed it along and took the best slot available, which was third place, and got $30,000 in prize money.

When he couldn't win or when his car wasn't working right, he went on to make the most of things. He passed Parnelli in points and, without capturing the Indy 500, he racked up his third national title.

He took first place in ten other races that year, in midgets and sprinters and stock cars and even in a sports car, startling the stars of that circuit by capturing the Nassau Trophy Classic in the Bahamas at year's end. He earned more than $100,000 during the year.

6

By 1964 A. J. Foyt had become the master of his profession and a master of the Indianapolis Speedway. He had driven thousands of miles testing tires at the track, first for Firestone, then in 1963 for Goodyear, an opportunity the better contract drivers get—and they are repaid not only by the tire companies but by the knowledge they gain.

"I know this ol' track pretty good now," Foyt said. "It's very tricky and it takes time to get to know it. I know every bump in the road. I know just when to slow going into each corner and just when to speed up coming out. I know the way the wind blows different places. You can only get that running here, and not just in races.

"I can never tell exactly how I'm going to drive until the time comes. If I get ahead, I simply follow the groove of rubber that the cars have laid down in practice. If I'm behind, I work my way up to the front the best way I know how. The groove depends on conditions that day and on your car. There are different lines you can take. There are places where it's good to make your passes and places where it isn't. These things are true of every track.

"Concentration is the key. And horse sense. You have to get to know your car, what it can and can't do. The car is different every year. Either it's new or it's changed. You have to drive it to find out about it, and not just in a race when there isn't room to experiment. You have to know the other drivers and figure out what their cars can and can't do. You have to figure out what the track is. You can only get these things by working at them and paying attention to what you're doing.

"I used to think I got home first. I used to think I carried my cars across. Now I know better. I know they carry me. I have to get the most out of them to get the most out of myself. If I think I'm a better driver than the next guy, I have to prove it by out-driving him, by making more of my car and of myself. That means if I got the fastest car, I can just go. And if I don't, I have to stay as close as I can without wearing what I got out so if the leader breaks I'm in a position to take over.

"If it's a short race, you got to sprint. If it's a long race, especially like a 500, you have to stay in it. Things break on these cars all the time. All you can do is do your best to get them right before they break, then not drive them so hard they're bound to break. You can lay back, but you can't let the leaders get too far from you. There's a fine line there and you use your judgment, if you've got any.

"The easiest races are 100 miles on pavement, but no race is easy. The toughest is 100 miles on dirt. Those babies bounce around and bruise you black and blue and you have to use all your strength to wrestle them around and by the finish you're just exhausted. But I like them because it's more a test of a driver than of a car. You have a better chance to wrestle a bad car home on dirt than on pavement.

"On pavement, the guy with the fastest car just has to keep it together and keep it on the track. I may be able to make better passes than he and I may be able to get through the corners cleaner, but if he can pull away from me down the straights, there's not much I can do about it.

"But 500 miles on pavement tests a man and a car. These races are long and run as fast as the cars will go, and you have to keep making passes and get through traffic all the time. The cars stretch out and you're never out of traffic. It takes three to four hours to run these races and that's a long time to be bearing down, especially if it's hot and you're roasting inside those tight cockpits in those hot cars.

"My hands get tired hanging onto the wheel. Sometimes on the straights I open my hand and push down on the wheel with my palms to rest my fingers. If things are going real well, I might drive with one hand. Your legs get cramped, especially in those new little rear-engine cars. Those are awful small for big men like me.

"They take a lighter touch than I'm used to applyin'. It's hard to change something you grew up learnin'. It's hard to teach an old dog new tricks. But the cars will teach you if you'll listen to them. You have to learn if you're going to keep up. You've got to keep up if you're going to stay ahead. If I have to, I'll handle 'em.

"I run scared. But it isn't exactly scared. More a kind of tight feeling. It's not exactly fun, but I enjoy it. It's you against the other guy. If you're good and you feel you can beat the other guys, it's a helluva challenge to go out there and do it. It's just that when you're out there you can't take it lightly. It's no laughing matter. There's plenty of other time for laughing."

He started the 1964 season by beating the best of the sports car drivers in the American Challenge Cup Classic road racing event at Daytona. He won a sprint car race in Phoenix and a couple in Pennsylvania—one at Reading and one at Williams Grove—and he took championship car races at Phoenix and Trenton before he got to Indianapolis.

The Phoenix event was the first test over a new triangular track and A. J. appropriately paced it. Parnelli paced qualifying, but A. J. streaked from the outside of the front row into the lead on the first lap and led Jones and Roger McCluskey the rest of the way.

At Trenton, Foyt broke the track record with a trial at 110 miles per hour, saw Ward get the jump on him at the start, but beat him through the backstretch of the first lap and went on to another wire-to-wire triumph. He arrived at Indianapolis undefeated on the new year. However, he faced formidable problems in the 500.

The European invasion was on in full strength now. Of 61 cars entered in Indianapolis, 24 were rear-engine lightweights, either built overseas or copied from the European cars. Fifteen would make the starting field. The best drivers had them. Even the Indianapolis establishment had swung over. Chapman had two new ones with Clark and Gurney driving. Mickey Thompson had several new ones, though he did not have established stars in the cockpits. Marshman had a Lotus. Ward had one, built by Watson. Sachs had one. Jones had another, Foyt another.

Foyt and Jones also had old front-engine heavyweights, originally built by Watson. Jones had trusty Ol' Calhoun, now almost an antique at the age of five, but a car that had won the race in 1963 and the pole position in 1962 and 1963 and had led every race in which it had been entered. Pouelson had reshaped it and Parnelli took pride in it. Foyt had a car that had barely made the race and finished far back when driven by a teammate the year before, but it had been improved by Bignotti and would be even better with Foyt.

Foyt and Jones practiced the "funny cars," as they called them, but were not comfortable in them, had no confidence in them, and finally went back to the cars that had carried them to the top. Stubbornly, they resisted change, allying themselves against the new wave. Foyt even went back to Firestone tires, although he now was being paid handsomely to test and drive Goodyears.

"I'm sorry, but I have to run what can win for me," he explained.

"Loyalty only goes so far. When the new stuff catches up, that'll be something else. Right now, there's just too much at stake to stand on ceremony."

In practice, he could not keep up with the new cars. Marshman moved at a speed in excess of 160 and Clark and Gurney came close to this speed. However, the Chapman Lotus-Ford team continued to commute between the United States and Europe throughout the month, still skeptical that they needed the full month to outrun the opposition, and they did not take the time to sort out their problems. For one thing, most of the new cars contracted to run Ford engines and these newly developed power plants appeared unreliable. For another, the Chapman cars were contracted to run on European Dunlop tires and these threw rubber in practice. Chapman shrugged and said, "We'll stand by our commitments. I'm sure they'll be all right in the race."

Two weeks of practice had produced intense competition for speed supremacy with cars spinning, sliding, and crashing with frightening regularity, though no one was injured seriously. An enormous crowd of more than 200,000 packed the Speedway to see men race the clock on the opening day of time trials, a tribute to the magic of this classic and to the European-American rivalry, which had produced a duel of new cars versus old.

Coolly, Clark captured the pole at above 158 miles per hour. Marshman came in behind him at 157. Next was Ward at 156, completing the front row. Fourth in line was Parnelli at 155. Foyt was right at Parnelli's heels with 154. About one mile per hour separated each of the fastest cars from the next fastest, and over the span of three hours running time of the race itself, this difference might be translated into a margin of more than a lap from car to car.

Hard men, Jones and Foyt, now the old guard, publicly puffed up their chests and in a display of bravado insisted the foreign forces and funny cars could not come through in competition. They said race day would be different.

"Come race day," Jones said to Foyt, "we might just have to run over some people."

"Well, buddy boy," replied Foyt, "we'll just put our foot down and, vroom, if those guys in the funny cars can't stay ahead of us, they better just get out of the way."

Privately, Parnelli grew pessimistic, prophesying, "Next year, this whole damn field will be full of funny cars, you watch. We're beating a dead horse. If they don't break down, I don't know how we can beat them this year."

Foyt shrugged and said, "Maybe my old gray mare has a race left in her. I'll let 'em test the new cars some more until they show me they can beat me. If I have to go over to them, I will."

"The Grand Prix guys simply know more about these new cars than we do," chimed in Bignotti. "But we know more about this race than they do. Maybe we can catch up on their cars before they catch up on our race."

Watson was sad. He said, "It's tough to work like hell and get to be king of the hill and then have to start over again with something else you know nothing about."

Sachs admitted he was not comfortable in the new cars but said, "We'll lose to 'em if we don't take our chances with 'em."

Late in the 1963 season, Sachs had crashed, cracking his jaw. His face was put together again with plastic surgery. He returned to Indianapolis in 1964 with his optimism intact. He had a new sponsor, Red Ball Express, which had given him a job off the track and a new car on it.

Once again, he tried to get his car on the track first the first day of practice, but it stalled on him and Len Sutton beat him out. Then in practice during the month he lost control of his car and slid 700 feet with it. Later, in practice on the first day of time trials, he lost control again and skidded his car into a wall, damaging it severely. He stayed up with it all night as his crew repaired it and sleeplessly put it into the race on the second day of qualifying.

At thirty-three, Eddie remained determined and optimistic. He said, "I want to win this race now more than ever and I think I'll win this year. Somehow, I feel this year is special." He had a two-year-old son now. Added Eddie, "I used to want to win this for myself. Now I want to win it for my son. Some day my son will stand in a school playground somewhere and he'll be able to say to the other kids, 'My daddy won the 500.' "

Losing the first day had left Eddie far back in the field, in the middle of the sixth row, directly behind Dave MacDonald in his Mickey Thompson rear-end novelty. The car was Mickey's lowest, widest, and shortest yet. It was the car of the future at this track, but no one then realized it. In fact, the radical car was suspect. MacDonald admitted he was uncomfortable in the car and on the track.

A sports car driver, the youngster confided, "In sports car racing there are escape routes, but here there are only the walls. If I get in trouble, I won't know what to do. My car is handling a little funny I just can't seem to handle it coming in and out of turns. But Mickey says I'm just here for the ride, to learn this year, so I can take it easy. I hope it goes all right."

Married and the father of two, he was, at twenty-seven, the youngest driver in the field. Thompson predicted a fine future for him and on the morning of the race was speaking of commercializing him with a line of Dave MacDonald T-shirts and similar products.

Before the race, Foyt spoke unhappily of the new cars. He said, "These new cars just seem like a bunch of sticks strung together with chicken wire. Instead of tucking the tanks away from you, there are fuel tanks all around the cockpit and they're full of gasoline, which is a lot more explosive than alcohol. They surround you with stuff that can blow you to kingdom come in a split second. I just don't think they're safe."

Although Ford had ordered that gasoline be used in its engines, Watson secretly loaded the Ward tanks with the less expensive alcohol blends such as the Offies were using. Alcohol might not work as well in the Fords, but it might be safer, he reasoned.

This was the first Indianapolis classic to be offered nationally on theater television. Hundreds of thousands of people crammed into movie houses across the country to witness it on Memorial Day, while more than 250,000 customers streamed into the Speedway to see it in person.

Clark accelerated his little Lotus into the lead at the start, followed by Marshman, Jones, Foyt, Ward, and Gurney. As the Scot completed the first lap, the field had begun to string out behind him. As he completed the second, hell blazed up behind him.

Coming off the fourth turn and into the mainstretch, MacDonald lost control of his car, sliced directly across the track, scraped an inner wall, splitting a side fuel tank, and slid back across the track toward an outer wall. His car exploded into a blazing, smoking inferno that obscured the entire area and brought observers screaming to their feet.

Following directly behind MacDonald, Sachs had no way to avoid the burning car as it caromed into his path. Sachs' car rammed into MacDonald's, picking up burning gasoline from it to form a funeral pyre, and slammed like a flaming arrow to the foot of the wall a few feet away. Great clouds of black smoke rolled up from the awesome accident.

Barreling along behind them, other drivers steered blindly through the smoke and debris. Some of the cars spun and crashed and some caught on fire. Johnny Rutherford's car vaulted MacDonald's car but landed on all fours and Johnny kept it going. Driving through, Ronnie Duman caught fire and tumbled from his car and over a wall, putting out the flames on his clothing as his car scraped to a stop.

As the leaders headed toward the second turn, the yellow caution signals blinked on, alerting them to the accident and warning them to slow down. When they passed through the corner and into the backstretch, they were stunned to see the enormous smoke rising in a huge black column across the track. Then, as they moved cautiously through the third turn, the red light flashed on, stopping them. Only once before in the history of this race had it been stopped completely, and that time by rain. Previously the drivers had to make their way carefully through the debris of an accident until the track was cleared. The drivers stopped, leaped from their cars, and stood around on the edge of the disaster.

Safety officials, firemen, and fire-fighting equipment had been rushed to the scene of the wreckage. They arrived within seconds of the accident and did what they could do. Nothing could be done for Sachs. Pinned in his car and probably knocked unconscious in the collision, he had been killed by the smoke and flames. He and the skeleton of his car were covered with a sheet. MacDonald was lifted from his car alive but unconscious and badly burned, and rushed by helicopter to a hospital. There he was found to have inhaled flames into his lungs. Other drivers were helped away and those who needed it were taken to hospitals or first-aid facilities for treatment.

The crews of the ill-fated drivers stood by their pits until they were told what had happened. When the full extent of the tragedy became known, one of MacDonald's mechanics sobbed heavily and toppled over a spare tire to the ground. Sachs' crew quietly picked up their gear and walked back to their garage.

The wives of both drivers were at the race, and were escorted to the infield hospital. When a slightly injured Johnny Rutherford came in for treatment, Nance Sachs pleaded, "Have you seen Eddie? Is he all right?"

Johnny lowered his eyes and said, "I don't know. I didn't see him. I'm sorry."

When Eddie's body was wheeled in, covered with a red woolen blanket, Nance sagged in shock. She was given a sedative and led away. "Just let me lie down," she pleaded.

Friends hurried to the Sachs motel room and took down the race decorations. Outside, a maid wept. "I cry," she said in a foreign accent. "They were so nice to each other."

Mickey Thompson led Sherry MacDonald stumbling and sobbing to a first-aid tent. She was given a sedative. Then, with Thompson by her side, she was driven to the hospital. She begged permission to see her husband which was denied. Soon she was told he had died.

In soft sorrow, she asked, "What am I going to do? How am I

going to tell the kids? He was such a good father. I don't want to go home."

At home, MacDonald's father and Dave's seven-year-old son had been at a theater, watching the race. When Dave was injured, the elder MacDonald rushed his grandson home, then hurried to the airport. There he was informed that it was too late. He sank to a bench.

"This was the first time Dave ever drove a car he didn't think was right," he murmured. He pressed his hands together hard, as though in prayer.

In the darkened theaters across the country as the fans waited for the race to resume, Sachs' face was flashed on the screen in an interview that had been taped earlier.

"I have never been afraid in a race car," Eddie's voice said. He was smiling. He had been about to begin the race he loved more than life and wanted to win most of all, as much for his son as for himself.

The race was suspended for 105 minutes. While the track was cleared, the drivers waited. Their cars were pushed into the positions they had occupied when the race was stopped, and the drivers sat or stood by them. They did not go back to examine the scene of the accident. Few even asked what had happened. They did not then want to know. They still had a race to run.

Parnelli Jones was one of the few who asked. Somebody said it was Sachs and MacDonald. Jones asked if they had a chance. The guy said, "No way," and walked off.

"So I just sat around and waited for the race to start again. But it was inside of me," Jones said later.

Ward did not ask. He sat in a sprawl, like a rag doll. Clark did not ask. He was hunched over, as though from the horror of it.

Foyt did not ask. He said later, "I didn't want to know. There would be time for me to know later. That wasn't the time to know. That wasn't the time to be thinking about it." But he couldn't help thinking of it. Perched on a corner of his car, his face almost expressionless, set taut, he said, "I feel awful. I didn't think those cars were safe. Damn it, it's like sitting in a bathtub of gasoline." He stopped talking about it. And he waited. Later he was described as "the one man most immune to the smoke of death," and it was said he drove "icily, with unbent nerve."

The race was resumed with the 26 cars starting in single file. Marshman drove past Clark on the seventh lap and led for 90 miles until he ducked low to pass under Johnny White's car, ventured too low, bounced roughly through the infield at track edge, scraped the bottom of his low-slung rear-engined racer on concrete, and knocked out an oil plug. His car swiftly started sputtering and he had to stop. He had been 25 seconds ahead and on his way to winning. Later that year he would be killed in a crash while testing tires at Phoenix.

Clark reclaimed the lead and he was pulling away, seemingly on his way to winning, when his tires started to throw off rubber, setting off violent vibrations in the chassis. As he completed the 47th lap, the rear end of his car collapsed, but the skillful Scot strained to keep it under control and got it onto the infield grass, where he parked it. He emerged to study the tire. He had tried this unforgiving place twice now and failed twice. He conferred with Chapman, who called in Gurney, whose tires were chunking away, too. For safety's sake this car, too, was through.

Suddenly, then, the race was between two of the old guard— Foyt and Jones—in their prehistoric monsters. Jones' car seemed faster and he was in front when he pitted for fuel on the 55th lap. As the fuel cap was screwed down and he was shoved away, fuel leaked onto the hot radiator and the car caught fire.

Alcohol fires are almost invisible except for shimmering heat waves, and Parnelli did not know at first that he was on fire. Others saw it or sensed it and ran to him, yelling and waving at him to stop. Instinctively he realized the nature of the trouble and dove from his car, his uniform aflame. He rolled on the ground while rescuers rushed to help him beat out the fire on his uniform and still others caught his car. He was not badly burned, but he was finished for the day.

Finally, then, Foyt led, far in front of the rest. He drove hard, almost too hard, pushing himself past the point of painful thoughts that might intrude on his concentration, as if to prove to himself that he could not be influenced by what had happened. Gloom hung heavily in the arena. The crowd watched the race quietly. There was no race. Foyt pressed farther and farther in front, seemingly on the verge of losing control of his car a few times but always hanging on.

Ward was second, but he fell farther and farther back. Foyt pitted only twice. He did it swiftly, sliding in and out in a hurry, taking on fuel but never changing a tire. Ward pitted five times. "It was at least three times more than necessary," he admitted later. "I made mistakes. I was shaken by what had happened. I was seeing ghosts, I guess." Once he thought he heard something rattling in the back of his car. But there was nothing. He pulled into the pits and told Watson.

Angrily, Watson asked, "What do you want me to do, overhaul it here?" and sent him on his way again.

Hurtubise was third going into the 145th lap, but then he lost oil pressure and had to stop. Branson was third then, but his clutch caved in and he was through at 190 laps. By that time, Foyt had lapped Ward and everyone else, the first time the leader had lapped the entire field in ten years. He passed Ward to lap him late to no purpose, except just to lap him. He was not even slowed when the return spring on his accelerator snapped and he shut it off by hand in the last part of the race. He came home under the checker more than a minute in front of his closest follower, Ward. A. J. had led the last 360 miles and for the 500 miles had averaged a record speed of better than 147 miles per hour. At the age of twenty-nine he had won his second 500.

He drove into Victory Lane where his wife, his father, and the rest of the crew—Bignotti, Frank Catania, Leroy Neumeyer, Bud Moyer, Bill O'Sullivan, Andy Miller, and Mac Mitchell—waited happily. For a moment, the horror was forgotten and there were no tears. Bignotti laughed boisterously. He leaned in to hug a smiling Foyt as A. J. pulled up, unstrapping himself, stood up in his cockpit, and took a seat in front of his roll bar.

He pulled off his helmet. His thinning, curly hair was matted with sweat. His face was sweaty and greasy. His coveralls had been torn to tatters in spots by the wind. He was surrounded by bedlam.

His father leaned in to hug him. His wife, Lucy, leaned in to kiss him. The queen was brought to him to be kissed. He kissed her. Twice. Then he kissed his wife again. He was handed a bottle of milk. He pushed it away. He said, "I don't want that. I want water." Then he changed his mind, took the bottle, and drank deeply from it. The milk council pays a bonus to the winner if he drinks their stuff in Victory Lane in front of the cameras, which were running and snapping now. Raymond Firestone was there with an aide, prepared to pay off the winner with a $7,500 check for using Firestone tires. Still in Goodyear coveralls, Foyt refused.

A microphone was shoved into his face as he was interviewed over the public address system. It was wonderful to win this race a second time, he said. He felt wonderful. His car had worked well. Everything was great. Bignotti was great, he said. He didn't know about the new cars. He knew about the old cars. They were still the greatest. Everything was great. Everything was wonderful, he said, smiling. Then someone handed him a copy of the Indianapolis *News*, which reprints its front page at the track for fast distribution. The ink on the headline was still wet. The headline read:

FOYT WINNER IN 500;
SACHS, MACDONALD DIE

Foyt's smile faded. He looked at Lucy, who was by his side. "Are they dead?" he asked her softly as though he did not want to believe it.

She could not answer him. She put her hand on his arm and squeezed it and pressed her lips together and looked at him through moist eyes. He hung his head, looking at the headlines of the newspaper, which lay in his lap. He was silent a few seconds. Then he gathered himself. He looked up. He said, "I'm sorry. I'm sorry those guys died." Then he was silent. No one wanted to press him on it just then. This was his moment of victory.

He was taken to the pace car, Lucy on his arm, to be driven around the track on a lap of triumph, smiling and waving at the cheering crowd. His was a popular triumph. The fans did not know him. Few of them had been touched by his temper. They were all moved by his ability and awed by his determination. They admired him. He was what a race driver should be—tough and fearless. He was a winner. It took a lot for him to lose. He drove around the shadowed track and smiled and waved at the fans. He drank champagne from a bottle that had been given him.

Afterward, he went to the Firestone headquarters in Gasoline Alley, carrying the empty champagne bottle in his hand, still in his uniform, sweaty and greasy and weary. The press waited for him there.

Lucy waited outside. "It's wonderful," she said, "but I'm relieved it's over." Wistfully, she added, "I hope he quits." He had said he might retire if he won this classic a second time."

Later he was asked about this. He laughed and said, "I'll retire when all my hair has fallen out. The way it's going, that may not be long."

He was asked first about defeating the new cars. Had they worked as hard at winning as they might have? Was he lucky?

"It might be true that the Lotus-Ford boys took the race too lightly," he stated. "I don't know. If they did, they were only ribbing themselves because of the money involved. People may think I was lucky today, but I say you have to make your own luck. If I have to stay up 24 hours a day the whole month of May to win, I'll do it. We worked over every part of the car that could break and we were ready to go 500 miles. George Bignotti deserves a lot of credit. He's some mechanic. We fight and argue a lot, but we've got the same spirit—we like to win.

"A lot of guys made fun of me for driving an antique car with an antique engine. Well, all I've got to say is these antiques have made me an awful lot of money around here and they made me a lot more today. We knew the Lotus-Fords would pull away early, but we also knew they'd have to stay in it or we'd be knocking on their door. They didn't last long. That left it between me and Parnelli in our old antique-ees.

"If he had stayed in it, we'd have had some race. If he had stayed in it, we'd both have had to turn some mighty fast laps. He didn't and I wasn't pressed after he fell out of it, so I didn't run as fast as I could have. But I pushed. I may have been pressing a little. I've always prided myself on being a smooth driver, but I felt sloppy today. I was slipping and sliding all over the track. But I had the best car and I never was in any serious trouble."

He was asked if he would go over to the new cars. "I'm not so sure," he replied. "They're the fastest cars, all right. But they're not the strongest cars. Those guys are good. Maybe they can make those cars better. If they're the best, I guess I'll have to go to them. But I'm not ready yet. I'm not ready to say I'll go to one next year. I had one this year and didn't go with it, and I'm sure as hell glad I didn't. I doubt that I'll go to one next year."

Bignotti, standing to a side, confided, "We'll probably use a rear-engine car next year. They're too fast for us. As soon as they last, they'll win. Maybe I can make them last. The way they pulled away from us today, you could see it's only a matter of time before they take over. And I think the time is now. I don't think we should wait until it's too late. You can't let anyone get ahead of you."

Then someone asked Foyt about the fatal accident and all the enjoyment went out of it for him. He said, "I hate to see Eddie and Dave lose their lives. They were my friends. No one likes to see someone get killed. Even if you don't know somebody, you still have a big enough heart to feel sorry for that person if something like this happens. And these were my buddies. I knew them both well. I didn't travel with them, but I liked them. Eddie was good for racing. We all got mad at him at times, but he had more guts than any of us. I always pray before every race that The Good Lord will take care of all of us. These are all terrific drivers and good men.

"The accident affected all of us. But we went on. The race goes on, so you go on. If it had happened to us, they'd have gone on. If you're a racer, you go on. I didn't know what had happened to them. I knew, but I didn't want to know. I knew I had to go on."

He went on with it, with the interviews, which were as painful as anything, talking to the writers as long as they wanted to talk to him, gracious in victory, patient with the same questions asked over and over. Eventually they left, and he was alone.

At nightfall, still in his suit with an elbow hole that had been ripped by the wind, rumpled and unwashed, he said, "I'm afraid of those rear-engine cars. I'm scared of having all that gasoline around me in that type of chassis. Well, damn it, you're sitting on gasoline, you have gasoline on each side of you."

He sighed. "I'm sorry those guys dead. We're all sorry they died. That is racing. Looky here, you can't let this get you down, about those guys getting killed. You got to carry on in racing. Maybe you haven't noticed it about me, but I haven't got any close friends in racing. You can't let anyone get too close to you in this game. If they get killed, it breaks your heart. And if you're going to race, you've got to race alone."

That night, A. J. and Lucy stopped at the funeral home in Speedway to pay their respects to Sachs. Lucy didn't get to see Nance, but she telephoned and talked to her for a while.

A. J.'s father and mother had been at the race. His sister, Marlene, had watched at a California theater. His son Tony, who was eight, had watched at a Houston theater. Tony looked a lot like his dad and showed a lot of his sort of independence. Terry, who was five, looked more like Lucy, but you could see A. J. in her, too. Jerry, who was only one, seemed likely to fit the Foyt pattern.

A. J. and Lucy called home and talked to the kids on the telephone. They were thrilled their daddy had won. They wanted to know when he was coming home. He would when he could, he promised. They missed him and their mom when they were away, but they were just too young to be taken to races like this and the long stay in Indianapolis would take Tony away from school too much. Lucy always fretted when she was away from them. She was with them more than she was with her husband, of course. She was home and he was away from home much of the year. Thus, she was more mother than wife much of the year. That was the life of a racing wife.

She didn't really enjoy being a racing wife, but she accepted it. "It's our life," she said. She shunned the spotlight. But she accepted it in May in Indianapolis. "Sometimes it's the closest we come to a vacation," she laughed. It was a working vacation for A. J., of course. And the pressure never let up. But she could share it with him. And it was a time they could be together. And when A. J. won, the pleasure was great.

With the car owner Shirley Murphy and his wife, A. J. and Lucy went to two parties but arrived too late for the food at both. Finally, the Foyts and the Murphys, all dressed up for fancy parties, went out to eat. "We went to that fifteen-cent hamburger joint down

Sixteenth Street, and I had my banquet," A. J. laughed. "Lucy had on her mink stole. She hesitated a little about eating in a hamburger joint. But at midnight on Memorial Day there aren't too many places open."

So Foyt supped on hamburgers and toasted his triumph with a soft drink.

He had made a date with two newsmen for breakfast at nine o'clock the next morning at the Speedway Motel and he made it on time. He confessed, "I didn't sleep too well last night. I tossed and tumbled all night and was up by six o'clock this morning. I couldn't get the wreck off my mind." Wistfully, he observed, "I'm thinking of selling the sprint cars I own and spending more time at home. I'm getting a little weary of being gone away from my family so much. Lots of nights I work on the sprinter until three, four in the morning. If I sell it I might have more time for other things. And I might concentrate more on other kinds of racing. But I'll be back at Indianapolis next year. I don't know what kind of car I'll have, but I'll be back."

That night he went to the Victory Banquet at the Murat Temple and collected a record first-place prize of $153,650, which was part of a record purse of $506,620. Ward got some $50,000 less for second place. The next day, Lucy went home to Houston to take care of her children while Foyt went on to New Bremen, Ohio, to resume racing in a sprinter.

He had come a long way from his first victory at Indianapolis, when Sachs so narrowly lost in such heartbreaking fashion. Once Foyt spoke of it. If Sachs had gambled and gone on in 1961 he might have won this race he wanted so much to win and retired and then not even been on the track in 1964. If he hadn't thrown a wheel in 1962, he might have won the race and still retired before 1964. If he hadn't crashed in practice this year, he might have qualified higher and would not have been right behind MacDonald at the start. If . . . if . . . if.

"You can't live on ifs in racing," Foyt said. "If you want me to be completely honest, I'd have gone on if it had been me. But maybe the tire would have gone and I wouldn't be here today. All any of us can do is the best we can do. Eddie did that."

At Sachs' funeral in Bethlehem, Pennsylvania, a floral spray sent by Dave MacDonald's wife was placed at the head of the casket. At MacDonald's funeral in Whittier, California, his two children put symbolic checkered flags across his casket. No resentment of racing was expressed. Friends and family spoke, instead, of the love these drivers had had for racing. But Mickey Thompson, who had designed the kind of cars other drivers would be driving at Indy a decade later, returned only once more to race cars at Indianapolis. His spirit had been sapped. Some condemned his radical cars at the time and it hurt him.

The next championship trail race following Indianapolis in 1964 was at Milwaukee. At the midway point, Ward, Foyt, and Hurtubise were running one-two-three close together. Ward's car wobbled from rear end problems and he slowed abruptly. Behind him, Foyt had to brake sharply. Hurtubise ran right over one of Foyt's rear wheels, sailed through the air, and rammed a wall, ripping off a wheel and a fuel tank. His car caught fire as it spun across the track and the bouncing wheel came into the cockpit and struck Hurtubise on the head and chest before it bounded on. Hurtubise's car settled to a stop in flames. Before he could be scooped from his cockpit, his face, hands, and much of his body were badly burned. He also had broken a rib, which punctured and collapsed a lung.

Hurtubise was treated first at a Milwaukee hospital, then later at Brooke Army Medical Center in San Antonio, where specialists are skilled in the care of burn cases. Through the long year he would struggle for survival. Despite plastic surgery, his face and hands would be extensively scarred. When doctors told him one of his hands had to be set in some permanent position, he had them set it in the shape he needed to grip a steering wheel. He not only would survive but return to racing. He would even win some major races. He still is driving, though he seldom wins now.

Foyt won the race in which Hurtubise was hurt at Milwaukee, remaining undefeated. "I hated to see Hurtubise hurt. He is a buddy," Foyt said. "I think he'll be all right. He's tough. You have to go on."

As he went on, everywhere he went he was asked about the serious accidents of the year, about the new cars he had suggested would cause serious accidents, about deaths in racing, and he began to pull back, resenting the persistent queries as an assault on his senses. He was also annoyed by the suggestion that he was a fool for following the trail, that he was afraid of the new cars and of accidents. He started to defend his sport. He contended auto racing was no more dangerous than boxing, skiing, football, or other sports, only its accidents were more spectacular and treated more sensationally by the press. He pointed out that his profession was only one of many dangerous occupations men engage in, such as bridge-building, tunnel-building, mining, deep sea diving.

New rules were being brought into championship racing by USAC. These would strengthen the rear-engine cars, reduce the amount of fuel carried by the cars, and require the fuel to be carried in rubber bladders within the tanks to minimize the possibility of explosive fires in crashes. Foyt indicated that if the new rules were carefully observed, he would be more inclined to go over to the new cars.

"I always want to keep up with the times, to stay ahead of the other guys," Foyt said. "If I have to turn to one of the new cars, I will. I would have at Indianapolis if the car had been better."

Sold back to its builder, that car had been driven by another driver and had broken down early in the race. But Bignotti was convinced the new cars were the coming thing now. He wanted to get one before they began to beat him, and he wanted to begin building them. Foyt resisted strongly because he was winning with his old-style cars, but Bignotti was sure he could not continue to win with them. They argued about it.

Foyt stepped off the title trail only long enough to shock the NASCAR crowd by winning the Firecracker 400 at Daytona. Back on the trail, he won his fifth straight championship event with a rugged run at Langhorne. It was a cruelly hot Sunday afternoon in June. The temperature on the surface of the track was 132 degrees. The temperature in the cockpit of the hot cars was even higher. A number of drivers dropped out and others drove erratically and admitted later that they felt dizzy. But the tough Texan kept going inexorably. Even when his power steering went out, he just wrestled the car around through thick clouds of dirt kicked up on the dry oval.

Weary, grimy, and soaked with sweat, he later asked, "Have you ever had power steering go out on your passenger car? It gets so stiff it's hard to turn. I really had to work for his one."

He had passed up a ride in a Ferrari in the prestigious 24 Hours of Le Mans to participate in this routine event at a track isolated in the Pennsylvania countryside, but he had won $7,500 for less than one hour's work at a speed of more than 102 miles per hour. "That's dangerous over there," he said. "You drive night and day against guys you don't even know. Here, this is what I know. Where else could I make so much money for the time I put into it? The championship trail is the road I know best."

He went on to his sixth straight of the season with a triumph in the Trenton 150, setting a new track record of better than 105 mph. The heat wave continued. It was 140 on the track at Trenton, and his brakes failed at 75 miles. He couldn't go as fast as others, but he kept on. Marshman in a rear-engine car led but broke down. Then Ward in a rear-engine car got out in front until he dropped out before he fainted, collapsing in the pits from the heat.

After that Jim McElreath forged into the lead, but he got so groggy he parked his car with only 25 miles to go. That left it to Foyt. He won it all by himself. In Victory Lane, his face was so red it looked as though it had been roasted. He was bathed with perspiration.

"Was it hot out there?" he said with a triumphant laugh. "I'll have to ask some of the boys 'bout that."

At Springfield he had trouble in time trials and was slotted 16th, the farthest back he had ever started a title event. He drove harder than the others, often slipping through the loose stuff up high. At 25 miles, he was tenth. At 50 miles, he was fourth. At 55 miles, he passed Parnelli. At 60 miles, he got by Don Branson. At 65 miles, he drove past Jud Larson to take the lead. Marshman moved up to challenge him, but Foyt fought him off, lap after lap. By less than one second, Foyt won his seventh straight race on the title trail, setting a new record.

Bill Horstmeyer was killed at Springfield when he ran his car into a wall and was trapped in it when it rolled over and came to rest aflame. He was thirty-five and had driven unsuccessfully for a dozen years.

It was a savage season. In a sprint car race at New Bremen, Jimmy McGuire, a twenty-three-year-old rookie of rare promise, flipped over another car and landed upside down. His right arm was crushed and had to be removed. But he got an artificial arm and resumed driving, though back in the bushes. At Terre Haute in another sprinter, Johnny White, the 24-year-old "rookie of the year" at Indy, vaulted a retaining wall, barrel-rolled down an embankment, flipped four times, and came to rest with a crushed spine. He was paralyzed from the waist down.

Banged from behind in a highway mishap, Foyt observed, "Sure, racing is dangerous, but no more dangerous than driving on the highway. At least on the track we don't have a bunch of drunks to contend with. We got people behind the wheel who know what they're doing. If you get in trouble, and it happens, you may get hurt, but you'll try not to take others with you."

Heading for Milwaukee and a 200-mile race on a paved mile that would work for the rear-engine lightweights, Parnelli Jones asked Colin Chapman for the loan of Jimmy Clark's Indianapolis Lotus-Ford and accepted an offer to run it under Chapman's sponsorship. If Panelli had gone over, Foyt couldn't let him get ahead, so he asked for a similar deal for Gurney's Indy Lotus-Ford and got it from Chapman.

Clark and Gurney were tied up in Europe with their Grand Prix cars. So, finally, the most prominent of the old guard had made a move. And it paid off for Parnelli, who captured the pole and won the race with record times. However, Foyt's car broke down on the very first lap, ending his undefeated streak on the trail and frustrating him. He blamed Bignotti as if it had not been A. J.'s own choice.

In front-engine cars on dirt tracks, Foyt won at Springfield and at DuQuoin and at the Indianapolis Fairgrounds, the latter his ninth title trail triumph of the season, surpassing the existing standard of eight in one season, which had been set by Tony Bettenhausen more than 20 years earlier. But when he got back into a new car on a paved track, it was another story again. In a 200-mile event at Trenton, Foyt dueled Jones for almost half the race, but then his clutch failed and his Lotus-Ford dropped out while Parnelli's went on to lap the rest of the field in winning.

It wasn't clear that Parnelli was driving better than A. J., but it was clear that Parnelli's Clark Lotus was better than Foyt's Gurney Lotus.

Back on the dirt at Sacramento, Foyt won his tenth championship car race of the year. He almost didn't make the race. During qualifications, he suddenly pulled into the pits. He told Bignotti something was going wrong in the engine. Bignotti checked and found out the fuel mixture had been too lean and a piston was beginning to burn out, which would have ruined the engine.

Bignotti replaced the fuel pump and thickened the fuel mixture and Foyt got back out in time to qualify to start sixth. He picked off the cars in front of him until he nailed Parnelli on the 30th lap and went on to win by ten seconds.

Exuberant afterward, he said, "My mechanical ability came in handy in time trials. A few drivers wouldn't have noticed the trouble until it was too late."

Back in the new cars in a 200-miler on the newly paved Phoenix track, Foyt paced Parnelli for 55 sizzling laps until A. J. spun out, breaking his gearshift. This time Parnelli's car failed, too. After lapping the field, his engine blew. Lloyd Ruby, a tough old Texan, went on to win his first championship event. The season was over. But a month later at Phoenix, in tests, the brilliant young Bobby Marshman cracked his new car and later died.

Foyt had won his fourth national driving title. He had won 10 of the 13 events on the championship trail, including his second Indy. It was the best record that has ever been put together on this trail. He had won every event he had finished, every event he had entered in front-engine cars. He had failed to finish and lost only the three in which he had driven rear-engine cars. However, he had begun to achieve truly high speeds in those cars and he could see they were the cars that were going to go the fastest so he would have to switch over to them.

"I'll have to go into the new cars now," he sighed. "I want to stay on top."

He was on top. He'd had his greatest single year. He'd won sports car and stock car classics as well as title trail tests. And in only five years, he had emerged the victor in 28 of 62 starts on the title trail, an incredible record on a circuit in which cars break down regularly, accidents often are unavoidable, and competition is intense. The previous record for victories on the championship trail had been 26, established by Ralph DePalma 50 years earlier. Ward had won 25, and he would win only one more. Foyt would win many more.

After winning the pole position for the first time at Indy, Foyt's number 1 car, a Lotus Ford, his first rear-engine lightweight, sits in the front row inside Jim Clark's number 82 and Dan Gurney's number 17 on a splendid spring day at the Speedway. (*Photo by John W. Posey*)

Like a man past his time and out of place, Foyt sits high in his erect front-engine sprint car, which he used when his championship car got lost in shipment, and leads rivals in low-slung lightweight rear-engine cars at Milwaukee Fairgrounds in 1964. (*Photo by John W. Posey*)

A. J. Foyt, driving a rear-engine Ford, spins coming out of the second turn (top); jumps from his car (middle); and rolls in the grass (bottom) to extinguish blaze when his clothes caught fire during the accident in the middle of the 250-mile Indy-type car race at Atlanta International Raceway in August 1965. (*Photo by United Press International*)

Top: Foyt's racer spins out after smashing into a retaining wall at the Wisconsin State Fair track in Milwaukee in 1966. *Middle:* Foyt prepares to jump from car as it bursts into flames. *Bottom:* Track firemen wash racing fuel from remains of Foyt's $40,000 Lotus Ford racer. Foyt suffered second- and third-degree burns. (*Photos from Wide World*)

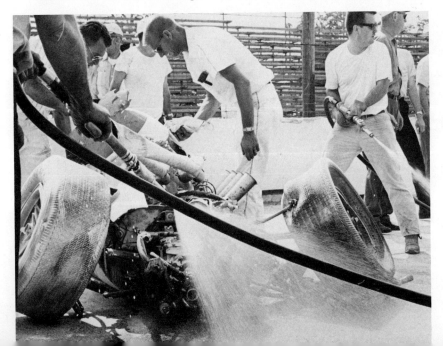

Winner of the pole position for the second time in his career, A. J. Foyt
in number 6 Sheraton Thompson Special, inside front row, brings the
field down the mainstretch for the start of the 1969 Indianapolis 500.
Moving ahead from the middle of the front row is eventual winner,
Mario Andretti, in number 2 STP Special. On outside is defending
champion, Bobby Unser, in number 1. In second row, right to left, are
Mark Donohue, number 66; Gordon Johncock, number 12; and Roger
McCluskey, number 82. (*Indianapolis Motor Speedway photo*)

Foyt in number 14 flashes inside Bobby Unser in number 6 on the way to
winning the 1967 Indianapolis 500. (*Indianapolis Motor Speedway
photo*)

Fuel is hurriedly pumped into two tanks of Foyt's racer and his large Goodyear tires are checked during pit stop in 1967 Indy 500. (*Indianapolis Motor Speedway photo*)

Foyt sneaks through smoking five-car crackup that occurred right in front of him on the last turn of the last lap en route to the checkered flag. (*Indianapolis Motor Speedway photo*)

Foyt takes a turn whipping his Ford sports car around tricky course at night during grueling French endurance test at the 24 Hours of Le Mans within one week after his Indy win in 1967. (*Photo by Ford Motor Company*)

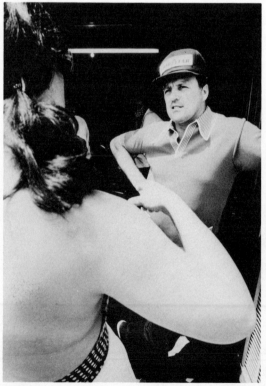

Foyt chats with fans at Indianapolis and Ontario Motor Speedways. (*Photos by George Rose*)

Foyt skillfully broadslides his dirt car sideways through a turn during a dirt car race in 1968. (*Photo by John W. Posey*)

Foyt fighting for the lead in 1968 Hoosier 100. Billy Vukovich is in number 98, Gary Bettenhausen in number 11, Bobby Unser in number 3, and Foyt in number 1. (*Photo by John W. Posey*)

A maturing A. J. Foyt in a happy, wistful moment (*Photo by Bob Tronolone*)

Waiting his turn, Foyt stands behind his car at Ontario Motor Speedway in California and talks to crewman Jack Starnes. (*Bill Libby photo*)

7

By the middle 1960s, A. J. Foyt seemed to have all a man could want. He had a beautiful and loyal wife, three handsome and healthy children, and he was the pride of his parents. His father even worked with him. Foyt had a large and lavish home in Houston worth more than $100,000 and an expensive vacation house on a nearby lake. He owned three cars—a hardtop, a convertible, and a station wagon—and five motorcycles. He had a boat. He even had his own private plane—an Aero Commander—that he flew, himself, to some of his races.

If he wished, he could live a life of luxury, and he had helped his parents achieve a comfortable mode of existence. He was young, still healthy and handsome. He still had most of his hair. He still had a sense of humor. He had begun to be hardened by pains that had to be endured in his profession, but he had not yet been bent by them. He had not yet been frustrated by years of failure. He had won almost everything a man could win in his sport and he was proud of his importance and prestige. His place in history was assured. And he knew as well as anyone that to go on in his cruel sport was to risk death or a crippling accident. But he wanted to go on.

"It seems I've always raced," he says. "As I see it, if you can't race, what else is there to do? If I wasn't racing, I don't know what I'd do with myself."

He was approaching the peak of his earning power. For winning his first 500 at Indianapolis in 1961, he had earned $117,975 for his team. For the entire year in racing, he earned close to $200,000. In 1964, he collected $153,650 for capturing his second 500. That year he garnered nearly $250,000 in racing, a record for one driver in one year. Later, in 1967, he would pick up $171,227 for winning his third 500. That year again he would earn nearly $250,000 from racing.

By the middle 1960s he had earned nearly $2 million from racing. The drivers usually collect 40 to 50 percent of their purses. Foyt collected 50 percent, plus contracted guarantees just to race.

His team backers contracted Foyt for more than $100,000 just to carry their colors each year, and Foyt kept switching backers to better himself. In time, he began to put his own team on the track and his backers budgeted the operation generously.

His business manager, Chuck Barnes, states, "The few drivers on Foyt's level are assured of a quarter of a million dollars a year before they even turn a wheel."

Firestone had been paying Foyt an annual amount to test and race its tires. When Foyt went to Goodyear, this sum jumped above $100,000. When he went to Ford, the company started him at a similar sum and wound up paying him so much to test and race its engines that it eventually sold the entire operation to him. Other commercial manufacturers of car products contracted with him to use their products and added bonuses whenever he won with them. He was paid to endorse products. And he put all his money to use.

He made investments in stock, real estate, and oil wells, which produced. He had a native intelligence, was shrewd with his money, and received smart advice. He bought a chicken ranch first, then a cattle ranch. He was a millionaire before he was thirty years old. No one would ever have to throw a benefit for him. Nor would he have to sell pencils to get by. He would sell cars, but that would pay off. His kids would never have to tap-dance on street corners for spare pennies. He invested in trust funds for his wife and children. He paid his taxes. Keeping up with his bills posed no problem.

There are a lot of poor racers struggling on the circuit. Racing is an expensive proposition. It pays off for a fortunate few. But if you are not a winner you do not get a large piece of the pie. Many winners go broke. Some champions go bankrupt. It is a hard, fast life and there is a temptation to live high while you can, to spend what you make because you can't take it with you.

Foyt was not so tempted. He had his toys, but he didn't play with them much. The gals who love racing heroes loved him, but he refused to put himself in a position where he had to pay off broads. If he was less than a saint, he was more than most men in his position. He spent most of his time on the road with his crew. He traveled with them, ate with them, slept with them. When he wasn't working all night on a car, he was staying up half the night playing cards with his crewmen, careful not to gamble away his hard-earned money. He won more often than he lost. He never went in over his head.

He and Lucy had been married since 1955. They'd had three children over the next seven years, handsome, healthy, lively youngsters. If A. J. was tough with others, he was not tough with them. He was gone most of the summers and home most of the winters.

The Foyt home in Houston is a three-bedroom house on four lots. Outside, there is a swimming pool. Lucy loves to swim. A. J. likes to water-ski at their lake house. Inside their main home, the furniture is a mixture of French provincial and early American. It reflects Lucy more than A. J. If it had been up to A. J., it would have looked like a bunkhouse. He doesn't spend much time there, anyway. He confesses that one year in the early 1960s he spent 185 days away from home. Whenever he is home, he is restless. Lucy said, "He has to keep going all the time. I don't guess there's such a thing as a day off for him."

Scene: The Illiana Speedway in Schereville, Indiana, on the Illinois border. It is a tiny town and a tired little track. It is a half-mile around and almost flat, with wooden guard rails. It looks like a throwback to the barnstorming era in racing.

It is a midweek afternoon and the grandstand is deserted. But on the track racing men are testing two brand-new stock cars. Among them is A. J. Foyt. It seemed strange to see him there, back in the bushes, but he had work to do.

"You never know how good you can get a race car to feeling unless you try everything possible," he said. "You put more weight on here, raise this side, lower this side, and pick up a little time. Then you try to do something else to squeeze a little more time out. Sometimes it works and sometimes it doesn't. A lot of people get their car feeling right and running fast and quit fiddling with it because they're afraid they'll slow it back down if they make any more changes. I can't do that, not as long as there's a little time."

He grabbed a wrench and twisted some nuts and bolts. Then, tape measure in hand, he made some mathematical calculations. He got into the car and took it out on the track and ran a lap at just above 24 seconds. The fastest the track had ever been toured was listed at 23.8 seconds. So Foyt was not satisfied. He brought the car in and helped the crew try some more things. They changed tires. They changed springs. He took it out again. Close to 24, now. The hours were passing, the afternoon fading fast. In and out, in and out. He made some more changes. He went out and turned a lap in 23.4, the fastest it had been run.

Observed a crewman, "Now the boys have another of Foyt's records to shoot for." Crew chief Ray Nichels added, "He doesn't mind working, which is one of the things that makes him the greatest. He'll try anything and he'll go from sunup to sundown to get the job done. If it's not finished then, he'll work around the clock."

It was sundown now and the crew chief was packing up. "We might run some tests in the next day or so," he said.

"If you do, call me. We might get a little more corner speed if we change a few more things," Foyt said.

And then he drove back to Indianapolis for the night.

At Salem, Indiana, they offered a $1,000 bonus to the first driver ever to turn a lap on a half-mile track at above 100 miles per hour. Foyt went right out and ran 100.1 mph.

Scene: Ascot Park in Gardena, California, a small town outside Los Angeles. The track was dirt turned almost into the consistency of tar by years of absorbing rubber and oil. There were open, wooden bleachers, a surrounding wooden fence covered by faded advertising, and some small, old light towers for night racing. This was daytime. It was before the track was renovated and improved, but even then good drivers drove there.

Foyt was scheduled to drive a sprint car race there on a Saturday night and he was at the track every afternoon all week to prepare for it. It wasn't a big race and it didn't pay a lot, but he was in it so he wanted to win it. He and George Bignotti and A. J. Watson were working on his car. They'd make changes and Foyt would take it out and fish-tail around the quarter-mile of dirt.

J. C. Agajanian, who promoted races in Gardena and eventually would take over the old track and make something of it, was watching and he said, "This is why Foyt is the best. Do you see anyone else out here today? No, you don't. If Parnelli were running the race, he'd be here. But not many would be. Parnelli is my boy, so I'm partial to him, but anyone who's in racing has to be partial to Foyt because he gives so much to racing."

Watson said, "Ward wouldn't even drive the little dirt tracks after a while. They're rough and dangerous. But Foyt will drive them. He will drive anything. That's how he got ahead of Ward. It isn't easy, you know."

Foyt came in and stood in the shade for a few seconds. "Why shouldn't I be at a race track I'm going to race on?" he asked, shrugging. "As long as racing is how I make my living, you'll know where to find me."

In 1962, when he broke down in the Indianapolis 500, Foyt ran back to the pits just to drive another car. It was a car without a chance, a car he'd never driven. It was dangerous. But there was still a race going on and he didn't want to watch—he wanted to be in it. Two days before he raced for more than $100,000 at the Indianapolis Speedway, they ran a sprint car event for $800 at Indianapolis Raceway Park, a new track not yet completed, not yet paved over. It was dangerous and rutty. The racers sent up showers of dirt that obscured the drivers' vision. Roger McClusky hit a hole and cartwheeled in the air, smashing himself heavily. Foyt drove daringly all the way and won the race. The dust was so bad most drivers admitted later they were afraid to make passes for fear of hitting a car they could not see, but Foyt ran flat-out and made all the passes he ordinarily would have.

"Just like a Texas sand-storm," he laughed later.

In 1964, after the track was paved over, they scheduled a stock car race there one Sunday early in May, right after practice had begun for the 500. The stock car race wasn't slated to start until 2 P.M., so Foyt got to the Speedway early in the morning and was the first driver on the track and practiced his championship car hard until he had set up some things for his crewmen to work on. Then he rushed over to Raceway Park and practiced his stock car and got it ready.

In the race, he dueled for the lead until a rock ripped through his radiator, ending his run. He parked his car, not even waiting for the race to be finished, and drove hurriedly back to the Speedway. He reached the pits at 5:40, just 20 minutes before the track was to be closed for the day. He drove his car on the track and got in some more tests on it before they closed down.

Bignotti later remarked, "It is typical of Foyt. He is so competitive he scares you."

The 1964 season illustrates his competitiveness as well as any. He was winning almost all the big races, including Indy, getting wealthy, but driving the small races, too. He would drive as hard for dimes as for dollars.

Early in the year, he agreed to handle a Corvette in the Daytona Sports Car classic for John Mecom, a wealthy fellow Houston sportsman. The car arrived at the track late, improperly prepared. Weary of waiting for it, Foyt was furious. He cussed everyone out, then went to work. For three days he drove himself and everyone around him at a furious pace, supervising the mechanical detail himself and doing the driving, too.

On race day the car would not start. Everyone else got going ahead of him. He was ready to pound it to pieces when the engine finally turned over. He roared off and in one lap passed 51 cars.

He lost a wheel and his engine went sour, but he kept going for the full 12 hours. He finished 23rd. Not many others would even have finished.

One week before qualifying began at Indianapolis, "Wide World of Sports" decided to televise nationally a 40-lap sprint car race at Terre Haute. Foyt decided to go racing. He drove the 73 miles from Indianapolis, towing his sprinter. He qualified far back. The start was delayed several times as Foyt charged through the field before the green flag was unfurled.

When the race did start, his engine sputtered and he fell back to last place before he got it going. Then he began to move up, driving hard. The crowd packing the ancient stands and the infield area cheered for him, but then his engine soured and he couldn't get any power and everyone else started to pass him. Though he was being lapped by lesser drivers, he kept going until his car finally quit completely. A. J. parked it in the pits, went into his garage, changed to civvies, and drove back to Indianapolis to resume practice there, where he won the race.

It rained heavily before another sprint race at Terre Haute that year. The track grew so muddy that even after it stopped raining the drivers did not want to race. First place was worth only $600. It just wasn't worth the risk. But a big crowd was on hand and the promoter needed the dough. He pleaded with Foyt to qualify, hoping it would lure the others to follow. Foyt shrugged and said he would. He ran as fast as he could, sliding all over the slick surface, and got a slow time. Then, just as he finished, the sun broke through the clouds and began to bake the soggy earth. The other drivers told the promoter that if he would wait a while for the track to dry, they would run. He agreed. By the time they went out, conditions were much improved. There were only 24 starting positions called for, and 24 cars qualified faster than Foyt had.

Foyt was raging. He went to the 24th and last qualifier and offered him $100 for his ride, which was more than the driver had any real hope of earning. Eagerly, he took it, turning his car over to Foyt. Foyt rode the outside on the first lap and passed seven cars. Driving like a madman, he soon passed everyone. He ran out of gas on the last lap, but was so far in front by then that he could coast in with the victory.

"Boy did that burn the boys up," Foyt chuckled.

Later in the year, he entered a 100-mile stock car race on the dirt track at the Indianapolis Fairgrounds. His car's engine blew in practice, which seemed to put him out of the race. But when team-mate Len Sutton qualified a sister car poorly, he turned it over to

Foyt "in the best interests of the team." A. J. tried to put his own number and name on his new car, but officials refused and he raged at them. Taking over a car he had not qualified, Foyt was forced to start 30th and last. He passed 13 cars in the first mile. He was fourth after 18 miles, third after 19 miles, second after 39 miles, and passed Parnelli to take first at 60 miles. He finished first and took his $4,300 check and laughed all the way home.

It was not just that year that he did such things. The following year, for example, he won the 100-mile championship test on the dirt at Springfield, Illinois, in his dirt track car on Saturday, then went to Milwaukee to run his new rear-engine lightweight racer in the 200-miler on the paved track the next day.

The car was supposed to be waiting for him there. It wasn't. It had been mistakenly shipped to Indianapolis instead. Taut and furious, Foyt turned to his crew, pointed to the dirt car on the trailer, and said, "Men, we came here to race and this little car is all we've got. Let's get unloaded and go to work." They unloaded it and went to work.

A dirt car is not designed for paved tracks and should not work on them. But with new tires and a new chassis setup, Foyt made it work. Pushed off by a worn-out crew, a weary Foyt led all qualifiers and led the race for awhile. Because the dirt car carried an undersized fuel tank, Foyt had to make an extra pit stop for fuel, but he still finished second.

When someone tried to compliment him, Foyt angrily asked, "What the hell for? We didn't win." He won the next race.

"My attitude is this," he said. "I'll blow the other racers over until, my beard is down to my knees."

If he had quit when it first became reasonable for him to quit, which was a long time ago, it would not have been because he had grown weary of blowing the boys down, of racing, which he pursued with a passion, but because the pressures of his passion were beginning to pursue him. Basically, he was a simple person who enjoyed cutting up or playing cards all night with the boys, who felt most at home with his fellows on a race track, who was comfortable only with racing cronies, who thrilled to the excitement of his sport and the singular sort of prestige it brought him.

But success spoils, prestige pales. Promoters wanted him to run every race because he was the one who pulled in the paying customers. He was worrying because he was running too many races, not taking the time to prepare properly for them. It was dangerous and he knew it. He wanted to win too much and suffered losing too hard. His friends had become his enemies. Everyone wanted to beat him. Beating him had become almost as important as winning the race.

Wherever he went, he was a marked man. People he didn't know sought favors from him. They tried to sell him things, to get him to invest in businesses, to pose for pictures with him, to get his signature on pieces of paper. In restaurants they'd interrupt his meals. He'd stay in his motel room and take the telephone off the hook. Writers and broadcasters were always after him for interviews. He didn't like giving interviews. He didn't like talking about his life and his family. He valued his privacy. He was basically a private person. He felt singed by the spotlight. He didn't enjoy his prominence.

Motels can be lonely places. He wasn't seeing his kids grow up. He knew his kids, his wife, and his parents worried about him. He was fully aware that they wanted him to quit, even if they didn't say it. Even his father, who traveled with him, suggested to others that it might be smart to quit. The rest of the family waited by the telephone for his calls after races telling them he was safe.

Lucy's first words weren't, "Did you win?" They were, "Are you all right?" This disturbed him, making him conscious of the continual risks he ran. Death rides with every driver anyway. O'Connor was gone. Bryan was gone. Sachs was gone. And so many others.

It all came together to bother him. "After awhile, there is too much pressure on you from every side. I get homesick. I just want to go home and let down," A. J. admitted one day.

At home in Houston, Lucy was open about their problems. "I don't ask Tony to quit," she said. "I knew he was a race driver when I married him. My family knew. But if they minded, they didn't say. They love Tony. We all do. We have confidence in him. But we worry, of course. This is what he wants to do. Let him do it. But it is a difficult life to live. You know he's doing a dangerous thing and you don't know how he's doing. You wait to hear. The kids wait, too, even if they're not aware of it.

"Jerry, the baby, is too young. Terry, who is five, went to one race and wants to go to them all. She knows what he's doing. She wants to be the first to know how he made out. She's very proud of him. Tony, Jr., who's seven, is proud of his daddy, too, but he doesn't want to go to the races like he did when he was younger. He stopped driving the quarter-midget we bought him. He's seen things happen. He knows enough to be afraid for his daddy and he wants him to quit. I know that hurts Tony. He tries to explain it to the boy, but it doesn't help.

"We're not with Tony enough. Since we're married, Tony has

been gone most of every summer and a lot of every winter. He's only home a few weekends, it seems like. He's hardly used the lake house or the boat. I travel with him some. I go to the big races. But I do have to care for the children. It's easier not going, anyway. I can't help worrying every minute when I watch him race. Things happen in races that scare me and depress me. It's easier to just stay home and get that phone call from him telling us everything is all right.

"I'm a lot like Tony. I'm a private sort of person. I don't like the spotlight. I don't like to give interviews. It's his spotlight, anyway. He's the one that works so hard for it. I don't deserve it. He doesn't like it any more than I do, but he can't help it, he has to live with it. I'd like to think that some day he will retire and we will have a more private life. But now I don't know if that will ever be possible. He's become too important.

"There are a lot of little things I'd like for us to do together that other families do that we never seem to do. But much as I want him to quit, I can't ask him to. It has to be his choice. He loves it so. He's so good at it. And he'd miss it terribly."

Foyt sat on an oil can before a race one day, squinted up into the sun, and said, "Everyone wants me to quit but me. I don't want to quit. Racing is my life. When I quit racing, it will be like ending my life. It's a lonely life. And I'm sorry for the worry I cause my family. But I can't help it. I don't worry. If I worried about the risks, I'd never have gone into racing in the first place. I know the longer I race, the greater the risks, but I'm no more worried about it now than I ever was."

Stories about his family worrying about him, and about his living his lonely life bother him. He figures that's his business, his and his family's, the racing business.

"People who don't even know me write about me," he says. "Writers who have never even interviewed me write about my feelings and about my life. I live the life I live because it's the life I want to live. If it's a little lonely sometimes, I can take it. I don't want anyone feeling sorry for me. I don't need anyone's sympathy.

"I'm a racing driver. I lead the life of a racing driver. Some of it is bad, but you got to take the bad with the good in anything. Basically, it's a good life. It pays real well and has made a good life for my family. If you run some risks for it, that's all right, too. Nothing is worth much if you won't run some risks for it. A lot of people have a lot tougher life. I like my life. I don't need any bleeding-heart of a writer telling people it's a bad life. That's why I get uptight with writers. Why can't they just let me race?"

It was in its way a plea. It was the racing he wanted, more than the racing life. It was the racing he wanted more than the money he made racing. He didn't want to be denied a dime he felt he deserved. He bargained for the most money he could make. But it was not money that motivated him.

"If he was running for 10 percent, he'd still give 100 percent," said Barnes.

Foyt had his vanities. "I've won more championship races than any man ever. I'm proud of that," Foyt said flatly. But it was not prominence he sought. It was success. Going faster than the other guy. Running the risks, not giving in to fear, surviving and winning. "I've known him many years and I can't remember a single day when he hasn't gone fast and hard in some way to better himself," said his stock car builder, Ray Nichels.

"I got to get better because I don't want to get beat," is his contention. "I got to be the best and I want always to be the best. And those hot kids are always coming at me. I'm king of the hill and they want to knock me off. It takes hard work to get to be king of the hill and harder work to stay on top. That's why I work so hard. I probably work harder than any other driver. They gripe about how hard they work, but that's a bunch of bull.

"Most of them don't work on their cars at all. They don't even hang around to help when they're being worked on. When they're ready, they drive them. In my book, that makes them chauffeurs. I'm a racer. I don't want anyone doing anything to my cars I don't know about. I want to be there and I want to be working. That's why I don't have much time for the press. Some nights I'm around my garage until three or four in the morning tinkering with my cars. I'd rather race than talk about racing.

"I've always got time for the guys I know. It's just that so many strangers come around, and they usually want you right then and they're not even polite about it. Well, the hell with them. If they ask me when I can give them a few minutes and they meet me then and they ask intelligent questions, I'll give 'em an interview. No one ever accused me of not talking. I'll tell it as it is. But I'd rather race than talk. If you don't work hard, you don't win. Winning, whoooeee, that's what it's all about. There's nothing on earth like it. It makes me sick any time I lose. I blow off steam and people criticize me for it. But I'm human. I can get mad just like anybody else. . . . Anybody gets in my way, I get mad."

He was understanding his case. No one else seemed to get quite as mad as A. J. did when he lost or other things went wrong. Aside from his rhubarbs with sponsors and mechanics, he has fought with promoters, officials, fellow drivers, and even fans. At Milwaukee in 1962, Foyt won a 100-mile championship car race and a first-place prize of $7,600. When he picked up his check, he saw that appearance money, which the national champion receives just for running, had not been added. The promoter, Tom Marchese, explained that it was a guarantee, not paid when it was covered by the purse.

Foyt didn't understand this and thought he was being cheated. He argued angrily with the promoter and they exchanged hard words. Then the twenty-seven-year-old driver invited the sixty-three-year-old promoter outside to settle it with their fists. Marchese refused and other officials came between them.

Later Foyt apologized, calling it a misunderstanding. "I was angry and said a lot of things, most of which I can't remember now, and I am sorry. I have apologized to both Tom Marchese and officials of the United States Auto Club," he explained.

Foyt was fined $1,000 and given a stern reprimand. He shrugged and said, "I got a fair shake. I'll see that it doesn't happen again."

He was too temperamental to keep that vow. He felt he was a target for rough riding and was getting more and more upset at the tough tactics of his foes.

In a minor race at Ascot Park in Gardena, California, a young driver, seemingly determined to pass the great Foyt, tried to pass him in a turn by going in so hard and so high Foyt wouldn't dare stay with him. He got by, accelerating sharply past him at an angle that carried him across the path of Foyt's car. He had made a move that was beyond his ability and he lost control. As a result, the rear end of his car slid out, he braked too hard trying to stop the slide, and the car spun directly in front of Foyt. Angrily but coolly, A. J. picked his spot, aimed just above the spinning racer, accelerated, and managed to get by with inches to spare.

He just let it go, but the next morning at breakfast he said, "He hit the panic button. He never should have spun out. He tried to pass me in a place he shouldn't have. He got out of shape and he lost it. Some guys driving today have no business being out there. They'll do anything to knock you off. They bump you, you got to bump 'em back. Sportsmanship, hell. These are rough guys playing rough. It's dangerous to duel out there. They'll run you off the track if you let them. I can't give anyone any breaks because they don't give me any. I'm the Indianapolis champ and everyone wants to pass me now and they'll run right over me to do it if they have to."

He was not alone in his feelings. Parnelli Jones said, "This is no sport for gentlemen. Every time somebody gets near you, you can't just move over and let him go past—you've got to stand up in your seat and drive her a little harder."

At a sprint car race at Williams Grove, Pennsylvania, young Johnny White passed Foyt on the outside at the end of a straight and angled over to drop right in front of him, cementing his lead, as they went into the turn. Foyt had to brake so hard his car's rear end started to cut loose, and he had to wrestle the steering wheel skillfully to keep it from coming around and throwing him into a spin. He managed to regain control, but he had been pushed to a point of fury.

The minute the race was over, as the drivers parked, Foyt pulled to a screeching stop, yanked off his harness, jumped out of his car and ran to White's car while White was still in it. He went right at White and a crowd of racing people around the pits swiftly surrounded them, obscuring them. Foyt was pulled away and the fans, on their feet in the stands in an attempt to see what was going on, booed him. Foyt seemed to make an angry motion and stalked away.

Tommy Nicholson, eastern supervisor of competition for USAC, who was on the scene, reported to his official body later that Foyt charged White while the latter was still strapped in his harness, threw a punch at him, struck him in the forehead, and applied a headlock on him before others intervened. He said Foyt made an obscene gesture at the fans when they booed him.

Foyt said, "I didn't swing at the guy. I was just holding him. Sure, I had him around the neck. I thought he was going to hit me. But I didn't punch him. I had his mechanic around the neck at the same time because I thought he was going to hit me, too."

Henry Banks, USAC's competition supervisor, suspended Foyt pending a hearing on the charges. Saying that after the story broke, even Foyt's seven-year-old son had wondered why he had hit the other driver, Foyt offered to take a lie detector test to support his statements. USAC had its lawyer at the hearing, while Foyt defended himself. When his mechanic, Barney Wimmer, and a rival, Roger McCluskey, testified to the truth of Foyt's version, and when Nicholson admitted he had not actually seen Foyt hit White, when no one turned up who could say he had seen Foyt hit White, and when White didn't even turn up at the hearing, USAC's nineteen-member board of directors dropped the suspension.

USAC President Thomas Binford admitted to Foyt, "There was not sufficient evidence to substantiate the charges against you." Then he added, "The board asked me to caution you that as a champion and gentleman, you should direct your complaints to the officials."

Foyt never has ceased directing his complaints to officials and has made it clear he does not consider USAC always right in its actions or rulings. He has had many squabbles with racing's governing body. And he has had many with others in racing. The White incident was not the first or last time he had a physical confrontation with a fellow racer. Racing men tell stories of a fist fight he had with Ed Elisian in Clint Brawner's garage in 1959. And of a fight he had with a mechanic at the Holiday Inn over the invasion of turbine cars into the Speedway in 1967. But he frequently cools off fast and doesn't carry a grudge. When White was paralyzed in an accident later and an auction was held for his benefit, Foyt put his helmet up. When the helmet didn't bring the price he thought it would, he bought it back himself for $500.

However, he does heat up in a hurry. The Speedway surrounds a golf course. One year a tournament was held during the practice period on the track. Golfers and golf fans being dedicated to golf, they were bothered by the booming sounds of the racers echoing over their course. One of the favorite stories around tracks is that when Foyt heard several of the golf crowd cursing racing and drivers as they returned to the motel from the tournament, A. J. blew his top and tore into them.

A witness recalls, "Two or three of them tried to take him on, and they were big guys, too, but Foyt took 'em apart. He belted them bad before others got in between them. Right then and there, I decided I never want any part of him. He's a heavyweight and he hits hard. In an alley fight, he's on my side."

At the first 500 run at Pocono, Foyt's crew members had pushed his car onto the pit apron and were starting to maneuver it into position. It was pointed forward and most push their cars backward until they reach the right row. Foyt's father started to turn the car around to push it head-first. For some reason, a guard objected. He put his foot in front of A. J.'s car and pushed A. J.'s father back. Foyt had been posing for pictures for some fans and in as good a mood as possible, but when he saw that this fellow had laid a hand on his dad, he blew up. His neck tensed and seemed to swell several inches. He moved right at the guard, grabbed him, and shoved him aside. For a split second it appeared he was ready to wade into the guy. His father called him off. It turned out his father had twisted his knee. Foyt threatened to find the guard's father and break his leg before he was calmed down.

A writer says, "If you saw it, you know how overwhelming it was. His temper is on a hair-trigger. He's a tough guy. All right, it's a tough business. He belongs. No one shoves him around."

One of his former backers has stated, "He's the greatest driver of them all, but he'll drive you crazy." Said another, "He's very moody, extremely unpredictable. He's up and down, hot and cold. He changes with the wind. One minute he's telling a tall Texas story and bragging and laughing, and the next minute he's telling someone off and cursing and snorting. He can't stand for any lack of enthusiasm among his crewmen. He wants to feel they're putting all they have into his car."

Said a racing official, "The best time to talk to him is after a victory. He doesn't enjoy it long, however, because then it's time to start worrying about winning the next one. And if he lost, forget it. Then he has to win the next one more than ever."

Said Rodger Ward, "I don't know any driver who wants or tries to win any harder. You can just see it building up. Early in the week, he's free and easy. Then the change starts. He starts getting a little edgy. By Friday, he's walking around with a look that says, 'Just let me at 'em.' Before Sunday, you can hardly hold him back."

A former member of his crew summed up his working relations with Foyt in this manner: "One minute he's funning with you, laughing and kidding around, and you say to yourself, 'goddam, he sure can be a good guy,' and then the next minute he's scowling and snorting and cussing you out and telling you to get lost, and you think, 'son of a bitch, what a bastard he is.'

"Well, there are only two ways to do things for Foyt—his way or the wrong way. You go his way or you go away. Everyone else is wrong. He won't tolerate a mistake. That's okay. This is not a business for making mistakes. But the more scared of him you get, the tenser you get, the more mistakes you make. When you lose, you know there's going to be hell to pay until he wins. Well, I quit because I couldn't take the tension."

Foyt's answer is simple and direct. "I know only one way to do things—my way. I don't say it's the only way. I don't even say it's the right way. But it's my way and it's the only right way when you're working for me. It's the only way to keep me happy. I'm happy when I know the crew and myself have put everything together right. I'm happy when the car is performing well. If the car works, I know I'll win.

"To be a winner, to be successful, you have to pay attention to detail. I won't allow sloppy work in my garage or at the track. There is no room for errors either by the driver or his crew. You're alone out there in the car. A mistake back in the garage or in the pit could end it all for you. I'm not anxious to hurry death along. Since I'm the one that has to go out there and drive the car and run the risks, I have the right to have things my way."

With Foyt, his backers work for him instead of his working for them. He is big enough to get away with this arrangement. He doesn't have to beg rides. He is offered the best rides. Backers want him because they can win with him. But if Foyt feels he can get more help from someone else, he'll make the move. He makes demands and drives tough bargains.

Former backer Bill Ansted said, "He may not have had much education, but he sure knows how to read a contract. Even when he leaves you, however, you feel he has been fair. You always know where you stand with him. As long as he's with you, he gives you your money's worth."

Foyt frequently has switched from backer to backer. One year, he switched sponsors three times—from Bob Bowes to Lindsey Hopkins to Bill Ansted and Shirley Murphy. But he stayed with the latter a long time because he felt they were the best of the backers. With Bignotti, it seemed almost a matter of, "All right, you've done a lot for me, but what have you done for me lately?" Foyt fired Bignotti many times and Bignotti quit many times before they fell out for the last time.

Foyt won Indy with Bignotti in 1961 but fired him shortly after Indy in 1962 when his wheel wasn't tightened in that pit stop and fell off on the track. Foyt won Indy with Bignotti in 1964 and went on to have his greatest year, but after failing to finish the first five races with Bignotti in 1965, Foyt fired him again and for the final time. Bignotti was as big as Foyt within the fraternity by then, and he was not about to go back, even if he had been asked.

Foyt then hired and fired Parnelli's ex-mechanic, Johnny Pouelson. That lasted less than a year. One night in 1966, the team was working overtime to prepare for two consecutive championship events—on a Saturday at Springfield, Illinois, and the next day at Milwaukee.

One car wasn't working right, so Foyt said, "We're gonna stay right here until we get this thing straightened out."

Pouelson agreed but said he wanted to run out to grab a bite to eat before continuing.

Foyt glared at him and snapped, "I said we're staying until we get it fixed."

Pouelson shrugged, went out for food, returned for his gear, and resigned.

Well, what Foyt really wanted was to run his own show himself and he has done that ever since. He has good mechanics working for him, including his father, but he is his own boss.

He sets his own sponsorship deals. He will not run anything or endorse anything he does not believe in. But circumstances compel him to make moves here, too. He as much as any other man talked

Goodyear into going into the racing game in the early 1960s, and he more than anyone else helped Goodyear end the monopoly Firestone had held on winning publicity at Indianapolis and along the championship trail. He was convinced Firestone wasn't doing all it could for him. But when he felt new Goodyears weren't right at Indianapolis in 1964, he switched to Firestones at the last minute. As the first winner who had not had to make a tire change, he brought Firestone tremendous publicity and he held his post-race press conference in the Firestone room, but he wore a Goodyear uniform and refused to accept Firestone's bonus check.

When someone asked him where the Firestone decals were on his car, he smiled and said, "I guess I went so fast they just plain blew off."

He helped Goodyear get racing tires good enough to win the big races and he won with their tires and made them competitive as a racing company with their rival—and was paid well for it.

He reluctantly switched from the Offenhauser engine to the Ford when he shifted to rear-engine cars, but he got a good contract from Ford to help them improve their product and he remained loyal even when the Offy was altered to the point where it worked well in the lightweights.

Eventually he took over the Ford racing engine operation, improved the engines enormously and started to sell them to rivals, though he doesn't sell as many as he might because rivals are wary he won't give them as good as he takes for himself.

This worry may not be totally unfounded. One of the tire company officials says, "Foyt will take any edge he can get and always is looking for an advantage. His pride is at stake so I seriously doubt he would give a guy anything but the best engine he could make. He'd be almost as happy to see an engine he built win the 500 as he would to win it himself, just as he was doubly happy when he won Indy in 1967 because he won in a Coyote car he built himself. But he can be tricky. He tests tires and when he finds something that works especially well he'd like to keep it for himself without telling someone else about it or giving it away to his rivals.

"When you get a tire that's working just right with the car and the speed it's going and the track at a given time, it's a helluva advantage. Nothing is more critical to the performance of racing cars than the tires and we have to keep improving them. Foyt is always asking for something special. But you can't keep faith with the other drivers who drive your tires if you give him something you won't give them. A company will assign a man to work closely with an important driver like Foyt and Foyt is always asking for a new guy or a young guy because he figures he can bully the guy, who will be in awe of him, and maybe sweet-talk him into saving something special for him. He's very slick, Mr. Foyt."

In 1964 Foyt was driving for Ford in the Firecracker 400 stock car classic at Daytona, but when he saw the Dodge was going to go better, he jumped into a Dodge and won with it, which frustrated the Ford people to no end. On the other hand, he was winning NASCAR Grand National races in Ford's Mercury cars in the early 1970s but switched to Chevrolets because by that time he had a Chevrolet agency in Houston and figured he should drive the car he was selling, and he has stuck to Chevies though he has not won as steadily in them. This does not mean the Mercury is a better car than the Chevy, but that for the time being the Mercs that are being raced are better for racing or are getting better help.

Such a situation can frustrate Foyt. In the late 1960s, the Plymouths that were being raced had a hot engine that was outclassing the Fords Foyt was driving. At one point in the Daytona 500, Foyt brought his Ford into the pits and said something to the effect that the thing wouldn't run right and either he parked it there or on the track. The team manager pleaded, then demanded that Foyt return to the track. So Foyt returned to the track, but within one lap he had grazed a wall with his car, drove it into the pits, parked it, shrugged, and departed.

Would a driver deliberately scrape a wall? In the first California 500 at Ontario, California, in 1970, Foyt had long since dropped out of the competition for the lead when Art Pollard took over the lead not far from the finish with Jim McElreath, driving a Foyt team car, running second. The best chance McElreath had of catching Pollard was if an accident happened on the track. That would bring out the yellow flag, slow the field down, and bunch it up, with the cars permitted to close in on but not pass the cars running in front of them.

Foyt, who had spent much of the day in the pits and had no chance for a good place, scraped his car on a wall. The yellow came out, the cars slowed and bunched up. After Foyt's car was removed—with Foyt himself helping, to hurry it up—the race was restarted and McElreath roared past Pollard to take the lead and eventually came home ahead with the winnings for the Foyt team. Some people suspect Foyt's actions were deliberate. He denies it.

The rule is unfair anyway, even if it helps produce close, exciting races with extra changes of the lead for the fans, because a driver can work hard and risk a lot to gain almost a lap lead on the next car and then have it taken away from him by the cars being allowed to bunch up under the yellow. The original rule was changed partly because during caution periods many drivers often refused to hold the margin that existed just before the caution period began and were continually catching up to or passing other cars whose drivers were trying to hold their positions. Foyt was one.

In the 1967 Indy 500, rival crews contended that Foyt sneaked up steadily under the yellows, sometimes making up as much as 12 seconds on leader Parnelli Jones. Even the public address announcer spoke of it to the crowd. In any event, Jones eventually fell out, while Foyt went on to the victory.

Parnelli admits he should have known better than to let Foyt take advantage of him. He knows all too well that Foyt is one of those like himself who wants to win at anything he does, whether it is playing cards or climbing mountains.

Once Parnelli and Foyt were talked into taking a lap race around the Indiana Fairgrounds track in the sulkies of harness horses in an exhibition between the regular races.

Parnelli recalls that Foyt went to him before the race and said, "Hell, buddy, we don't know anything about these things. We could get killed. Let's play it smart. Instead of taking a lot of chances, we'll just stay together most of the way, stroking 'em nice and easy, and after we come out of the last turn and hit the homestretch, we'll give our horses a whack of the whip at the same time and go from there and let the better man win."

Jones said, well, all right, sure, it made sense to him. So that's the way they went. Until they entered the fourth turn. And then there was Foyt suddenly giving his horse a shout and whacking him with the whip and shooting away from Jones, who went to the whip himself then, but too late.

"I couldn't catch up. The so-and-so slickered me," Jones laughed admiringly.

In the Ontario 500 stock car race in California in 1971, A. J. made a move Buddy Baker has not forgotten. "I guess he wanted to get around me. Anyway, he pulled up alongside me and he kept motioning to his right tire and signaling me as if to ask me if it was going flat. Like a fool, I took a long look at it and said, no, it was okay. At that moment he took off right away from me and left me behind like some sucker."

Another odd incident involved a serious accident in a championship race at Phoenix that compelled officials to call a temporary halt. Conditions on the track were bad. Foyt was leading, but his engine was going sour. Foyt went around to other drivers suggesting the race should be called at that point. Many others were willing to go along with him. They did not know about the condition of his engine. But when Foyt talked to Eddie Sachs, the later said, "A. J., there's no way we're going to hand you this thing on a platter. We're gonna go right on running."

Foyt argued angrily while the other drivers and other people around the pits watched in amusement. The race was resumed. Foyt soon fell out of it with a sick engine. A driver says, "Well, what the hell, if you can sweet-talk your way into an easy win without risks, why not try?"

Al Unser smiles and says, "Foyt bends every rule in the book. He may even break a few. Hell, he rewrote the book himself. But we admire him for it. Hell, you got to admire a man who knows how to win."

Some rules bug A. J. In the 1970 California 500, a directive was handed down to the effect that drivers had to have metallic sensors on the hoods of their cars to trigger electronic equipment each time they passed the finish line and provide fast, accurate information as to the number of laps each car had run and where it stood in relation to the other cars.

It was a system desperately needed in racing. In long races cars pass and repass and are passed and repassed and go in and out of the pits and after awhile no one is sure who is where. Time and again a situation has occurred in which no one knew if the car in front was in the lead or a lap behind. In addition, there have been times when two or three drivers drove into victory lane at a race's end each thinking he had won. This, of course, resulted in official rechecking of the scoring later, and even the recheck often failed to resolve this critical matter to everyone's satisfaction. It is racing's major failing and not enough is done to correct it.

The pylon "scoreboards" at Indianapolis and Ontario are inadequate, for example, but they build new grandstands instead of new scoreboards and do not invest in improved scoring systems, so all the people who have spent so much and exerted themselves so much or risked so much to make this a race are seldom sure of the precise lap position of each car while it is being run and who has won when it is done.

Well, Ontario tried it in 1970 and Foyt's car wasn't running right, so he got it into his head that the sensor had something to do with it. Accordingly, during a pit stop he grabbed a hammer and knocked it off, which ruined the entire system, of course.

In stock car racing, you are not allowed to tape up your windows. In a 500 at Pocono, in 1973, Foyt was practicing for the time trials in a Chevrolet Malibu that had tape on its back windows. When a rival, apparently Butch Hartman, called him on it and the officials black-flagged him into the pits and told him to take off the tape, Foyt was so furious he started to haul his car away, ready to pack up and take off and forget the race.

But cooler heads prevailed. They talked the hot-headed Foyt into removing the tape and forgetting it and showing them up by running fast. So Foyt did just that. Richard Petty looked like a cinch for the pole until Foyt went out and qualified faster, driving like a demon.

Gordon Johncock said, "Shoot, they just made A. J. mad. He hadn't been practicing within a mile of the speed he turned on."

But as sweet as revenge was, it turned sour in the race when Foyt's car could not maintain such speed and was unable to keep up with Petty and Hartman. He was visibly upset when his pit crew informed him on his helmet radio receiver that he was a lap down to the leaders in the late going. He figured the officials were wrong about his position. When Gary Bettenhausen had an accident and the yellow caution signals went on and the pace car drove onto the track to lead the pack around at slowdown speed, A. J. roared past the pace car and pulled his car to a halt at the start-finish line to give the officials a piece of his mind.

While he was hollering at them, the pace car returned, the green signal returned, and Hartman, Petty, and the rest resumed at top speed and Foyt took off with his tires screeching. When the checkered flag fell, he was listed in fourth place, still a lap behind the leader, Petty. But USAC stockcar supervisor Bob Stroud promptly penalized Foyt a lap for passing the pace car in the caution period and Foyt dropped to seventh in the standing but skyrocketed into orbit in anger. He charged into the USAC office in the garage area and had a few things to say before departing in a dark mood. He'd threatened to file a protest fee to try for a reversal of the ruling, but after his stock car chief, Banjo Mathews, checked the scoring sheets and approved the official version, the matter was reluctantly dropped.

Foyt will use the rules to help him, too. The outstanding example of this came in the last race of the championship circuit season in 1967 when A. J. entered holding only a slim lead of 340 points over Mario Andretti. A. J. could not let Andretti finish much higher than he did or gain many more points if he was to hold his lead and win another title. This was a 300-mile race at Riverside Raceway in California. Foyt not only entered himself in his lead car but entered Jim Hurtubise in a backup car. Quietly, he arranged with Hurtubise to surrender his car to Foyt if Foyt's car failed. He also arranged with a rival, Roger McCluskey, to surrender his car to Foyt if the second car also failed. The rules at the time permitted relief drivers to gain the points of the car's final finishing position. So Foyt was prepared. Andretti was not.

Andretti's car was faster than Foyt's. Most of the way Mario dueled Dan Gurney and McCluskey for the lead. Just short of the halfway point, Foyt was pressing to catch Andretti when Al Miller spun his car right in front of A. J., who ran off the track in a desperate maneuver to avoid him. The attempt failed and Foyt's car was racked up by Miller's wildly careening racer. Angrily, Foyt jumped out of his wrecked car and ran from the first turn back to the pits. He got there just in time to see Hurtubise's car being towed away. It had been black-flagged out of the race for throwing oil. Foyt swiftly signaled McCluskey, who, though he was in the lead at the time, pulled in to put his car under Foyt.

Roger jumped out, Foyt jumped in and took off. The car had lost the lead during the stop, but Foyt drove relentlessly after Gurney and Andretti. With 17 laps to go, the clutch in Foyt's car started to slip. When he tried to let it out all the way, the rear wheels spun. On a road course, this is ruinous. Foyt fell back. In fact, it is considered a miracle of sorts that he could keep his car going. He hung on desperately. Andretti ran out of gas and had to make an emergency stop, which dropped him from first to third place at the finish, behind Gurney and Bobby Unser. Foyt hung on to finish fifth in McCluskey's car.

The public address announcer informed the crowd that Andretti had won his third straight driving title.

Worriedly, Andretti asked, "Is that official?"

"No way," insisted Foyt.

And it wasn't. When the officials added up the points, Andretti had 420 for finishing third, while Foyt had 160 points for finishing fifth in McCluskey's car. Andretti had a total of 3,360 points for the season while Foyt had 3,440. Thus Foyt had won an unprecedented fifth title by 80 points.

Foyt turned over the $3,625 fifth-place money to McCluskey and reportedly gave him a gift for Christmas that made up for the $16,000 first-place prize Roger might have earned.

Foyt denied that he had "bought off" Roger. "You don't buy off McCluskey," he said. "Roger and I have been friends for a long time. He came to me before the race and said that if anything happened to my car, I could drive his. That's all there was to it."

McCluskey shrugged and said, "Foyt loaned me his sprint car last season and I won the national championship in that class with it."

As for Andretti, his reaction was, "I should have friends like that." He noted that he and Foyt had had breakfast together that morning.

"He didn't let me in on any of his secrets," Mario said drily. "What did we talk about? We talked about our eggs."

Angry but awed, he drove A. J. away in a dune buggy. He drove it hard. Hitting a bump, he set Foyt bouncing in his seat. "Hey, take it easy, man," screamed Foyt, laughing. "You're scaring the hell out of me."

Ironically, Andretti tried the same trick the following season during the last race of the season, again at Riverside, when he started with a slim lead in points over Bobby Unser. Andretti not only entered a second car he could take over if his car broke down but he made deals with just about every driver around to take over their cars if he had to. He began by sharing the lead with Gurney while Unser spun out on the first lap, fell far behind and had to come back a long way to get near the lead.

Around the halfway point, Andretti's car had to be parked in the pits with a broken rod bearing. His second car already was out with engine trouble. Andretti ran to his pal Parnelli's pits. Jones brought in Joe Leonard's car and replaced Joe with Mario. Andretti raced out, went to pass Art Pollard in a turn, ducked inside of him, drifted wide, and hit Pollard. The impact sent both cars spinning into the wall and out of the race.

Mario jumped out and started to run back to the pits, but Parnelli met him with a motorcycle, picked him up, and drove him to Gene White's pits, where Lloyd Ruby's car was called in and turned over to him. Andretti roared away and took the car from fourth to third place but was passed by Unser, who took second, behind Gurney.

When they added it all up, Unser had prevented Mario from taking his third title by just six points.

"It works for Foyt, but not for the rest of us," sighed Andretti, who wound up driving for pal Parnelli's team.

The rules were subsequently changed. From then on a driver could get points only in proportion to the part of the event he had raced.

The start of the colorful Daytona 500 race in 1972 (*NASCAR photo*)

Foyt in Purolator car shoots inside and roars past Bobby Allison in Coca-Cola car to eventual victory in 1972 Ontario 500 race. (*Photo by George Rose*)

Wood Brothers pit crew moving fast to service Foyt during pit stop in this same race (*Photo by George Rose*)

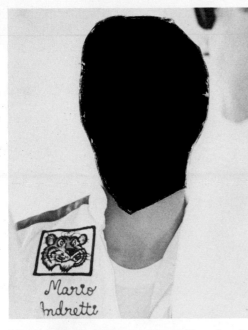

Mario Andretti (*Photo by Darryl Norenberg*)   Al Unser (*USAC photo*)

Mark Donohue (*USAC photo*)   Richard Petty (*USAC photo*)

Race officials at DuQuoin Fairgrounds in DuQuoin, Illinois, use a fire extinguisher to put out flames on A. J. Foyt. The fire started when fuel was spilled on Foyt as he pitted during a USAC race. (*Photo from Wide World*)

Foyt barrels his number 14 Coyote through a corner in the 1973 Indianapolis 500. (*Indianapolis Motor Speedway photo*)

His number 14 car having caved in, Foyt jumped into teammate George Snider's number 84 Coyote. But it, too, collapsed and he pushes it himself during 1973 Indianapolis 500. (*Indianapolis Star photo by Frank H. Fisse*)

Typically furious, Foyt argues with USAC official Bob Stroud over tape and sheet metal on his car that had been declared illegal at Pocono stock car race in 1973. (*Photo by Peter West*)

A jubilant Foyt celebrates his victory in his Coyote in the 1973 Pocono 500 race in Pennsylvania. (*Pocono International Speedway photo*)

Foyt chats with rival Bobby Unser. (*Photo by George Rose*)

Foyt's father looks down as Foyt eases himself into cockpit prior to time trials before race at Ontario Motor Speedway in California. (*Photo by Bill Libby*)

As he is today—battle-scarred, hair thinning, tough as ever—A. J. Foyt
(*USAC photo*)

8

Foyt is not indestructible. Bent too far, he breaks. He is admirably tough, almost awesome, but he is human. He can be hurt. He hides from it, but he knows it. He lives with it. He is brave, which does not mean he is never afraid.

Going to Riverside to race stock cars the day after his thirtieth birthday in January 1965, A. J. Foyt had a premonition of impending danger. He recalls, "Usually I like to run there, but that one time I just didn't want to go. Before I left the airport, I called Lucy and told her where I'd parked the car and where to find the keys. That's something I'd never done before."

It worried her. Foyt says, "I told her I was phoning just in case I got held up, or weathered in, or something."

On the 171st lap of the 15-lap race, Dan Gurney, Junior Johnson, and Marvin Panch were running one-two-three. As the large, gaudy cars roared into the second corner of the twisting road course, Foyt closed in at 140 miles per hour on Johnson and Panch, planning to pass them to make a run at the leader. As he tried to slow down to take the turn, his foot drove the brake pedal to the floorboad. He had no braking power left. Foyt had a fraction of a second to decide on a course of action.

"You don't exactly reason it out," he recalled later. "Hellamighty, there's no time for debate. If you've been doin' this thing for awhile, you get the picture right away and you react, almost by instinct.

"I didn't see how I could get by them on the high side. Maybe I could have missed Johnson, but not Panch. If I'd of hit him from behind, I'd have rode him up into the wall. I might've gotten away with it, but I don't think he could've.

"I didn't think I could cut underneath them and stay on the track, but that's what I figured I had to do, so, wham, away I went."

It is not that Foyt is the ultimate sportsman. He will take any advantage of a rival he can get. If he can trick a foe, he will. But he is a real man. Put to the test, he comes through as a real man would.

He has said, "It's a tough business and you have to be tough to survive in it. You don't give anyone any breaks because no one will give you any. But there comes a time when you have to show the respect you feel for your rivals. If you've gotta go, you do your damnedest not to take anyone with you. If you're gonna live, you're gonna have to live with yourself."

Foyt wrenched his steering wheel hard to the left, cutting down to the inside of the track. Desperately he tried to straighten out, hanging on the rim of a sharp incline for a moment, then he slid off and hurtled down a 35-foot embankment, bouncing end over end, as high as 40 to 50 feet at one point, in a wild plunge before settling into a steaming, crumpled heap on the infield grass. Fortunately, his car did not explode or catch fire.

A rescue crew rushed up to pull him from the twisted metal. He was trapped inside and it took them 14 minutes to pry him from the tangle. He was conscious but groaning with agony. They lifted him out and set him carefully on a stretcher and raced him by ambulance to a nearby hospital, where his condition was first listed as "fair."

He had a fractured vertebra in his back and a broken left heel and his body was rubbed raw and bruised badly. He later reported, "Flesh was torn from my neck and my right hand. All the skin was scraped off my left ear and the left side of my face. My ears were slightly cauliflowered. My chin was badly bruised. My lips were swollen almost double. My feet, elbows, and rear end were bruised so bad they turned black. My whole body was a mass of bruises."

The force of the terrible tumble was so great that the brand new coveralls he was wearing simply split apart and his crash helmet was dented in. It appeared that the heavy roll-bar protection built into these big stock cars had saved him from being crushed, but he said, "Just a hair faster and I'd have broken every bone in my body." Other drivers have failed to survive much less serious accidents.

He was doped up and treated, placed in a cast and hospitalized for long weeks of painful mending. But on the first day he was described as "cheerful and alert" and the second day he was taken from the intensive care unit and he was joking, "Now I got to order me some new crash helmets."

Soon he was spending his time studying for his test for his airplane pilot's license. And all the while his shattered body was mending he was forced to live with deep, nagging pain, yet he refused to yield to it. His wife worried by his side, confiding hope to friends that this might be the end of his racing at last, all the while knowing better, knowing him too well for that, knowing he would resume racing as soon as possible.

"I'm going back to it, sure," he said. "Shoot, you can't let things like this get you down. This is part of it." Logically, it was time to quit. But A. J. is not a logical man.

He was flat on his back for a while before he was able to sit erect for brief periods. Then he was allowed short trips away from the hospital before he was finally discharged. At first he had to use crutches in order to get around, and for some time after that he had to wear braces on his back and heel. But gradually his body knitted together again.

He had lost 25 pounds by the time he was released from the hospital, but he began to swim daily in the heated pool at his Houston home and take walks and build up his weight and strength. Near the end of March, less than three months after his smashup in California, he flew to Arizona and limped into Phoenix Raceway. Friends and foes in the fraternity were surprised to see him and rushed up to slap his back and welcome him and to kid him about his accident.

"I flew like a bird," A. J. chuckled.

No one said much about how stiffly he moved around, though someone remarked, "Looks like mebbe you broke a wing, boy." It was clear he was still hurting. But there was a race and he was ready to race. He lowered himself painfully into the cramped cockpit of a little Lotus-Ford rear-engine car and streaked around the one-mile paved oval in less than 31 seconds to lead all drivers in qualifying trials. And he remained the frontrunner until his car began to leak oil and overheat and finally sputtered to a stop.

"Anyway, I'm back," he said afterward, never happy with a loss.

"It was one of the most incredible comebacks any man has ever made," stated Chris Economaki, editor of *National Speed Sport News,* the car racing newspaper, and an ABC-TV commentator. "These are tough guys, these drivers, but they were amazed."

One week later, still strapped up beneath his coveralls and unable to completely disguise his limp, the tough Texan moved into Atlanta to drive a high-powered new Ford in a 500 mile stock car race over a one-and-a-half-mile paved high-bank track that stands in the Georgia countryside.

As the big cars boomed noisily around the oval in practice, Foyt was asked why he was there. "I'm a racing driver. Where else should I be?" he replied. His face, usually suntanned, seemed pale. A smile spread over it. "I feel okay, though I admit I feel older than I did a year ago at this time," he said.

Stuffing his hands into his leather jacket, he moved off to watch the work that was being done on his car.

Sitting nearby, one of Foyt's friends and stock car racing rivals, Freddie Lorenzen, said, "He's hurting bad but you can't get the sonofabuck to admit it. They tell me his back hurts so bad he can't sleep at night. I know his foot hurts. He tries not to show he can't walk right, but you can see it. But that doesn't mean he can't still drive better than almost anyone else."

The race was run on a scorching southern Sunday. One third of the way through it, Foyt came charging up on his old friend from Riverside—Panch—who was his teammate in Atlanta and driving a sister car. As Foyt went to pass Panch, the throttle on A. J.'s car stuck. As they headed into a turn, he could not slow down. It was chillingly similar to that moment at Riverside, only now Foyt saw some room on the outside.

"I thought, uh-oh, here we go—Riverside all over again. Only this time I had a place to put her. I went flying high, wide, and handsome," A. J. recalled later.

Panch said, "I saw him go past me out of control and I felt it when he hit the wall and I just didn't want to think about what might have happened."

This time, however, Foyt escaped unhurt. His car scraped to a stop along the wall and he was able to walk away from it, cursing his bad luck. He walked back to the pits, stewing. When they towed in his bent-up car, he threw his helmet in it. He sat on a pit wall watching the race for awhile, then began to pack up to leave to fly to Phoenix, where he was wanted to test tires.

By then, however, on this steaming, suffocating day, Panch, though in the lead, was suffering from heat exhaustion and neck cramps and signaled that he had to come in. He needed relief and when he got into the pits and was helped out of the car, the Wood Brothers team called to Foyt to jump in. A. J. grabbed his helmet and went to work. Slumping wearily against the pit wall, the sick Panch said, "I was never so glad to see anyone in my life as I was to see ol' A. J."

There were 122 laps left of the 334-lap marathon. Foyt drove hard to hold the lead. Aside from the heat, five accidents in the last part of the race removed most of the field. Of 44 starters, only 14 still were running at the finish, but Foyt was one of them, holding off Bobby Johns in a bitter battle to take the checker and the $18,000 first-place prize, the cheers of more than 50,000 fans, and the backclaps of his happy crew.

"If you can't beat 'em, join 'em," he grinned as he threw an arm around Panch's shoulder in Victory Lane. Privately and with some relief, A. J. admitted to a friend, "I was beginning to think I'd used up all my luck."

He still was hurting all the long month of May in Indianapolis as he prepared for the 500. He had two rear-engine lightweights to test. He would run one. He had gone over to the new-type racers.

"I held out as long as I could," he said. "I may be the last guy ever to win this race in a front-engine car. Maybe I can be the first to win in a rear-engine car. They're gonna win. You gotta go with what is gonna win."

On the fifth day of the month, Foyt was practicing his "funny car" at just under 160 miles per hour going through the second turn when the left rear hub-carrier broke, wrenching off a wheel. He spun out of control for almost 1,000 feet, narrowly missing the outside wall but careening from there front first into the inside wall. Meanwhile, the bounding wheel flew up to meet him, rolled across his back and across the top of his helmet, and then away again. The car plowed to a stop on the infield grass along the backstretch. It was the first time he'd struck a wall at Indy.

As aides rolled up in a pace car, Foyt was stomping around his bent racer, kicking at the ground, shaking his head and asking, "Am I all right? Am I all right?" He said, "Man, I thought that blank-blanker would never stop spinning. I was in that long, long spin, and, man, I was reaching up and unhooking my shoulder straps at the same time. Then that old tire came rolling up over my head and I thought to myself, 'Well, this car is going to catch fire for sure, but one thing it ain't going to burn up is old A. J.' When it started to slow down, I stood up in the seat and bailed out."

He had only a cut on his nose where it had struck the windshield and a cut on his knee suffered when he scrambled out of the racer.

He crouched by his car, inspecting it. He thought something had broken in his gear box, as had happened to him twice before. Muttering that he had ordered new gears, he swore he would not drive the damned thing until they came. However, it turned out to be the hub-carrier, which is only one of a thousand things that can crack on a car. He still felt the new cars were not safe and spoke about not running them.

Parnelli Jones had gone over to the new cars, too. Four days later he was hurtling into the backstretch on a practice run when his car's right hub-carrier broke, breaking off his wheel. But he was only going 125, and somehow as the car started to slide and spin on three corners he wrestled it to a safe stop. Getting out, he said, "Thank God, I wasn't standing on it."

The next day, the last Monday before time trials, Foyt stood with Jones in Parnelli's Garage 53 on Gasoline Alley looking longingly at Ol' Calhoun, the number 98 that had carried Parnelli to glory at Indy.

"Hey, where is your 'Old Faithful?'" Parnelli asked Foyt, meaning his 1964 winner.

"Gosh, I really don't know, but I bet I could get her real quick," A. J. smiled.

Laughing, they agreed they would be wise to return to these heavyweight roadsters. Foyt climbed into the cockpit of Ol' Calhoun to try it on for size. "Remember we've shaken hands on it," he said to Parnelli. "If you'll drive yours, I'll drive mine."

Parnelli looked away wistfully, silent for a few seconds. Then he walked over to his new car. "Well, I've gone 158 in this one and that doesn't look too bad now."

He knew and Foyt knew they were kidding each other. They had to race the new ones. Foyt studied Parnelli. "This is getting to be serious," he said quietly. "We're gonna have to do something about these little things."

Parnelli shook his head and grinned. "I know where I'd like to be on race day. High in the stands with a big cage around me. I don't want to get hit by all the flying nuts and bolts and stuff off these funny cars."

Foyt smiled and said, "Why it's gonna be more dangerous for the people in the stands than us. They have to worry about all that stuff off the cars flying up and hittin' 'em in the head. Of course, we haven't got it too good, either, with those little dudes strapped to us."

Others were laughing. Foyt turned to Bob Renner of the Indianapolis *News* and said, "Why look at Parnelli. He's getting bald, And me too. We've lost all that since coming here. You're really shook aren't you, Rufe?" He paused a moment, then added, "I know I'm really worried. I've been looking for a way to retire. Much more of this and I will."

Suddenly he got out of the old car and was gone from the garage. Parnelli sat for a few more seconds, staring at Ol' Calhoun. In practice later, he crashed his new car again, badly, but escaped with minor injuries.

USAC had removed the front fuel tanks from the rear-engine cars, reduced the permissible fuel load, and required rubber bladders within the tanks to contain the fuel in an effort to increase their safety. They turned out to be safer than the old cars, but the veteran drivers didn't know that then and they were worried about the new contraptions.

Drivers still would be killed racing, but drivers always would be killed racing. For some years fatalities would occur less frequently than in preceding years. And many of those that occurred would come in front-engine dirt-track cars or sprinters or midgets, not in these rear-engine lightweights. The lightweights broke up easily, but this proved to be a safety factor since the cars skidded to a stop on their bellies instead of running over other cars and vaulting into the air and turning over. Getting upside down is about the worst thing than can happen to a race driver. And for many years fires in crashes became infrequent. But it was awhile before drivers stopped dreading the new cars and blaming all accidents on them and wanting to turn away from them.

Foyt captured the pole position for the race, but his gearbox gave way just short of 300 miles and he left it and perched on a pit wall in despair. When someone asked him how he felt, he said, "Maybe I'll quit. Maybe it's time to quit."

Later, he spoke of accidents in racing. He said, "Sometimes I think the things that happen to other people are harder to take than what happens to you. You try not to get too close to the guys, but you can't help it. My first race at Indianapolis, Pat O'Connor and Tony Bettenhausen bought it. I was close friends with them. Pat was a nice man. So was Tony. He helped me get here and gave me a lot of pointers. I really felt bad when he died.

"That race at Milwaukee when Hurtubise went over me really bothered me. He got out of it okay, but he was hurt bad. I felt bad that I was involved. I had three close calls in that race and it really made me edgy. You have close calls in a lot of races. You stop counting 'em. I've been upside down five times. You go on your ear in one of those dudes and it shakes you.

"The thing is, I felt comfortable in the old cars. I don't feel comfortable in the new cars. They scare me. I know enough to be afraid sometimes. You can be too brave. I quit sprint cars because everyone said they were too dangerous to keep driving and I started driving stock cars more because they were supposed to be safer, so what happens? I have the worst accident I ever had in a stock car.

"Well, I get to the point where I think of quitting and then I know I really don't want to, so I don't think I will. I'm young as race drivers go. I'm still good at this. I guess I'll go on with it and try to push the other stuff out of my mind."

It was hard for him to do. During the 1965 season there were no deaths in racing, but Mel Kenyon burned fingers off in one accident and Norm Hall crushed a foot off in another. In 1966 Chuck Rodee was killed during qualifying trials at the Speedway and Jimmy Davies, Jud Larson, Red Riegel, Don Branson, and Dick Atkins all were killed while Johnny Rutherford broke both his arms in sprint car or midget car mishaps.

In 1966, on the opening day of time trials at Indianapolis, Foyt brushed the wall heavily with his car and severely damaged it, though he escaped unhurt. Examining Foyt at the field hospital, the doctor expressed astonishment that for the first time since he had been observing drivers after accidents he had found one whose pulse swiftly had returned to normal.

"Hurry up, Doc," A. J. growled impatiently, "I got to get back to fix my car." But it had made an impression on him.

He fixed his car and got it into the race on the second day, far back where he would be in the thick of traffic at the start. On the flying start, Billy Foster tried to move up from the outside of the fourth row by squeezing through a narrow opening near the wall, but he scraped the wall and slid off into Gordon Johncock's car. The two tangled in tight traffic, which distintegrated into deadly disorder.

Suddenly cars started spinning and crashing in every direction, broken parts hailed down on the careening cars, and at least a dozen wheels broke off and bounced about wildly, some so high they cleared the fences and injured 14 fans.

The cars skidded in showers of sparks on their undersides, caroming off walls and one another and, as they ground to a halt, the drivers hastily leaped from them. Foyt's car was caught in the melee and was cracked. He got it stopped alongside the outside main-stretch wall and wrenched from it, gashing an arm and a leg. Caring little for his dignity at this moment, Foyt climbed like a frightened monkey up the wire fence in front of the grandstand and hung there, looking back at the tumultuous commotion below him.

Some fans laughed at Foyt, regarding his climb up the wire as something funny. He did not find it funny. As the accident ground to a halt, he climbed down and walked angrily away through the debris.

Later he said, "Cars were crashing all around me. The only way out was up the fence. I'm satisfied to have escaped safely."

In fact, incredible as it may seem, his minor cuts were the only injuries suffered by anyone in the accident. But 16 cars had been involved in the multiple crash and 11, including Foyt's were eliminated from the race.

The following Sunday, he crashed his car in practice at Milwaukee —his third accident in three weeks. He was driving down the home-stretch when the left rear suspension broke, propelling the car into a spin. It backed into the outer wall, rupturing the rear tank and releasing fuel, which burst into flame. When he unfastened his safety harness and tried to get out by putting his hands on the edge of the cockpit to push himself up, the metal was so hot it burned his hands and he had to drop back inside.

"I knew I had to get out or just fry," he said later. "I gritted my teeth and put my hands back in the burning fuel to raise myself out. I could have broken a leg and never felt it because my hands hurt so much."

With a great exertion of will, he finally got out. His hands were burned. His face and neck absorbed lesser burns. These and his wrecked car forced him from the race. He had started 82 consecutive races on the championship trail, an all-time record for the circuit, but he missed this one, snapping his streak.

The accidents he suffered these years were not the first in his racing career, nor were they to be the last, but they were his worst and they made a mark on him.

His first serious accident had occurred in 1959 in a midget car race. He was in the thick of traffic when a wheel flew off his car. It collapsed in one corner, then spun to the outside, as Foyt fought to control it, and finally hurtled into a wall with terrific force. Dazed and struggling to keep his senses, he had to be helped from his wrecked racer. An ambulance rushed him to the hospital, where it was discovered he had suffered a brain concussion and a cracked back.

They say you can't tell about a driver for sure until you see how he reacts to his first serious accident. Foyt was fidgeting, anxious to get back into action. He recovered rapidly and was soon racing again.

"I remember it all right, but it never bugged me or anything like that," he said later. "It didn't slow me none."

At Phoenix, in tests early in 1968, his fuel injector jammed wide open as he was barreling into the first turn. He hit the brakes to slow down, locked them, and both front tires burst.

"The left front popped first, turning the car to the left," he stated afterward. "This is what saved me from going into the wall head first."

The car sideswiped the crash wall and ripped off the front wheels, which flew back over the chassis, peeling off a fuel tank cover. The chassis crumbled from the impact. Fuel ignited and entered the cockpit, burning Foyt's right hand, but he scrambled out before further damage was done.

That same year, at that same Phoenix track, Foyt and Andretti were swapping the lead back and forth when Foyt skidded on an oil slick, slammed into the homestretch wall, richocheted 250 feet down the track sideways, and was rammed in the fuel tank by Andretti's car. The tank split, the fuel ignited, and Foyt was burned. He had to be helped from the car, but the injuries were not as severe as they might have been. He just went right on immediately after his recovery. It sometimes seems there is steel instead of sinew in these men.

In 1969, on the dirt at Springfield, Illinois, Foyt smashed up his car, but again got out with minor burns.

In 1971 he tore a tendon in one arm, which made it painful for him to steer his cars. He tried cortisone so he could carry on, but it was ineffective. Finally he applied the same liniment he used on his quarter-horses. Surprisingly, it worked and he was soon back in business.

The next year, following the Indy 500, Foyt ran a dirt race at DuQuoin, Illinois. He was ahead when he had to make a pit stop to take on fuel. As he was pulling away, fuel that had splashed on hot metal ignited and caught fire. The flames blazed into the cockpit. A. J. dove out of the moving machine. As he hit the ground, the car rolled over his left foot, which got tangled in the wheel and twisted.

"It was torn up pretty bad," Foyt recalled later, "but it was better than staying in that hot seat."

His foot was encased in a cast and he was put on crutches. He missed three months of the season, but before the year was over he was back in action, limping heavily but driving hard.

At the end of the 1973 season, in November, Foyt was hospitalized with infectious hepatitis, missing the final race at Phoenix. A man of simple tastes, he seemed embarrassed to discover it stemmed from eating bad oysters.

"I never did like them until about two years ago," he said, "and then I got to really liking them, but it will probably be a long time before I eat them again. I'd never missed a race due to illness. I've raced with pneumonia, flu, and even while I was on crutches, but this was the first time I couldn't make it."

Infectious hepatitis has lingering after-effects and usually four to six months elapse before a sufferer recovers his strength sufficiently to engage in heavy physical exertions. Some supposed Foyt's work on his 1974 car would be slowed and he might miss the 500 at Daytona in February and the 500 at Ontario in March. But he was out of the hospital within two weeks and Lucy, who was waiting for him at their home in Houston, was not surprised to find out he had stopped off at the shop on the way. He had been ordered to rest, but she said there was no way she could keep him tied down. She said, "He's a big boy now."

Foyt swiftly went to work on his car, said he planned to test it at Ontario in January and would be racing at Daytona the following month and Ontario the month after that. He said a checkup showed he was almost back to normal in six weeks instead of six months.

"I feel fine," he said. "I'm rarin' to go."

He had clung to his spot at the top for a long time before starting to slip. Hot new heroes climbed over him and he found himself struggling to stay with the speed. The battle scars were showing, but he seemed as determined as ever.

When he was feeling good and things were going good, A. J. Foyt called George Bignotti, Big George Notti. He'd say, "George, you ol' dago, you're all right." And he'd turn to whoever was around and he'd say, "That Big George Notti, ain't he beautiful!" And when he was not feeling good and things were not going well, Foyt would say, "Goddam it, the wheels are jumping this far off the track. Now fix it or I'll do it myself." And off to a side he'd say to someone, "That damn Bignotti, sometimes he thinks he knows it all, but he doesn't. I have to drive the damn things, he doesn't."

He'd cuss Bignotti and Bignotti would cuss him back, and Foyt would fire him and Bignotti would say Foyt couldn't fire him because he quit first. Then they'd forget about their differences and go back to work together. They had come apart for a few months in 1962, but then they got back together again before the season ended. But it was always almost coming apart between them, they were always arguing.

Joe Leonard once said, "If Foyt had said some of the things to me he'd said to Bignotti, I'd have taken after A. J. with a monkey wrench." Bignotti simply smiled and said, "A. J. is not the easiest guy to get along with."

Parnelli Jones once said, "If you took a piece of paper and asked all the members of a racing team to put down what percentage of the operation's success they were responsible for, you'd come out with about 500 percent."

There usually are ten to twenty men on a racing team from the backer through the mechanics to the drivers. The backer is at the base of it all because if he does not hire good people or buy excellent equipment, even a team with good men on it will fail. Some backers have more money or are willing to spend more than their rivals, which gives them a proportionate edge. Some teams must operate conservatively because if they hang a car on a wall, they don't have a backup car to put on the track or if they blow an engine they don't have a spare to substitute.

Beyond the backer, the chief mechanic and the driver are, on the average, about equally responsible for success or failure, although they do not get equal amounts from it. Both must be skilled at their specialties. The mechanic does the hard dirty work in the shadows while the driver runs the risks in the spotlight. The mechanic's contract may call for a fourth the base pay of the driver. If the car wins, the mechanic may get 15 percent of the purse, the driver 50 percent.

Depending on the budget he has and his own preferences, the mechanic may have specialists building chassis and putting together engines for him. He may buy the basic units and rebuild them to his own ideas. If he puts together a good enough car, a driver who is less than the best may be able to win with it. If he does not, the best driver cannot win with it. The best drivers may be able to get a little more from a car than others can. The delicate balance between them sways unevenly with the rise and fall of their fortunes.

Despite their success together, Foyt and Bignotti were beginning to wear each other down as they entered the 1965 season. Foyt was sore from that terrible accident he'd survived at Riverside in a stock car and he was limping painfully and cussing freely as he moved into Indianapolis. At Phoenix he'd led, but his engine had overheated and failed him. At Trenton his car's rear end had gone out. By the time he got to Indianapolis in May he was getting edgy.

Foyt was rubbing rough spots on Bignotti. Bespectacled, calmer, less explosive but no less proud, perhaps even vain, Bignotti said, "A. J. is one of the few drivers in this business who understands everything about cars. He could build his own cars and they'd be competitive. This is both bad and good. He can tell you what's wrong with a car he's testing and how to fix it and a lot of drivers can't. He's always right about what's wrong. But he's not always right about how to fix it.

"Because he's a good mechanic, he won't let his mechanic alone. Because he's the best driver doesn't make him the best mechanic. There are differences between good mechanics just as there are between good drivers. A lot of us are good at what we do. Some are better. Some are more imaginative, some more conservative. Striking a balance is the big thing. You don't just want the fastest car or the one that will run the farthest, but the one that will run the fastest and finish.

"We always have to look ahead. We see what improvements are starting to work. We copy one another. We try to improve what's being done. But some guys always have to be fancy. If something isn't far-out, they're not happy. Well, I don't feel I have to blaze trails. I won't try something radically different until I feel it's better. The mechanic and his driver may be at odds on which way to go. Foyt and I are always at odds. But in the past we decided we could do better together than we would apart. I decided it's better to fight with Foyt all week and win on Sunday than have peace with somebody else and never win."

Despite having won at Indianapolis for the second time in 1964, Foyt was no less anxious to win in 1965. A third 500 triumph would be as many as any competitor had ever won. And he put himself under heavy pressure by deciding to abandon his beloved front-engine heavyweight in favor of one of the new rear-engine lightweights at Bignotti's urging. As far as Foyt was concerned, Bignotti was out on a limb on this one, but it was Foyt's final decision. He even decided to use dangerous gasoline because it would bring better mileage.

They were working with the Chapman-Clark Lotus from the previous year, rebuilt by Luiji Lesovski, a master craftsman, to Bignotti's specifications. Parnelli Jones and Rodger Ward also had new rear-engine lightweights. They were not at home in these new machines, which were smaller and more subtle than the car they'd taken to the top. But competition was closing in on them.

Chapman and Clark were back with a brand-new Lotus, better built than those of the past. And this time they came convinced that they would practice as hard and as long as necessary to get ready for this richest of races. They were without Gurney this time. Convinced that Clark got the edge from Chapman, convinced he could do better on his own, Gurney had bolted, bought a Lotus-Ford, built two similar cars himself, and hustled up support to form his own firm, patriotically called All-American Racers. Of the 68 entries, 44 were rear-engine cars and few of the old-fashioned forces seemed competitive.

The old lions such as Foyt, Jones, McElreath, Hurtubise, Ruby, Branson, and the rest were threatened by some young tigers. Among them were Mario Andretti, Gordon Johncock, Johnny Rutherford, and Joe Leonard. Two more were the Unser brothers, Bobby and Al.

Brothers Jerry, Louis, and Joe Unser were born in Illinois and reared in Colorado. They used to fool around for fun with motorcycles. They raced cars up the road to Pike's Peak before races were run there. Joe was the first to be tempted by Indianapolis and he was killed near Denver in 1929 testing a car for the 500. Louis never was tempted past Pikes Peak and he won nine titles there over twenty years before he was ruled off the road after forty-one years as too old at the age of seventy-two.

Jerry had four sons—twins Jerry, Jr., and Louie, born in 1933;

Bobby, born in 1934; and Al, born in 1939. Pop Unser ran garages, first in Colorado Springs, later on the highway through Albuquerque, New Mexico. Later, Bobby and Al moved into their own houses along the same route. Jerry, Jr., became the first Unser to race at Indy, but he crashed there in 1958 and died in another accident there the following year. Twin brother Louis won two titles at the Peak and had some promise as a driver, but was stricken with multiple sclerosis in 1964. He now builds engines and helps his brothers. Bobby reached Indy in 1963 but, stuck in the Novis, had lasted three laps in two years. Now, in 1965, brother Al joined him, but in a better car—one of the Foyt team cars.

Both had tremendous ability, but it was hard to pick between them. Bobby had a heavier foot. Al drove more with his mind. Bobby was a charger who had to run as fast as he could for as long as he could. Al was a waiter who could hang back until the chargers cracked. It was a matter of personalities. Bobby was more flamboyant, more extroverted, cockier. Al was cooler, more reserved, but almost equally confident.

Joe Leonard, out of San José, California, was one of the greatest racers motorcycles have had. He starved along the way. Even after he became a champion he never made much money. So he went into cars and now was seeking his fortune as a rookie at Indianapolis in one of Gurney's new cars.

"I've listened to the Indianapolis races on radio since I was seven years old," he said. "I was almost killed in my first motorcycle race when I was sixteen. I was in a coma seventeen days. I still don't remember what happened. But when I came out I remembered I wanted to race. Now, fifteen year later, I'm here and it's a dream come true." He was a bear of a man, dark-haired and handsome.

Gordon Johncock was a little guy, so small you wondered how he could handle a big car. A farm boy from Michigan, he dropped out of high school to plunge into racing. The crippling injury to Johnny White now had given him a ride in the big race. He took the vacated seat and swore he would win here sooner or later.

Andretti, too, was tiny, but he was the most impressive of all the newcomers. He was one of twin brothers born in Italy. Their father was a farm administrator of some substance until the war, which took everything from him. He wound up working in a toy factory. Growing up, twins Mario and Aldo had as their heroes in the sporting world, instead of baseball or football players, race drivers. They hung around racing garages.

At thirteen, without telling their parents, they joined a sort of little league for kids who raced miniature cars. When Aldo got injured in a race, they said he'd fallen off a truck. When he got burned, they said a box of matches had exploded in his hands. When Mario broke a kneecap, they said he'd fallen on the church steps. But so many boys were hurt that the program was disbanded and they were adrift.

Their dreams of becoming Grand Prix drivers when they grew up seemed dead when the family moved to the United States, to Nazareth, Pennsylvania, where the father's brother lived and where work was available in the mills. The twins' spirits revived when they found racing all around them. It was a different sort of racing than they'd known. This was rough racing in jalopies on dirt tracks. But it was racing and they begged into it. They kept it from their father until Aldo was hurt and had to be hospitalized.

Finding out, the father was furious. "Did I raise my sons to have them brought home in a basket?" he asked.

He would not speak to them for a long time. But they would not give it up. After Aldo recovered, he returned to it, but he crashed and crashed until eventually he did give up. Mario won consistently until he moved up to the title trail.

Now he was a rookie at Indianapolis, driving for Al Dean and Clint Brawner, following Foyt and Bryan and Sachs on this team. A little dandy with a little mustache, Dean sat in a hotel lobby and said, "I still think of winning Indianapolis. I had Bryan and Foyt, who won it after they left me. I had Sachs, who almost won it for me, who was killed after he left me. I still have nightmares about the time Sachs lost to Foyt. I wanted Sachs to go on, but I'm glad it wasn't up to me. I'm no bloodthirsty boxing manager sending out a palooka to get punch-drunk or hurt or killed. I send out safe cars. I've been with Brawner a long time and he's a mechanic who gives an owner and a driver a safe car.

"I hope Andretti appreciates that. I think Mario can be as good as any of 'em and I think he can win it for me. He's hungry. He's after something and he won't let go until he gets it. I mean for him to get it with me. We got him under contract. I've had it with the handshakes."

Brawner, rawboned and weather-beaten and wearing a straw hat and a red bandanna over his neck to save his skin from the sun, said, "I still think about '61. I'll never stop. But it's gone now and so is Sachsie. You got to go on. You go your own way. No one owes you anything. You give the guys what you've got. The drivers know they can count on me. These cars don't finish by chance, you know. A lot of knowhow and sweat goes into them. After all these years I been in this business, it's hard to believe, but I never had a driver killed in one of my cars. Sachs got killed in another guy's car, not in mine. Not that the guys are grateful. They don't think about getting killed. They think about winning. Well, if you don't live, you can't win.

"I win a lot of races with my cars. I've won everywhere but Indianapolis. Well, I'll win there yet. I had Bryan, who won there. I had Foyt, who won there. Now I have Andretti, who'll win there. I only hope I'm with him when he wins. I wouldn't be surprised if Mario leaves sooner or later. Others have—why shouldn't he? I may leave Dean myself one of these years. I've thought about it every year. Why? Money. If you get a better deal, you go. If Mario goes, maybe I'll go with him. But it'd be kind of nice if we would win Indy with Dean first."

Mario was a cool, confident young man. Small but handsome, he hid behind extravagant sunglasses. He held himself back from people. The ladies loved him, but he was loyal to his wife and children. He played it cool. He sat now at the track, adjusting the strap on his helmet. With him, everything had to be just so. His uniform was spotless. He held out a pair of soft leather gloves he used racing.

"They're made especially for me," he pointed out, proudly. "I'm not afraid of Indy. I got to learn things, I'll learn. I'd like to win it for Dean or Brawner. I understand they've been trying a long time. But I'd like to win it for me, mainly. And my family. As long as Dean gives me what I need to win, I'll stay. But I'm not married to him. Contracts run out. If I can do better somewhere else, I'll go."

At another time he said, "I figure everyone was intended to do something. I figure I was put on this earth to drive race cars." Asked what he would have been if he had been born another time, before race cars, he thought a moment and then said, "I would have been a knight."

Ward's marriage had ended. But he had begun another marriage, to a young beauty queen. Over the last six years he had finished first twice, second twice, third once, and fourth once at Indianapolis. It was a remarkable record for that cruel place. But now he was like a man out of place and out of time.

"I don't like these new cars," he said. "I think they're the cars you got to drive to win, but I don't like them. I don't know if I can make it with them. I want to, very much. Before time runs out on me."

He was asked if he wanted to win to show off for his pretty young bride. He smiled and said, "You've seen her. What do you think? I got to show her the old man's still got it."

But this was a tough time for the old guard. Foyt and Jones both cracked up in practice. And Ward went too slow on the first day of time trials and was called in to try again another day. Andretti went out and the rookie raced to new qualifying records, averaging almost 159 miles per hour. But even as Dean and Brawner were congratulating him, Clark took the Chapman car to new records that broke the 160 barrier. The previous year he had been the first foreign driver to capture the pole position in nineteen years.

Who could beat 160? Parnelli had fallen far short. Foyt always said he never shot for the pole at Indy, he just shot for a spot near the front. "You don't win the race on the first lap," he snapped. But Foyt often says one thing and does another. He always ran the first lap as if it was the last one. And now he went out and went after the pole.

Even as Clark was being interviewed and congratulated on placing on the pole again, Foyt was barreling around the track far faster than he had practiced, surprising everyone, bringing the vast crowd to its feet with a great din of applause. He clicked off the laps with incredible precision, a marvel of consistency, the slowest of the four and the fastest only 28/100ths of a second apart.

The fastest was just under 162 miles per hour and the average was above 161. He parked the car with a broad grin on his face and when they asked him about it, he said, "Well, ah just wanted to return the record to the Yew-nited States."

Heavy winds blew Ward and the others away from fast speeds on Sunday. The following week, in practice, Parnelli crashed once more. His qualified car had to be rebuilt again. On Saturday, the third day of qualifying, Ward crashed. Without expression, he walked back to his garage.

Watson patted him on the back. "Ward, you're fired," he said, smiling thinly.

Then he went to see the wreck to see if it could be salvaged for Sunday. They worked all night. And most of the next day.

Al Unser in the Foyt car joined brother Bobby in the field Sunday. The field was filled. Only a faster time could bump a car out. With one hour remaining, Ward was waiting on line, talking about his newborn daughter. He sat in the sinking sunlight and waited. Then he went out and raced too slow. He needed 154 and got 153 instead. Added up, he was just two seconds too slow over ten miles to make it. He parked in the pits and sat in his car with his head down for a long time before he got out as photographers popped flashbulbs at him. Watson watched him as he walked away. Then Watson walked away, too. It was getting away from him, too, and maybe he knew it.

Foyt had gotten Goodyear in this year. After 43 years out of the race, Goodyear had 12 starters. Of the 33 cars in the race, 27 were rear-engine lightweights, 17 powered by Fords and 10 by Offies. For now, the Lotuses were in the lead and Foyt and Jones, mauled in mishaps in them, were making sorry little jokes about them, knowing they could go fast enough in them but not sure if they could keep control of them and go 500 miles. Before the race Foyt admitted, "Oh, man, I'll be glad when this one is over."

It was over for him long before the finish. It was over for a lot of cars for only 10 cars were still running at the finish. Hurtubise in one Novi went out on the first lap with transmission trouble. Bobby Unser in the other Novi gave out at 172 miles with a sick engine. Granatelli held up a sign for his wife in the stands asking her to keep her chin up.

All three Gurney cars went out early. McCluskey's car collapsed with clutch trouble after 60 miles. Leonard's car limped out leaking oil after 70 miles. Gurney's own car surrendered with clutch problems just past a 100 miles. Jones' engine began missing at 150 miles, then his steering went haywire, but he struggled on somehow. Bud Tingelstad threw a wheel and hit a wall at 285 miles but was unhurt, and this was the only accident of the safest 500 in Speedway history.

Foyt tested Clark early. On the second lap, A. J. daringly drove high on the outside of the first turn and popped past him. Later, Clark said, "I let him go just to see what he could do, which turned out to be nothing, so I went by him and that was that." Clark reclaimed the lead a few laps later and started to pull away at a record pace of more than 150 miles per hour. Foyt pushed hard, but could not keep up the pace.

Having employed the famed Wood Brothers crew from southern stock car racing to speed up his pit stops, Clark was in and out fast on his stops and was almost a minute ahead of Foyt when A. J.'s gear box gave way near 300 miles. He pulled into the pits. Bignotti and the team went over the wall to service him only to see Foyt unbuckling himself and climbing out of the cockpit. Without a word, Foyt walked past Bignotti and back toward Gasoline Alley.

On the way Foyt met Gurney, who walked with him into Foyt's garage. Foyt slumped down on the floor near a clothes locker while Gurney went to a cooler and opened them bottles of soda pop.

A writer came in and asked, "Hey, Tex, what happened?"

Foyt stood up and said, "The gear box let go. That's all I have to say. Hey, will someone close the door? I don't want to see anyone."

Later, Bud Furillo of the Los Angeles *Herald-Examiner* cornered

Foyt. In response to a query, Foyt stated, "I don't know if I'll race any more. Everything has gone wrong for me this year. I was gaining on Clark. I had been holding back. My motor just got to running when the gear went out. Well, he's a good driver. He would have won last year if he'd been on Firestone tires. This year he is. My Goodyears were fine. My gears weren't any good."

Having led 190 of the 200 laps, Clark coasted across the finish line more than two laps in front of Jones, who wobbled home just before his sick car ran out of fuel. Right behind him came Andretti, finishing third.

At Milwaukee the following weekend with Clark absent, Foyt was fast qualifier but his gearbox again gave away a little past the halfway point and Jones won. Rodger Ward spun out but, despite his own troubles, took time to analyze Foyt's.

"He literally abuses a car," Ward said of Foyt, which did not make A. J. any merrier. He felt his car was abusing him. He felt Bignotti was abusing his car.

"I haven't finished a race on pavement since July last year," he murmured grimly. "Either George has lost interest in racing or he wants to get with a new driver."

At Langhorne for another 100-miler, Foyt told Bignotti he didn't even feel like driving the race in his car. Bignotti told him the defending national champion had a responsibility to run as advertised. They argued. Foyt decided to run after they agreed to separate after the race. Possibly if the car had held up and Foyt had won he would have gotten together with Bignotti again, but A. J.'s engine overheated early and he was finished. After the race, won by McElreath, Foyt and Bignotti broke up for the final time.

"I was going to give up racing, but I decided to give up my mechanic, instead," A. J. said. "I need to change my luck, somehow. We seem to have a problem. We can't even get halfway through a race without something falling off the car or breaking or going bad. I have to try something different or stop trying."

Bitterly, Bignotti said, "It's been brewing quite a while. When the car falls out, naturally I get the blame. But it's been something I couldn't control. A. J. likes to run things his way. And we've been running them that way for the last four or five races. And we haven't won. I set up a car one way and then he practices it and changes it all around. And then when we don't win, he blames me.

"He's sort of superstitious. He visited this old lady, this mystic, and she told him what to expect once and it happened and he sort of got to believe it. He believes in someone who believes in a Ouija board as the best way to forecast mechanical problems. I believe that's foolish. Well, I believe the best thing for us to do is to let him find another mechanic and I'll find another driver and maybe we'll both start winning again."

Most mechanics and drivers are satisfied to win sometimes, but these two had become used to winning all the time and could not easily settle for less. They had won a record 27 championship trail races together, including a record ten in one season, and including two Indianapolis 500s, and four national titles in less than six full seasons, but now they had broken up.

Pouelson had parted from Parnelli and, although Agajanian told Foyt he'd never win with Johnny, Foyt took him on. Meanwhile, Ward, Watson, and Wilke had come apart, too, and Bignotti joined John Mecom to form a team with Ward as their driver. The pressures of racing and the competitive instincts of racing men loosened alliances and drove teams easily apart.

Foyt shrugged and said, "I think I've got a good man in Pouelson. He's a veteran pilot and knows aerodynamics and discovered several things we wound up copying. As for Bignotti going with Mecom, I wish George and John and their drivers the best of luck. I'll be out there trying to beat them just as they will be trying to beat me. There's no hard feelings."

Bignotti grinned wistfully and said, "Before I finished my first season with Foyt I needed pills to calm my nerves. He's not an easy man to beat, but maybe it'll be easier to beat him than live with him."

Having lived with Foyt had made it impossible to live with his wife, Bignotti suggested. Foyt took up too much of his time and sapped too much of his strength and destroyed his disposition. Now he was living alone. George later said, "He cost me my happy home and $183,000 in settlements."

At Trenton, at 150 miles, Foyt finished and he won. And he was elated later. "I finally finished in a rear-engine car. I finished and I won, thanks to John Pouelson," he said pointedly. But at Atlanta, after taking the pole and leading by a lap late in the race, his racer conked out with a broken rear suspension.

Back at Langhorne Foyt nursed an overheating car into second place, finishing, but barely, without winning. At Indianapolis Raceway Park he was ahead until he ran out of fuel the last lap. Andretti won.

Back at Milwaukee, Foyt spun out early. In the Springfield 100, Foyt won. But at DuQuoin he wore out a tire, had to change it, and settled for third. At Milwaukee with his Lotus lost in shipment, Foyt put his dirt track car on the pole, led early, lost a tire, and settled for second.

Other drivers had been getting in their licks. Rutherford, Leonard, and Johncock had scored their first victories on the title trail. But Foyt and Pouelson were getting it together. At the Indianapolis Fairgrounds, Foyt won his fourth straight Hoosier Hundred dirt track classic, nosing out Andretti. At Trenton, Foyt triumphed again, though Andretti won enough points to clinch his first national title.

At Sacramento, Foyt, already aggravated by having had another title slip away from him, was further frustrated by his car's failures in practice. The race should have meant little to him. The purse was small. But he was brooding bitterly about the business through the long morning. The sun was bright and hot, the track dry and dusty, and Foyt worked hard pushing his car past its performance potential in practice, bringing it back to the pits dissatisfied time after time, and angrily barking orders to his crew.

As the morning turned into afternoon and time trials drew near, Foyt lost his temper and physically pulled a crewman out from under his car and crawled under the car himself. For half an hour he worked on his back in the dirt, sweating heavily, while cars started to take their time trials.

Finally it was time for his trial. His white uniform soaked with sweat and soiled with dirt, his face sweaty and greasy, Foyt jumped up, stretched to straighten his cramped back, grabbed his helmet, pulled it on, jumped into the cockpit, and was pushed off in his car. He qualified ninth fastest. He was in, but not in good shape. As soon as he got back to the pits, he slid under the car and resumed his mechanical labors.

When the field went on the track, Foyt was on line. Immediately, from the start of the race, he drove with great daring. Posted in ninth position, he quickly moved up to eighth on the first lap, seventh on the second lap, sixth on the fourth lap. He blew by Bobby Unser to take fifth place on the eighth lap. He was fourth by the 20th lap. He lunged by Jud Larson to take third on the 27th lap. Then he ran right over the rear wheel of Carl Williams, almost crashed, kept control, but dropped back and had to start the hard climb all over again. The crowd was all for him and making a lot of noise.

At 72 laps, Foyt got by Larson again to take fourth. At 82 laps he roared by Andretti to take third. But then Williams spun out and the yellow flag was unfurled, and the drivers were held in their positions at reduced speed and Foyt's chase was curtailed. After the green flag went up, Foyt charged into second, but before he could catch Branson in first the checkered flag flew and it was all over.

A writer tried to compliment him on his showing. "What the hell for?" Foyt asked. "I didn't win."

At Phoenix, in the last race of the season, Foyt did win. Andretti led for 185 miles, but Foyt passed him near the finish of the 200-mile event to take it. This made it five victories for Foyt in the last half of the season and moved him to second place in the final driving standings behind Andretti, who had won only one but had high finishes in almost all the races.

"Well, he's consistent," Foyt commented. "He picked up a pack of points at Indy and ran real strong all season. But if we'd gotten going sooner we'd have beaten him out. I think with Pouelson we can go good next year."

He was riding a wave of optimism for the moment, but time turned him unhappy again. He'd won 19 races in 1961. After winning nine in 1962, he'd won 16 in 1963 and 19 in 1964. Despite his troubles, he'd taken top honors in 10 races in 1965, including his second straight Firecracker 400 at Daytona on the southern stock car circuit. But he won only two races in 1966, both minor events—a midget car race in April and a sprint car race in November—and in between he suffered and came apart from Pouelson even as he had before with Bignotti.

There was one race before the 500. Foyt and Andretti were dueling for the lead when they tangled and spun out. Mario said, "We were racing. Don't blame anybody." Foyt said, "The next one is the one that matters most."

He had two cars for Indy. He had his old Lotus-Ford. And he had a car he called "The Mongoose," which Lliji Lesovski had built for him from a Dean Jeffries design with Pouelson's help. Foyt fashioned a Ford engine for it, although Dale Drake had taken over the Offy and developed a supercharged engine that was more powerful but less reliable than the Ford. Eventually, Ford would have to go to superchargers, too.

The old guard was getting into the new thing. Parnelli had built a couple of new cars he called Colts. Backed by Dean, Brawner had built a new car called The Hawk for Andretti. Dan Gurney had built no fewer than five cars called "Eagles." He kept three for his own team but sold two to other teams. Granatelli was back with two Novis. Chapman was back, but Granatelli had taken over sponsorship of this team, too, for STP, with Clark and Al Unser in Lotuses. John Mecom bought three Lotus-like Lola-Fords for Bignotti to fashion for the new Scot Grand Prix star Jackie Stewart, sports car driver Walt Hansgen, and Ward. When Hansgen was killed in practice for Le Mans, Graham Hill was hired to return to Indy as a replacement.

Watson and Wilke were back with three cars. Two were assigned to Don Branson and Chuck Hulse. The third, which would have been Ward's, went to Chuck Rodee, a veteran who had been waiting a long time for a good race.

"You wait all your life for a year like this," he said.

On the first day of time trials, Rodee crashed and was killed. He was only the second driver to be killed during a qualification attempt. The other was Stubby Stubblefield in 1937.

Andretti had been the fastest all month and he remained the fastest with new records of a lap above 166 and an average of close to 166. Clark came closest to him at 164. Snider surprised in Foyt's second car with a 162.5 to complete the front row. Jones hit 162.4 to make the second row. In all, 18 made it, including Hill and Ward, both well back. Gurney burned out a couple of clutches. Foyt curtailed one run at 161, went out again and crashed, wrecking his car.

The next day Foyt took a brand-new, untested Lotus-Ford out of its crate, set it up, and put himself into the race in the seventh row at 161. Snider sent him a note: "Congraulations to the second team from the first team." Foyt laughed hollowly. The same speed the day before would have put him in the second row. Gurney, Mc-Cluskey, and Leonard all made it in Eagles. When Ruby and Jerry Grant made it in Eagles purchased from Gurney it put in the race all five cars Dan had built. On the following Saturday, both Unsers made it. On Sunday, Parnelli's second driver, young Dick Atkins, was bumped from the field. Thompson's cars failed to make it. Granatelli's Novis both were wrecked out of it and laid to rest at last. Only one front-engine car made it, and it was an antique that would not last a lap.

Well, 11 cars failed to last a lap. There was that terrible accident that converted the track into a wrecking yard. After Foyt fled his wrecked racer up a fence, climbed down, and walked away, he said, "What a damn, stupid waste. I'll never start in the back again. If I don't make it on the first day, I'll go home."

Gurney was one of the others with a year's work wiped out in one minute.

Soon after the survivors got going, many of them dropped out. Snider crashed out at 55 miles. Andretti dropped out short of 70 miles with his valves fouled. Brawner and Dean drooped in despair. Ward parked in the pits at 185 miles. Asked what was wrong, he said, "Everything's wrong," and walked away. Later, tearfully, he announced his retirement.

Clark led for a long time but spun twice within 22 laps and lost his head, though he managed to keep going. Ruby forged to the front and stretched out. At 365 miles he led by 50 seconds. Then he began to throw oil, black smoke began to blow from the rear of his car, and he was black-flagged off the course.

Suddenly, Stewart led by a lap with only eight laps to go. Then his oil pressure dropped, he slowed and pulled over on the grass, and he, too, was out of it. Now Clark led again. Thinking he was a lap ahead of Hill, Clark let Hill pass him. Now Hill led. From 15th starting spot, he had fallen into it. Taking the checker, Hill came across, then Clark. They continued on around the track coasting into Victory Lane, first Hill, then Clark.

Confusion reigned. Bignotti embraced Hill. Backer Granatelli, thinking he finally had his first 500 triumph, and Chapman escorted Clark to the officials to protest. But after a review of the scoring records, Chapman and Clark had to settle for second.

With Hill in a car that could not go fast but could go far, Bignotti had his third Indianapolis 500 triumph. The team collected more than $150,000. Foyt's team picked up pennies. Someone asked him if he might retire. He said, "I always say I will, but I don't seem to be able to do it."

Having had three cars wrecked at Indianapolis, he bought Clark's Indianapolis car from Chapman for $50,000, took it to Milwaukee, and promptly wrecked it. Something seemed to break in the back end, which swerved out, sending Foyt into the wall. The car burst into flames and he was badly burned before he could get out, but he seemed more bothered by the loss of the car. "I didn't get much for my money," he mourned.

It was that kind of year for him. He fixed up one of his cars but it wouldn't work right. At one point, after a valiant effort in one race, someone said, "No one could have won with that car. Anyone else would have quit on it."

Foyt snapped, "I don't quit on any car. I'm not a quitter." Then he stalked off.

A rival racer smiled and said, "It bothers him that he can't blow the boys down any more."

A. J. got the car working in the Hoosier Hundred and seemed a certain winner until the brake pedal broke.

"Had it given way gradually, I could have backed way off and babied her and there still would have been no way I could have been beaten, but it just went and I went with it," he said sadly.

Foyt finally decided to build a new car for the following season at his Indianapolis garage. He saw no sense in running much of the rest of the season. Testing the new equipment would take up most of his time. He'd broken with Pouelson in August, got back with him in September. Soon, at season's end, they parted for good. In June of the following year Pouelson was killed in the crash of a private plane.

Over the winter, Andy Granatelli called to tell Foyt he had a new car, a turbine, and asked Foyt if he wanted to test it and maybe race it at Indy. Foyt said he thought turbine engines were for airplanes, not cars. Granatelli insisted this one would work in a car. Foyt knew Granatelli had tried new things before without their working and he wasn't much for experimenting with something like this anyway, so he turned Granatelli down, pointing out that he already had two new cars he'd built for the 500, was his own boss now, and really didn't want to work for anyone else.

So Granatelli called Parnelli and Parnelli said he'd give it a try. Later, after a brief test, he said he'd go with it if Agajanian approved. He went to Aggie and asked for his release from their operation. Aggie said okay, so Jones went, guaranteed $100,000 by Granatelli. Jones had been thinking of quitting but the turbine tempted him to go around just once more.

Granatelli had begun to think of a turbine racer in the early 1960s. A turbine ran on kerosene-type fuel, which burns cooler and slower than other fuels. The engine also runs smoother than others, yet produces enormous power. It cost about half and weighed about half as much as other racing engines. It was permissible under existing rules, but it did pose problems. Being a large engine, it would require a big chassis. There were time lags between acceleration and speedup and between braking and slowdown. Braked hard, the brakes baked. And the engine required cool temperatures to be at its best.

Turbine cars had been tried a couple of times before at Indy and had failed. But Granatelli was convinced he could put one together that would work efficiently in the hands of a very good driver. He commissioned various concerns to build him the sort of engine, chassis, and other components he felt would fit together right. The turbocar began to take shape in 1964 and was ready early in 1967. It was a fat four-wheel drive car with the engine alongside the driver. It took a lot of work, which was done in secret and cost $600,000. When it got to the track, it turned the establishment topsy-turvy.

Foyt arrived feeling fit. He'd built two new cars, called Coyotes, restored his father to his team with the title of chief mechanic— he'd been on and off it a couple of seasons while A. J. jumped from mechanic to mechanic—and felt better prepared than in the recent past.

He told Ray Marquette of the Indianapolis *News*, "A lot of people don't realize that in the last two summers I have been hurt for a total of eight or nine months. I came back too early after breaking my back at Riverside and the doctors didn't want me to come back as soon as I did after being burned at Milwaukee, but I wanted to race so I did.

"When I was laying in the hospital hurting so bad I did think for awhile that maybe someone was trying to give me a message and my morale was low, but that was only when I was hurting so bad. Then I realized we had gone to Indianapolis with two new cars and we weren't ready. So we kept on hurrying to catch up and never were ready for a race.

"Now I feel we're ready for this season. After last year there were a lot of people who thought Foyt is through, but I certainly don't feel that way. It was the worst year in my career, yet I consider myself fortunate in getting through the year alive.

"I'm not superstitious, but it was my thirteenth year in racing, I finished thirteenth in the USAC national championships, and the only sprint race I won was on the thirteenth of the month. Now my car number is 14, it's my fourteenth year in racing, and I'm feeling great. Our operation is going smoothly. My dad has joined our team and taken a lot of decision-making and detail work off my shoulders.

"The first goal I had in racing was to win more races than any other United States driver by the time I was thirty years old. I achieved this and now my goal is to become the first man in history to win four 500-mile races. I'm in good shape and whether or not I do win the 500 four times I've still set some records that are bound to stand for a long time.

"Right now I'm not thinking of anything else but winning my third 500. That would put me one step closer to my goal. And if I do win a third and a fourth, I'm not even sure I'll retire from racing then. When I do quit, I'll stay in racing and run cars for other drivers. Racing is what I like to do."

He liked it a lot less when he saw the turbocar. It was so smooth and so powerful it awed the other competitors. Its engine ran so quietly it sneaked up on others in practice and rolled right by them, leaving in its wake a wave of shimmering heat. It used an airfoil on the tail, a forerunner of the wings that were to follow, and obscured the vision of the cars chasing it.

Foyt complained, "That engine is nothing but a jet. This place is supposed to be a proving grounds for cars, not airplanes. When it comes up behind you, it comes without warning. You can't hear it.

When you're running behind it, it roasts you and the heat waves blur your vision. When he cranks up that damn airfoil you can't see around it."

Everyone who had to beat it had complaints. Everyone was convinced it outmoded everything else at the track and if it worked would force everyone to junk all their equipment and start all over again at a collective cost amounting to millions of dollars. A lot of its foes started to suggest it should be banned.

"These guys are against progress," Granatelli retorted. "What they're really against is someone who is smart enough to come up with something better than they've got. They're against being beat."

Parnelli said, "No one knew what the car could do. They thought I knew. I didn't know a damn thing. I was just learning how to drive it. It was damned hard. No one knew the engine ate up the gears. The thing would pull apart above 166. But I found out I could go 166 all day. No one else could come close to that."

Few realized that the car had problems, but Foyt guessed it. He figured the gearbox would go. He said it before anyone else said it, before the car had qualified. When it qualified only sixth fastest, his spirits soared. "It won't last half the race," he said. "Sooner or later the engine will overheat or the gearbox will go and it will be gone. It may be the car of the future. I don't know. But no new car comes here and sorts itself out right away. It will take time to develop it. Its time may come, but it's my time now. I feel like I'm gonna win this race."

Andretti put Brawner's new Dean car on the pole at just under 169. Gurney slotted his new Eagle next at 167. Johncock slid in at 166 to fill the front row. Foyt had some problems but pulled into his pit at one point, jumped out of his car, rummaged around in his equipment for a spare part, handled the replacement himself, went back out on the track, and swiftly started turning in the speed he wanted.

When it was his time to qualify, he ran his laps at 54.13 seconds, 54.10, 54.03, and 54.23, a typically consistent Foyt tour. All four laps were within a fifth of a second of each other. He took the car to its maximum and held it there. It added up to an average speed of 166.289 mph, fourth fastest of the day, putting him in his orange car on the inside of the second row, right behind Andretti.

Joe Leonard in the Foyt sister car took the spot alongside his boss. Jones put the fat red STP Turbocar on the outside of the row. Ruby and the Unser brothers took the third row spots. Clark made it, but with a misbehaving car that landed way back in the sixth row. The others had caught up to and passed Chapman now. Defending champion Hill made it, but only on the last day and in the last row. No Watson car even made it. At the end of the last day Watson sat alone in his garage. Progress had passed him. There were no front-engine heavyweights in the field.

The night before the race, Foyt went to bed about 9:00. The phone in his motel had been turned off. He lay about an hour thinking about the race. He fell asleep at about ten, he said later, and slept soundly until about 8:15. Astronaut Wally Schirra came up to talk for awhile. Then Foyt had breakfast and left for the track. He hung around with the boys for awhile and didn't go back to his garage to change into his uniform until about 35 minutes before the start of the race. While he changed, he discussed strategy: You can go with a hot fuel mixture or a light load of fuel, both of which increase speed but require extra pit stops, or go with a cool mixture and heavy load and save time with fewer stops.

"I hope I guessed right," Foyt said. "I'm going with cool fuel and a full load. I hope I'll have to make only two pit stops. I walked down the line out there and a lot of the guys had their fuel 'popped up.' I guess a lot of them will go with light loads, too. I guess the turbocar has them scared. I don't think it will last. I still think you have to go 500 miles and that's just what I aim to do. I'm just going to feel out the field. If there's a hole, I'll go, but otherwise I'll hang back and watch how the rest of the guys are going. When the time comes, I'll move up. Maybe I've guessed wrong about strategy, but I hope not. Anyway, this is a game of percentages and gambles and I've made mine."

The place was packed, as usual. The approximately 300,000 spectators spread out over the arena, were more excited than usual because of the threat posed by the controversial turbocar. It was a gray, overcast day. Traditionally, while May was a month of rain in Indianapolis, it did not rain on this race. But luck has a way of turning sometimes.

At the starting command, 32 cars fired up. Defending champion Hill's car would not start. Ignominiously, he had to be pushed aside while his crew worked feverishly to get his car going. They finally succeeded. But he did not last long. Neither did Clark. As it turned out, after revolutionizing this race, the Grand Prix crowd had been caught and surpassed and soon would be staying home again during the month of May.

As the cars came down the mainstretch for the start with the checkered flag flying and Andretti accelerating, he glanced in his rear view mirror and saw Foyt rushing up behind him. Anxious to stay ahead, Andretti shoved in his clutch to gain added power and he singed it. He got into the first turn in front, but before Foyt or anyone else could get around him, the turbocar glided outside from outside the second row and swept past the entire first row as it started to string out. That fast, Parnelli had pushed his freak to the front. Andretti said, "The son of a bitch didn't even have the decency to wave." For 18 laps he pulled farther and farther in front, flying at record speeds. But by then it had begun to rain. And the race was stopped with Jones 12 seconds in front.

Andretti already was in the pits. The rest pulled in and their cars were packaged in plastic and tarpaulins and everyone waited and waited. After five hours Tony Hulman called it a day and said tomorrow was another day. The next day was a weekday, not a holiday.

Not all could wait. Those who could crowded the town.

Parnelli said, "I can wait. It was like a Sunday drive out there." He seemed cool and confident.

So did Foyt. He dined that night with Hulman and teased Tony about calling the contest just because it was a little wet out there. He said he couldn't wait to win. He told Tony, "I'm so sure I'm gonna win this race that I ought to charge you for keeping my money overnight."

But that night Foyt slept fitfully. He was disturbed. He had a sort of vision in which he was leading on the last lap when a smashup took place in front of him and he had to brake to beat it. Maybe the waiting and mounting tension were getting to him. He seemed a lot less loose as he readied himself to renew the race the next day.

They started single file in the order in which they had been running in the 19th lap. Jones was first, followed by Gurney, then Foyt. Ruby already was out, but overnight a new clutch had been installed by Brawner in Andretti's car and he was once more in the race, at the back of the field. But before long his car threw a wheel and that was it for him.

He kicked at his wheel and walked back to his pit. He said softly, "You dream about tomorrow and then tomorrow turns out to be like any other day."

Brawner said, "Tomorrow. Next year. You keep trying."

Al Dean didn't say anything. He sat staring into space. There would be no next year for him. In a few months his heart would stop and he would die.

From the restart, Foyt and Gurney could not keep up with Jones. At fifty laps Jones led by twenty-five seconds. But two laps later, however, as he was lapping Lee Roy Yarbrough, Lee Roy spun. Jones spun with him. Only their wheels touched and then just briefly. Side by side, they waltzed into the infield. Somehow, Jones kept his car from stalling. He got it pointed straight and returned to the track as Gurney blew past him. Accelerating, Jones blew right back past Gurney to regain the lead, and soon started to stretch out again.

Ultimately Gurney's engine went sour and he fell back. Foyt moved into second place. Jones was 16 seconds ahead at 130 laps when he pitted for fuel. While Parnelli was in the pits, Foyt buzzed past on the track. When Parnelli returned, Foyt was 30 seconds in front. But at 148 laps Foyt had to pit for fuel and Parnelli went past. When Foyt rolled out, gesturing obscenely at Granatelli in the Parnelli pit, Jones was 20 seconds ahead and pulling away again.

"I had been certain he was going to break," Foyt said later. "But when he got past the midway mark and kept on going I figured I was finished. I figured all I could do was keep going, keep as much pressure on him as possible to keep him running as hard as possible, and hope for the best, but about the best I could do at that point was stay in the same lap with him."

Running smoothly, the turbocar was clicking off the laps flying far in front toward the finish. Here and there a spin or a smashup occurred, but nothing serious, nothing to stop Jones. With 50 miles left, Foyt was 50 seconds back and the only car in the same lap with the leader. The next car, Al Unser's, was three laps back. The competition was completely outclassed.

Late in the race, Johncock spun out and stopped on the track and the yellow lights came on and the pace was slowed for awhile. When the car was cleared and the green signals flashed on and the pace picked up, Jones seemed to be a certain winner. Suddenly, on the backstretch of the 197th lap, with less than ten miles to go, Jones slowed. A six-dollar ball bearing had broken, crippling his gearbox. His jet car was abruptly without power. All he could do then was coast around toward the pits. It happened so abruptly it was shocking. Jones sat in his car, steering it, sick with despair.

The announcer screamed the news that Jones was coasting. The fans came up shouting. Granatelli and his crew stood as though struck dumb by disbelief. Foyt could not hear the announcer in his noisy car, but he could see the fans standing and shouting and waving him on before he could see Jones. In that instant he sensed something had happened to Jones and his heart jumped. He shot past Jones and then past his pits, nodding to his father and the rest of the crew that he knew what the situation was, and he drove into the last two laps now well out in front. Only his car betraying him or an accident crippling his car could beat him now.

He came through the next-to-last lap and into the last lap and around and into the last turn. All the while his mind was working hard and he thought about an accident and he slowed sharply.

"It was as though I had a premonition," he said later. "I had dreamed about it, and then I came around the last corner and there it was! If I hadn't already slowed down, there is no way I could have gotten through it."

At the head of the homestretch, the suspension snapped on Bobby Grim's car and he slowed, causing Chuck Hulse and Carl Williams to brake and slide into each other. Williams bounced into Grim. Behind them, Bud Tingelstad and Larry Dickson spun. In an instant, cars were spinning and sliding and crashing all over the track as Foyt moved into the chaos.

"I slowed down so much I could have walked faster," Foyt said later. "I threw her in low gear and went low and somehow I sneaked through. And there was that bee-you-tea-ful checker waving at me."

And so he had his third Indianapolis 500 triumph, which placed him with the immortals. He had given Goodyear a victory. He came into Victory Lane and there was Lucy and his father and the crew, who had been worried sick by the wall when the announcer shouted about the wreck and screamed he didn't know if Foyt had gotten through it. But he had, and now they kissed him and hugged him and pounded his back and a broad grin broke out over his face. Told that his teammate Joe Leonard had come in third behind Al Unser, Foyt replied, "Hey, now, that's really something, isn't it! My cars first and third. Hey, that's really something."

Which it was, of course. And not the least special thing about it for him was that he had won without Bignotti.

He said he sympathized with Jones and Granatelli, who sat in dark moods without speaking in their garage.

"It wouldn't happen again in a million years," growled Granatelli. "Well, we scared 'em. They'll try to ban it now. I'll sue 'em." Jones muttered an oath and got up and left.

At the Victory Dinner, Foyt collected $171,227 for finishing first and $43,527 for Leonard finishing third, and A. J. said something about the old dog not being dead.

At breakfast the morning after the race he said he had been so excited he could not sleep the night before. Dressed neatly in an orange sweater and tan slacks, looking handsome and healthy and happy, he ate steak and eggs and potatoes and toast and watched Parnelli driving off with angry force on the first tee of the golf course beyond the motel restaurant window. He smiled.

"I felt sorry for Parnelli, but I felt happy as hell for myself. I know how it feels to lose when you have the big one won. But, with all respect for Parnelli, he had an unfair advantage on us this year. That ol' jet car has twice the horsepower of anything here, and it just ain't fair to run it against piston engines. If they don't restrict it or bar it, I'll have to run one myself next year, but I don't want to. I could have run harder, but I couldn't catch Parnelli, so I didn't. You've got to make up your mind in this race whether you want to be a showboat at first or run strong all day and I feel I did the smart thing."

Later, he added, "They can say I fell into my three wins here from now to doomsday, but I say I outsmarted 'em, which is something for a guy who likes to lead, who has won most of his races by charging. When you win, it doesn't matter what they say. Ask Parnelli."

Parnelli didn't have much to say. He had a shirt made up that said "Indianapolis 490 Champion" on the back. He showed it to Foyt, who laughed and said, "I don't know about that, buddy, but they paid me off on 500."

Within a week Foyt had gone with Gurney to share a ride in a Ford in the famed 24 Hours of Le Mans, which they won—and that was something special. He not only won the Indianapolis 500 and the 24 Hours of Le Mans within a week but he was the first to have won both classics at any time. And within a few more months Foyt had taken more championship races, at Springfield, DuQuoin, Trenton, and Sacramento. By planning smartly in advance, by having alternate cars to jump into every time the car he was driving stopped, he finished high enough in the season's final championship race at Riverside to steal his fifth national driving championship from Mario Andretti.

Foyt's comback was complete. He was on top again. But the top is a hard place to stay.

This writer had written a book in which he called A. J. Foyt the greatest American race driver. The first time the writer saw Parnelli Jones after that, Parnelli was playing cards in an office at the Ontario Speedway.

Without seeming to look up from his cards, Parnelli said sarcastically, "A. J. Foyt the greatest American race driver!"

The writer said, "Well, P. J., if he isn't, who is?" Thinking Parnelli would probably suggest himself.

Very slowly, emphasizing each word, Parnelli Jones replied, "The greatest American race driver is George Bignotti."

There are those in the racing profession who feel that anyone who drives for Bignotti becomes the best because of what Bignotti brings to a driver. Bignotti did win 27 championship races in less than six years with Foyt. And Bignotti won 39 in the following eight years with other drivers, while Foyt won only 18. And through 1973 Bignotti won 66 championship races, including six Indianapolis 500s, two Pocono 500s, and two Ontario 500s, while Foyt won 46 title races, including three Indys and one Pocono 500.

However, Bignotti had won only one title race in four years with other drivers before he teamed with Foyt. With Foyt, he made a reputation that brought him the best backers and drivers. In addition, a mechanic can put more than one car in a race at a time, as Bignotti regularly does, and can go on at his peak for many more years than a driver.

The late 1960s and early 1970s took a lot from Foyt. He suffered severe injuries and many disappointing setbacks. A number of new challengers arrived on the scene while many veterans dropped off on the side of the road. Gurney would go through the 1960s but then would retire to concentrate on operating his team. Jones retired in 1968, also to operate his own team. Clark was killed in a crash in a minor race in Germany in April, a month before the 1968 Indianapolis renewal. Andretti was at his peak. Al and Bobby Unser were reaching theirs.

The sons of great racing drivers who had been killed racing—
Tony Bettenhausen's son, Gary, and Bill Vukovich's son, Bill—
were rookies at Indianapolis in 1968. Another rookie of note, Mike
Mosley, was the youngest driver in the field there that year at a
mere twenty-two. Two polished and scholarly young men from the
sports car ranks, Mark Donohue and Peter Revson, debuted there
the next year. Another from this background, Jerry Grant, had
raced there several years but made a splash there for the first time
the following year. The year after that, two hot kids came in—
Swede Savage and Salt Walther.

Donohue arrived as part of a package with Roger Penske, a retired
sports car champion and successful automobile dealer. Both were
1959 college graduates, from Brown and Lehigh, respectively. Both
were in their early thirties. Penske was called Captain, "as in
Bligh," reported Robert Jones in *Sports Illustrated*. Donohue was
called Captain Nice. Penske operated a racing team and ran a taut
shop. He was cold, confident, and calculating. Donohue drove for
him and was under the whip. He was warmer and a lot less confident.

Penske employed an Austrian, Karl Kainhofer, as his chief mechanic, but Penske was mechanically knowing, too, and Donohoue
had graduated with a degree in engineering, so the trio was tech-
nically superior to most rivals. The cars they prepared in their
Pennsylvania shop were superior to most machinery. Donohue lived
off the main line in Philadelphia with a wife and two sons.

Revson was something more of a swinger, a bachelor and Holly-
wood handsome. He came from a fine family and, although it was
not his father but his uncle who operated the Revlon cosmetics
fortune, Peter complained so often about being called the Revlon
Heir that he came to be called by his rivals Peter Poverty. He
bounced from college to college to college before he wound up in
auto racing. Beneath his sun-tanned blonde beauty were eyes that
gave off sparks and the heart of a hero. He wanted to do something
daring and he wanted to do it well and he wanted to make his own
way with it.

These were members of the new breed in racing, who had moved
up from sports cars instead of from sprint cars, from fancy road
courses instead of ramshackle dirt ovals.

Grant emerged from the Pacific Northwest, a fellow who tended
to fat, a lover of life who took to a toupee when he began to bald.

Savage emerged from Santa Ana in Southern California as a
young man yearning nearly recklessly for success.

Walther came from Michigan wealth. His father, a steel man,
sponsored racers at Indiana before he sponsored his son, David, who

picked up the nickname Salt racing boats before he began to race cars. He reached Indianapolis early and still young.

Mosley hit the top at a young age, too. He settled in Indianapolis, where racing is a way of life for some. He said, "I want to be where the racing is."

Vukovich and Bettenhausen inherited racing backgrounds. Gary Bettenhausen, whose brothers, Merle and Tony, were moving up, too, was a warm, affable fellow, as his father had been.

"Pop never pressed us to race, but we knew he loved it and we have loved it as long as we can remember," Gary said. "It has been a long time since he died driving, so it was strictly our choice to follow in his footsteps, but we know he died doing what he wanted to do and we want to do it, too. We're proud of him and we feel he'd be proud of us now. Mom understands. Pop won everything but Indianapolis. We'd like to drive there together and we'd love for one of us to win it for him."

Young Vukovich, much like his father, cold, tough, taut, a bit of a loner, said, "I resent that everyone assumed I was supposed to follow in my father's footsteps. Sometimes I feel I was driven into it. I'm not afraid of it, but I'm not in love with it. I could leave it, but I can make money in it. I look at a Foyt and I feel if you're tough enough you can get a lot out of it."

The tough Texan, Tony Foyt, returned to Indianapolis in 1968 with a new Coyote, which turned out to be one of the fastest of the piston engine cars after he ended an experiment with an automatic transmission and turned from an experimental turbocharged Ford engine back to a standard Ford racing engine. He put Jim McElreath and Carl Williams into spare cars. Gurney was working with a stock Ford engine in a new Eagle. He had sold another Eagle to Bob Wilke for Bobby Unser to drive. Jud Phillips, a clever veteran mechanic who never had won at Indy, had a turbocharged Offy to fit it.

Jones had formed a racing team with business associate Vel Miletich and had Joe Leonard driving for them. With Dean dead, Brawner and Andretti were operating on their own with some sponsorship help. Brawner had put a turbocharged Ford in his Hawk and Foyt bet Andretti fifty bucks it wouldn't last fifty laps.

If they lasted, the best cars seemed again to be Granatelli's turbines. Sports car master Carroll Shelby had entered turbocars. Veteran Indianapolis sponsor Jack Adams had entered one. But Andy's appeared to be the best. USAC officials had reworked the rules reducing the permissible size of the turbine engines in an effort to restrict the potential superiority of these cars. Granatelli had taken them to court but lost. Instead of giving up, he had Chapman build a fleet of Lotus-like tubs to hold the turbine, which was moved to the rear of these flashy four-wheel drive creations. Andy and his brother Vince and other engineers worked to solve the problem of producing the power they wanted from a smaller engine. Clark, Jones, Stewart, and Hill were set to drive four of these cars. Stewart withdrew, preferring not to run Indianapolis, which he called "unsafe."

Early in the month, Jones withdrew, saying, "These new cars are not competitive." He released his driver, Leonard, to join the turbo-car team and signed George Snider to replace him on his own team. Granatelli pleaded with Parnelli to reconsider. When he would not, Art Pollard was put on the team.

Jones said, "I'm not ashamed. I don't think the cars are fast enough. A few years ago when I was younger, I'd have skinned my bottom trying to make it go fast enough."

He helped Leonard and others master the intricacies of driving the tricky turbocars, but it was not easy because they were not as easy with a race car as he was. Leonard lost control of one and wrecked it and went into another.

Jones also aided Agajanian with his car. He tried to help Vukovich, who didn't want to be helped. At one point, after Vukey cut a hot lap, Parnelli ran to him enthusiastically. "Hey, buddy, you just did 166," he said.

"Baloney," Vukey said. "165½. That's what they had on the electric eye."

"Naw, lots of guys had you at 66," Parnelli insisted, wanting to boost the lad's confidence. He said, "You're looking smoother than an awful lot of guys out there. You're just a little slow picking it up coming out of the turns, but you'll get on to it. You know, this car is a lot better than most of 'em out there. You ought to be able to do 68 with her."

Vukey gave Jones an odd look. "You probably couldn't get it over 63," he said.

Parnelli looked at him a long moment. Then he said softly, "Why do you think I quit? I'm getting too old for this business." Then he walked away. He didn't bother the boy again.

Foyt admitted he had talked about taking a turbine car, but decided against it because he didn't believe they belonged in the race. His decision was set when new legislation limited them. "It may be that the engine will not be as powerful as our engines now. We'll have to wait and see. I honestly don't believe the turbocharged Ford will last the race. That's why I decided to go with the standard Ford, which is dependable. Dan Gurney's stock Ford may be dependable. I'm not sure the turbocharged Offys will last, but they're the ones to beat. Bobby Unser, Lloyd Ruby, Gordon Johncock, Roger Mc-Cluskey, and one or two others may be faster in their turbocharged Offys than I am in my Ford, but I work for Ford so I'm sticking to Fords. In time I think the turbocharged Ford will be a winner."

Shirley Murphy, one of the big guy's backers on the Sheraton-Thompson team said, "A. J. isn't the kind to throw grease on an owner. But if the turbines turn out to be the best and are allowed to return, he'll have to return in one."

They soon appeared to be the best, though they had their troubles. At the end of the first week of the month, Mike Spence crashed in one and was killed. On the heels of Clark being killed, Chapman was, he said, "hurt deeply." He said, "I have no stomach for this now," turned the cars over to Granatelli, and departed for England. A worried Shelby withdrew his turbines, saying, "I'm not sure they're safe." In time Chapman returned, but Shelby did not. The Adams turbocar never showed and its driver, Bob Hurt, went into another car. On the final day of time trials, Hurt wrecked his new car, broke his neck, and was permanently paralyzed.

It was only a few days before the first day of time trials that Foyt abandoned his attempts with the turbocharged Ford. He had to set up his standard Ford engine in a hurry so he was satisfied when he fit into the field ninth fastest at a high 166. He was worried that his relatively untested engine would not last so he took the green flag to start his run without a warmup lap and turned in four almost identical laps of 166.8, 166.9, 166.5, and 166.9 to fit into the third row between McCluskey and Johncock. Immediately in front of him were Andretti, Ruby, and Al Unser. But in the front row inside of Bobby Unser were Leonard and Hill in two of the turbocars. Farther back in the field was Pollard in a third turbocar.

First Hill broke the 170 barrier. Then Leonard bettered him with new records for one lap of 171.953 for one lap and 171.559 for four. Bobby got one lap above 170 for a record for piston engines, but the turbines were in the race, too. Foyt frowned and said, "They're in one race and we're in another. If they finish, they'll finish far in front." He did get Jim McElreath and Carl Williams in with team cars.

At the start of the race Leonard sped his blood-red turbocar to the front while Hill and Pollard in the other turbocars dropped back. As it turned out, they never were competitive. It was a hot day and their engines did not work well. Leonard's seemed to work though Bobby Unser had blasted by him and seemed able to hold him off. Andretti's engine went sour on the first lap. He parked in the pits after two laps and later paid Foyt his 50 dollars for the lost wager. He took over a sister car driven by Larry Dickson but soon that quit too and Andretti and Brawner had been beaten again. At 105 miles, Al Unser lost control of his car and he broadslid a barrier, the car twisting apart and throwing debris all over the track.

Bettenhausen drove over a chunk of the broken car, knocking out his own machine's undercarriage, and he limped into the pits. As Bobby drove by, Al gave him a prearranged signal that he was safe and the relieved brother returned to his race.

Three pit stops had been made mandatory this year. Emerging from a pit stop, one of the gears in Bobby's car began to come apart. Quickly he found himself in a struggle to hold his lead. Each time he emerged from the pits it took him a long time to regain speed. The rest of the field, led by Leonard and including Foyt, began to gain on him. Then, just past 200 miles, a connecting rod broke, disabling A. J.'s machine and ending his run.

Disheartened, he returned to the pits to help out with his cars that remained on the track. McElreath's car might have been competitive. Later, Foyt admitted, "Everyone wanted me to get in Jim's car. But that's not the way I do business. When I sign someone to drive for me, it's his car. I've won this race three times and a lot of guys have never won it." Later, however, the McElreath car broke down, then the Williams car broke up on a wall and the team had failed.

Around the halfway mark, Ruby had joined Leonard in the bid to catch Bobby Unser. They caught him and it became a three-way battle for the lead. After the three made their pit stops, Unser had taken so much time regaining speed that he seemed beaten. Ruby led Leonard by 12 seconds and Unser by 20 seconds with just 65 miles to go. And then a coil popped in Ruby's engine and he slowed and coasted toward the pits, having broken down while in the lead not far from the finish for the second time in three years.

Leonard appeared the likely winner then and in the pits Granatelli hugged Parnelli. With less than 45 miles to go, Williams whacked the wall, bringing out the yellow caution signals. The field ran at slowdown speed for 25 miles. The turbine engines are wound up to perform at top speed; they stiffen at slow speed. When the green came out again and Leonard hit his accelerator, his car lurched, the engine died, and he coasted toward the infield. As the vast crowd howled in hysteria, a startled Unser sped past, smiling broadly. For the second time in two years a turbocar that seemed safe in front near the finish had failed.

Leonard walked from his car back to the pits where he sat

wordlessly among Andy, Parnelli, and the rest. Granatelli had been trying to beat Indy since 1946 and he had failed every time. A promoter, unstylish and immodest, he was an unpopular person, but his persistence and pain almost made him a sympathetic soul now.

Unser ran off the remaining laps and slid across the finish line 55 seconds in front of Gurney, who had finished for the first time. Kenyon was third and Denis Hulme, in a Gurney team car, fourth. Gurney's family had broken up. He was about to be sued for divorce. The track had hurt his home life. But the track was his home. He had lost, but he was not entirely a loser. Cars he built had finished first, second and fourth.

"Maybe I should build cars and not race them," he sighed.

Unser said, "I was lucky. The turbocars are in a class by themselves. They should be banned."

They were. Further restrictions not only reduced their power unreasonably but outlawed the four-wheel drive they required. Regretfully, angrily, Granatelli had to give up on them, going back to more conventional racers for the future. Foyt spent a lot of the summer practicing the turbocharged Ford for the future, missing some races here and there. The races he ran on the title trail frustrated him.

His engine expired in the first lap at Phoenix. His chassis broke and he was the second man out at Trenton. His fuel-feed failed in three laps at Milwaukee. Ronnie Duman died in a crash there. Foyt's engine overheated at Las Vegas. His engine gave out in an event in Canada. And at Springfield. And in Michigan. Back at Trenton, a wheel broke off his car. Back at Milwaukee, a wheel locked on him.

He won a few, however. He beat the turbines that finished a race for the first and last time at Castle Rock, Colorado, near Denver, on a road course. He led the Hoosier Hundred almost all the way. He won wire-to-wire at Sacramento. He came from a full lap back to win at Hanford, California. This was the first-ever victory for the turbo-Ford. As he had for Goodyear, Foyt produced for his sponsors. He started eighteenth and passed 11 cars in 20 laps and 7 more the next 70 laps and finished fourth in a road race at Indianapolis Raceway Park. He had a few high finishes besides his four firsts. But it was a tough year for him.

In the first race of the season at Phoenix, Foyt's car broke down early. He was watching as a spectator when just past the midway point in the race Roger McCluskey's car skidded on oil into Johnny Rutherford's car and the two cars began to blaze as they slid to a stop along the wall.

Standing 100 feet from the accident, Foyt ran to it, reached right into the flames and helped Rutherford out of his car, pulled the burning shoes off the racer's feet, then sprinted to McCluskey's car and helped others who had rushed up to pull Roger from his racer. With such swift rescue work, none suffered more than minor burns.

In the final race of the season at Phoenix, Foyt himself was wrecked in a collision with Andretti and suffered severe burns.

Bobby Unser had captured five races on the tour that season. Al Unser, Andretti, and Foyt had won four each. But with the bundle from Indy, Bobby had enough points to take the driving title. Foyt also had won some stock car races along the way and it had been a fair year for him financially, but a frustrating year personally.

The next year was worse. He won six stock car races but only one championship contest—the Hoosier Hundred at the Indianapolis Fairgrounds. It was his sixth victory in this classic contest of dirt racing on tour. No other driver on the championship trail has ever won any one race more than four times. Taking a check for nearly $20,000 to run his earnings in this one race alone to nearly $200,000, Foyt laughed and asked, "When are you going to give me title to this place?"

But it was small consolation for the rest of the season when six stock-car triumphs and three thirds on the championship trail were all that he had to show for his efforts.

Indianapolis was the most disappointing of all. He brought a cigar-shaped Coyote to the track. It was strong, swift, and agile and considered a compliment to him as a car-builder. (He had also developed a powerful turbocharged Ford that was a tribute to him.) He practiced consistently at above 170 and captured the pole position with one lap at 171.6 and four laps at 170.5, the fastest piston engines had ever pushed a car, although not as fast as the turbines had turned the year before.

Andretti and Al Unser were the only ones who had practiced at similar speed. And Al, driving a Bignotti car for the Parnelli-Vel team, had cracked up cavorting on a motorcycle on the Speedway grounds and broken an ankle and was out of the race. Andretti had crashed his Brawner car heavily three days before the first day of time trials, suffering severe burns to his face and hands, and after it was repaired he fell short of Foyt in qualifying.

Bobby Unser filled the front row. Rookie Mark Donohue and veterans Johncock and McCluskey captured second row slots. Gurney, Ruby, and the rest of the regulars got in further back. Rookie Revson got in at the back of the field.

Lacking sufficient financing, Brawner and Andretti had accepted Granatelli's sponsorship. Brawner and young Jim McGee, who had become co-chief of the crew, had built the car and prepared it, but Granatelli had it painted his orange-red color and slapped STP stickers all over it and laid claim to it. Andretti's turbo-Ford was overheating in practice and Brawner and McGee asked for and received permission from chief steward Harlan Fengler to add an external radiator that might cool the engine. However there was a rule forbidding external changes between qualifying and race day. When Foyt, who had worked long and hard to rig up an extra internal radiator before qualifying, protested, Fengler withdrew permission, which angered Andretti.

When the race started, Andretti flashed to the front past Foyt. However, Andretti's engine soon started to overheat, he had to slow, and first Foyt and then Ruby roared past him. Andretti figured he was finished until, studying the gauges, he realized that if he didn't exceed 165 the oil and water temperatures held at a safe level. He couldn't keep up with Foyt and Ruby at that speed, but he could stay ahead of the others. Bobby Unser's car, meanwhile, was behaving erratically and Gurney's car was struggling.

Foyt flew in front for 78 laps, leading by a little more every lap, his car behaving beautifully. On one lap he went almost 166, the fastest any leader lapped all day. He was eight seconds in front and seemed well on his way to that fourth 500 triumph he wanted so much. And then he began to lose power and he found others roaring past him. He hung on awhile, hoping his speed would return, but it did not. He went into the pits, returned to the track, returned to the pits again. At 200 miles, he got out of the car and with his crew pulled off the hood and dug into the guts of the engine. Here, it was discovered a piece of metal had come apart in the turbocharger. Even then he refused to quit.

Crewmen took the broken part back to the garage, where it was welded back together. Waiting, Foyt paced the pits in a fury. A television commentator invaded the pits to try to interview him but was ordered out. It was almost 24 minutes before the part was brought to the pits and restored to the car and Foyt returned to the track. He was out of contention. So were McCluskey and Snider, whom he had gotten into the race in sister cars.

Ruby led until shortly past the halfway point. When he pitted for fuel, a member of his crew sent him away before a refueling hose had been disconnected from the car's tank. As Ruby sped away, part of his tank was pulled from the car and the fuel gushed out. Ruby slammed on the brakes and sat there as though the blood was rushing out of him. For the third time in four years he'd lost the lead through no fault of his own.

Andretti had it then. And he kept it. Charging as though he was in the running, Foyt raced him. But Andretti would not race him; Mario let Foyt catch him and pass him and go around and catch him and pass him again. "I knew how many laps he was behind. I wasn't going to let him get me into any trouble," Mario said later.

There was little trouble on the track throughout the race. Andretti came home first, followed far back by Gurney, Unser, and Revson. Placing next were Leonard, Donohue, and Foyt, who had charged all the way back up to eighth place by the finish.

Andretti's victory came too late for Dean but not for Brawner, who waited for him happily in Victory Lane. And not for Granatelli, who came on the run. Andretti's wife, Dee Ann, came on the run, too. Fat Andy and Fat Dee Ann, the one fat from good living, the other fat from being seven months pregnant, came huffing and puffing to kiss the winner, whose freshly scarred face was creased in a smile.

"I feel like Pancho Villa," murmured Andy, who acted as if he'd done it all himself.

"I feel like hell," Foyt said. "I feel like I lost when I should have won. Hell, it was a little ten-cent clasp that failed. I was almost hoping something else would break after I went out so I could say to myself it just wasn't meant to be my day, but the thing ran like a dream all the rest of the day. Everything else worked beautifully. I could outrun everyone else. I would have won my fourth one easily if that one little thing hadn't failed."

Mario went on to win eight races and his third national title. But Brawner argued with Granatelli and broke away from him at season's end. Mario stayed with him and stopped winning. Foyt had stopped winning. He won only that Hoosier Hundred. He was on his way to winning in Milwaukee when he ran low on fuel, went in, and stalled in the pits. He was leading in Colorado when he spun into a ditch to avoid a skidding car. He was leading at Springfield until he suffered a flat tire. He crashed and suffered minor burns. He was going for the lead at Indianapolis Raceway Park when he lost his brakes. Later, he lost control and crashed at Riverside. His car was severely damaged but he escaped injury.

He got four cars into the Indianapolis race in 1970. It was the largest team in the race in 25 years and a tribute to the car-building, engine-building, and all-around mechanical work of him and his father and the rest of the crew.

He got himself in third fastest, in his new Coyote under the

Sheraton-Thompson banner. He got George Snider and Donnie Allison in with Coyotes he had entered in partnership with J. H. Greer.

At Ford's request, Foyt had taken over from Lou Meyer the responsibility of building and supplying parts for their turbocharged engines at the track. With three cars in competition, he felt he had all he could handle. During the third day of time trials, he smiled and said, "If I had four cars in this race I'd commit suicide."

Then Jim McElreath came to him and asked if there was any chance he could get a ride in a fourth car Foyt had entered. It was a brand-new car that had been held as a backup car for use if anything went wrong with the others. It hadn't been run. It hadn't even been unpacked. A. J. said his crew already was stretched pretty thin and he'd have to talk to them and think about it. McElreath said he figured Foyt would say no, but he hadn't been out of the race since he first came to Indy and he was desperate.

Foyt liked the veteran and sympathized with his position. He got back to McElreath and said they'd give it a go.

They took the car from the crate and went to work on it well into the night. The following morning, Foyt took it out to test it, ran it for the first four laps of its life, and burned a bearing on it. They towed it back to the garage, removed the engine, put a new one in, and Foyt took it back out and ran it ten laps. He brought it in and said the front shocks needed changing, so they changed the shocks. The car was then turned over to McElreath. He took it out and sped four laps in it, brought it in, and said something was wrong with it. They changed the turbocharger. He took two more laps and it was working. Foyt told him to go out and qualify, and he did.

"That guy is fantastic," McElreath said later. "I'd been bumped from the field and I knew he had no business putting another car out there. But if he's your friend, he's a good friend. And if there's a challenge, he wants to meet it. They worked from six o'clock until after midnight. Nobody had to tell anybody what to do. Everyone just seemed to know. I sure wanted him to shake it down for me. He built the car, after all. I might have driven the car all day and not figured out it needed new shocks. But if he does a job for you, he does a job for you."

The car was one of only five that ran all day. In fact, it finished in front of Foyt's own car and right behind another Foyt car driven by Donnie Allison. That gave Foyt two of the first five placers and three of the top ten.

But Foyt himself did not win. And Bignotti won, with Al Unser. The Parnelli-Vel team with Bignotti fielded two fast cars, turbocharged Ford-Colts driven by Unser and Joe Leonard. Leonard's car failed, but Unser's did not. After taking the pole at above 170, Al drove a beautifully fashioned car flawlessly at speeds of around 166. Foyt led twice. He was running second and within reach of the lead late in the race when McCluskey crashed and Ron Bucknum barged into him and A. J. had to swerve to avoid them. The violence of the collision wrenched the gearbox apart and he lost power and wound up crawling pitifully the final 50 miles just to finish tenth.

Unser led the last 100 miles and won handily from Donohue, who was driving a McClaren car purchased from Team McClaren. Dan Gurney finished third, followed by Allison and McElreath. Andretti in an ailing Granatelli car limped in sixth. The purse passed a million dollars and Al collected $271,000 for Parnelli, Bignotti, and the boys.

Al Unser went on to win the national title. Sadly enough, Foyt did not win a race. His car failed him time and again. At DuQuoin, he lost control of his car, crashed right over the wall, and was brought back to the starting line in an ambulance. He got out and limped around on a bruised foot and the crowd, which had feared for his life, saw him and stood up and cheered him for a full five minutes. As angry as he was, he had to smile and nod. But it was a bad year—except at the first California 500 at the fantastic $25 million plant in Ontario. After he dropped out of contention with transmission troubles, he hit the wall, which gave McElreath a chance to catch Pollard and pass him and put a Foyt Coyote in front at the finish for a fat payoff for the Foyt team. His kindness to McElreath was repaid.

Foyt smiled and said, "He had a terrific car."

Foyt started 1971 by winning the Daytona 500, the classic contest of the southern stock car circuit. He had a shot at winning that fourth Indianapolis 500 though he didn't have the fastest car. Revson had that, putting a Team McLaren car, mechanicked by Teddy Mayer, on the pole at a new record pace of more than 178 miles per hour. Donohue practiced faster in a McLaren purchased and prepared by Penske, but he was only second swiftest in the actual time trials. Bobby Unser, in a Gurney Eagle prepared by Wayne Leary, was third fastest. If Gurney was going to win this now, it would be as a builder and owner, not as a driver. He had built a fast car that would set seven track records on the tour, but was not durable and would win only two races.

The McLarens had provided the latest revolution in racing. They were low and wide with wide tires that adhered to the tracks and the car moved through the air with aerodynamic excellence. Airfoil wings forced down by the winds that were whipped onto them increased downthrust. The cars cornered almost as fast as they swept through the straights. As with other radical designs that worked, these were widely copied and became the dominant design on the tour.

Hulme in another Team McLaren car took the inside spot on the second row. Al Unser in Bignotti's Parnelli-Vel car landed alongside him. Outside in his latest Thompson Coyote came Foyt. A. J.'s car ran all day, but it didn't run fast enough. Donohue ran fastest, reaching 174 on the 66th lap, but his engine stopped on the next lap. Bignotti's two Parnelli cars driven by Unser and Leonard then dueled for 50 laps, trading the lead seven times before Leonard's turbocharger failed. Unser went on from there to win his second straight Indianapolis 500, bringing Bignotti and Parnelli back to Victory Lane there. For the third straight year, there were no fatalities in practice, qualifying, or racing. But missing from the celebration in Victory Lane was Unser's wife, Wanda, the mother of his three children. Their marriage was failing.

He collected $238,000 of the $1 million purse for his team. Foyt picked up almost $65,000 for third place, plus another $25,000 for Donnie Allison's fifth-place finish.

"Forget it," he said. "Without winning, it's a disappointment. You win or you don't. The cash is only consolation. I was strong enough, I just wasn't fast enough."

It was the same story in the first Pocono 500 in Pennsylvania. Foyt's car went all the way, but it didn't go fast enough. Donohue's Penske car qualified fastest and finished first. Leonard's Parnelli-Bignotti car had problems in the pits but still was close enough to pass Donohue when he lost control on an oil slick and slowed briefly on the 191st lap. Seven laps later Donohue caught him, passed him, and went on to win narrowly. Foyt flashed across a close third.

Things got worse in the second California 500 at Ontario. Snider crashed a Foyt car on the fifth lap. A. J. who had led awhile, was running second to Al Unser when his car's rear end gave out at 157 laps. Had it held up, he might have won, for three laps later Al's gearbox conked out. Savage, back in action after a near-fatal crash in a sports car at the same track, crashed out without serious injury. This left it up to Leonard, who brought the Bignotti-Parnelli car a lap in front of Pollard and two laps in front of Bettenhausen. He picked up $135,000 of a $635,000 payoff.

It was a disappointing year for Foyt, who ran nine of the ten races and finished fifth or better in five of them to wind up second in the final driving standings. His only victory was a late one at Phoenix. There had been 41 races on the tour since the middle of the 1969 season when Foyt last had won one.

In 1971 Al Unser won five races including his second straight Indianapolis 500, but Joe Leonard won the California 500 and placed high so consistently that he took his first national title and the sixth for one of Bignotti's drivers. This was the year Bignotti moved into a $180,000 mansion in exclusive Rolling Hills in Southern California.

Foyt went back to work in his Houston shop. You could not rest if you were going to keep up with your competition.

Weary of losing with Granatelli, having brought Granatelli his first title trail victory, but not having won a title trail contest since mid-1970, Mario Andretti jumped to Parnelli's team and brought McGee with him. It was said McGee had become bigger than Brawner, who was wandering now and struggling. Bignotti remained to act as mechanic on the Unser and Leonard cars.

Rather than rest on their laurels, Parnelli and Vel ordered radical new cars from Maurice Phillipe, one of the brains behind the Lotus development. Rumors spread about these mystery machines. Foyt asked about them of everyone who might know. One night Parnelli got a stooge to telephone Foyt in Houston. He asked Foyt if he'd heard about the new cars. Foyt said he sure had and he wondered what they looked like. The stooge asked Foyt to swear he wouldn't reveal the source. Foyt assured him he would not. The stooge said, "Well, the biggest thing about them is the driver doesn't sit. He lies on his belly, like he's riding a sled."

Foyt didn't think it was very funny. Neither did Parnelli after he put the cars on the track. They weren't so radical; they just weren't very good. The fast cars remained the Eagles and the McLarens. Bobby Unser blazed a Gurney Eagle to new records of 196 mph for one lap and 195 for four. Revson and Donohue put McLarens alongside him on the front row. Foyt's engine blew and he had to wait until the second qualifying day. He had said he never again would go on if he failed to make it the first day and had to settle for a spot far back, but when it came to it he couldn't stick to it and he went on the second day and accepted a 188 and the 16th slot.

A couple of years before, Foyt had been fired by Goodyear for running a stock car race on Firestones. He thought that was pretty funny. They talked about it and got back together again. He now switched from Autolite to Champion spark plugs at the last minute before qualifying for the 500. In the Autolite office off Gasoline

Alley, Foyt's picture was turned to the wall. When he heard about it, A. J. laughed like hell. He didn't find a lot to laugh about through the month, however.

He was concerned about the speeds produced by the wings. He didn't like the wings. He felt they helped cars go faster than men could control them. Though they held the car on the track while it was pointed straight, he was convinced that they sent the car out of control when it got crooked. He said, "There may be no limit to how fast we can make a car go, but there may be a limit to how well a man can control a car past a certain speed, especially on a track that was not designed for any such speed."

Unser had surpassed the previous pole speed by an incredible 17 miles per hour. The field raised the average speed an awesome 12 miles per hour. While attempting to qualify, Jim Malloy, traveling in an Eagle far faster than he had ever gone before, crashed and was critically injured. He died six days later. It was the first fatality at the track since 1968.

"We can't afford to lose men like that," Foyt said.

Rookie Merle Bettenhausen hit a wall trying to make the race, failed, but walked away. Later in the season he scraped a wall, ripping an arm off. When he recovered, he returned to racing one-armed with brother Gary's help, back in the bushes but still speaking of winning Indy for his father.

Gary almost won in 1972. All who remembered his father rooted for him and he was leading with 45 miles left when his engine failed. Bobby Unser had led at first, running away from everyone before his engine cracked after only 75 miles. Mosley swapped the lead with Bettenhausen for a while but then Mike lost control coming out of a corner, crashed on the mainstretch, caught fire, and bailed out aflame, burned but otherwise all right.

After Bettenhausen dropped out, Jerry Grant led awhile. He had to make a late stop for fuel. Grant was refueled from a sister car's supply. Later Bignotti protested and Grant was penalized several places. Donahue took over and ran the last dozen laps in the lead to put himself and Penske in Victory Circle after some frustrating years. Separated from his wife, he had slept on a cot at Penske's place in recent months. Now he had won $218,000 of the millon-dollar payoff. Was it worth it? "I don't know," he admitted wistfully.

For Foyt the race was worthless. When the cars were sent away, his wouldn't go. Pushed to the end of the pits, his crewmen got it going just as the field came down the stretch for the start. Later, in a furious mood, he stated: "They started ahead of schedule. When my engine caught, I saw them coming at me and I was ready to move out and drop into position as they came past. They were moving slowly under the yellow. Everybody had their hands up signaling one more warmup lap to get in shape. Then it went green. They waved the flag all of a sudden and sent them on their way.

"I couldn't believe it. I almost pulled out, but I barely caught the green out of the corner of my eye. If I had pulled out, you would have seen the damndest wreck you'd ever seen. Suppose I had been a rookie and, seeing the yellow, had pulled out? They would have crucified me.

"I blame the starter, Pat Vidan, as well as the steward, Harlan Fengler. The steward gives the order, but the starter still has to throw the flag. I think we've got to have someone up there who will use good common sense. They saw me down there with my motor running and could have let me in line. I probably draw as many people to the race as anyone. It was embarrassing to me and my sponsors."

His turbocharger went out at ninety miles and he lost 21 laps making repairs, returned to the race but was out for good at 150 miles. Thus ended another attempt to win his fourth Indy 500.

They had removed dirt races from the championship trail and placed them in a short championship circuit of their own. Foyt went to DuQuoin for one, caught fire in the pits, injured himself severely, and was finished for most of the season.

He was leading when he stopped in the pits for fuel. Anxious to get going, he let the clutch out slightly before refueling was finished. They use a fuel can in these races where little extra fuel is required. When the car moved, the can flipped into the cockpit.

Foyt later explained, "It hit me right in the head and my whole head caught on fire. When I tried to get out, I must have slipped and the rear wheel caught my foot. It tore it out of the socket and twisted it all around. There wasn't a fireman around. Dad came over the fence and saved my life. He was right there with an extinguisher. I burned the roof of my mouth and my tongue."

His foot was in a knee-length cast for almost a month. He said it was weeks before he could move his top lip without it splitting open. He said his right wrist was slow in healing and it drove him crazy. He was in a wheelchair for a while and then on crutches, and that drove him mad, too. "The hell of it is," he said, "if I didn't like the damn game and the challenge of it, I'd quit like everybody is yelling at me to do."

As soon as he could walk he wanted to go to Pocono for the 500, but the doctors wouldn't let him. That was in late July, two months after the accident. Leonard brought the Bignotti-Parnelli car home in front and went on to bring Bignotti another national title, his eighth and Joe's second.

Foyt limped into Ontario for the California 500 in September. Donohue and Bettenhausen were sidelined with injuries. Grant broke through the 200 mph barrier to take the pole on the first day, but Bobby Unser, delayed by blown engines the first day, set new records of 201.965 for one lap and 201.374 for four on the second day. Both drove Gurney Eagles.

Despite pain, Foyt put his car in the race sixth fastest at 190. Grant's engine blew on the pace lap. Unser's engine went inside of 70 miles. So did Foyt's. Andretti's engine conked out at 130 miles. Bobby's blew just short of 200 miles. So did Revson's. The engines just couldn't sustain such speed. Ruby's went out late. So did Leonard's. And Johncock's. McCluskey was left in the lead, winning his first major race and about $80,000 of the $340,000 prize.

Foyt returned to DuQuoin, the scene of his accident, to win at 100 miles. With seconds in dirt races at Springfield and Indianapolis, he accumulated enough points to take the title in this new division. Later he pointed to it with pride. "Those people who say I haven't been winning any championship races lately don't know what they're talking about. They call it the championship dirt division, don't they? And I won it, didn't I?" It wasn't the same thing and he knew it, but he wouldn't face it.

At motels, homes, saloons, and restaurants near tracks before big races, drinks flow freely, music blares loudly, and the ladies act lively. Race drivers are involved in a hard, demanding occupation by day, though one can hide from it at night. It is an exciting thing they do; it gives them glamor and attracts to them hangers-on of improper persuasions. Not all drivers drink heavily, love or live loosely, but there are those who do. Some are wound so tightly that they must cut loose before they snap. Others easily handle the pressures of their profession. There are those who prefer their families to trackside friendships, who would rather be home than away from home. Admittedly the temptations along the auto racing trail are tremendous. After a race there are always celebration parties. There always are women waiting. The women chase the drivers. There is a certain entertainer who frequently turns up on the trail who wants to make it with the winner in a garage somewhere—anywhere—right after the race while he is still hot and sweaty and dirty because then she feels really a part of this exciting thing he has just done.

There are women like this—famous, infamous, and unknown— who trade their favors for favors at every stop along the road. And even if you do not care for these women, even if you do not have to get drunk to forget your fears, even if you can sleep through long, lonely nights in strange rooms—if you are a driver, you lead a life that frustrates your family life. And even if you have a wife who is not constantly torn by apprehension, you have made life difficult for her.

It is a fact that four of the last five winners of the Indianapolis 500 through 1973 have been divorced, most of them after winning. The exception is Mario Andretti. Before these five an exception was A. J. Foyt. The four are Gordon Johncock, Mark Donohue, Al Unser, and Bobby Unser. Another before them was Rodger Ward. One who fits with them is one who was second twice, Dan Gurney. They are all nice guys, but all of them state that the pressures of their profession provoked problems that could not be overcome.

Their life is simply not normal. Most of them struggled to hold their marriages together before they broke up.

Gurney has remarried and the Unser brothers are keeping company with lovely girls they may marry. Parnelli Jones traveled with a lady as his wife most of his career, which he discussed openly in his book, *Parnelli*. He was so intent on achieving success in racing that he did not want to be distracted by the demands of family life. She says he married her; he says he never did. She sued him for divorce and he settled with her out of court. When his career was coming to a close, he married a bright and beautiful girl and began to raise a family. He seems content. He is heavily tied up in racing still, but he himself rarely races anymore.

Whether or not A. J. Foyt is a saint, it is clear he is not about to get entangled with the ladies who lie in wait for him, finding the big, good-looking, heroic, and famous figure fascinating. Foyt is faithful to Lucy, who seems to be an ideal racing wife. She has admitted she is afraid for his safety, has confessed she wishes he'd retire, but has learned to keep her fears to herself and let his wishes govern his life. He still wants to race, so he races. She is there if he needs her. When he is hurt, she nurses him, as much as he will let her or anyone nurse him. When he is racing, she usually stays home and takes care of the kids. He calls after races to tell her what has happened.

She goes with him to some races, such as a big event like the Indianapolis 500. They opened expensive, special luxury suites behind the motel overlooking the track in 1973 and Foyt bought one for $10,000 and she was his hostess there, often making meals for his friends and business associates.

Sometimes, but not often, one or more of his kids has gone to his races. His daughter Terry was taken to the 1973 Indy race, which turned out to be a deadly event and traumatic to anyone who watched it, much less a youngster. They really are no longer kids. Terry was fifteen in 1973, a lovely young lady, apparently more interested in racing than Tony, who turned seventeen in 1973. Tony apparently was more interested in horses. Tony, Terry, and Jerry, who was eleven in 1973, all like horses and love the Foyt ranch. They were in school and were growing up rapidly and their father protected them from the sort of publicity he disliked but had to endure by keeping them in the background. He is devoted to them.

He spends as much time with his family as his racing allows, though theirs is not the typical family situation. He is away from home a lot. They take vacations together when they can, perhaps a visit to the lake or a camping trip. They spend time together at the ranch. He is basically a family fellow. His father heads up his crew. His sister works in his business office. His brother-in-law has helped him with his business interests.

Some years ago when his daughter was thrown from a horse and hurt severely, Foyt flew from the road to be by her side. And he shot the horse. Some supposed this was his temper. He said it was simply because the animal was dangerous. To his relief, his daughter recovered.

His personal wealth has been estimated at $10 million. A. J. Foyt Enterprises in Houston is an elaborate operation. He has investments in oil wells, race tracks, real estate, shopping centers, and motels. He has the biggest Chevrolet dealership in south Texas. He advertises that all they have to sell is their good name. He has won awards for his advertisements as well as his sales. And his service is excellent. When he took over the agency he told his 130 employees, "I will demand the same excellence here in the service departments as I do on the racetrack." Among his associates in some of his various enterprises have been Jack Valenti, former White House aide to Lyndon B. Johnson, and various oil millionaires. Foyt is on the board of directors of the Greenway Bank in Houston. He deals now in high finance.

After many years with Ansted, Murphy, and the Sheraton-Thompson or ITT Thompson sponsorship, Foyt went with Jim Gilmore as his sponsor in 1973 and began to bear the Gilmore Broadcasting banner. Gilmore, from Kalamazoo, Michigan, is a wealthy fellow fascinated by racing, and he has been in it for eight years. It has cost him a considerable amount of cash.

"I love competition in life," he states, "and racing may be the last great individual competitiveness in our country. It's unpredictable. I can forecast what will happen in business, not in racing, and that intrigues me. It's a great 'out for me.' It stimulates me in my other businesses. My wife loves it as much as I do and we're fortunate that our children do, too, so it gives us a chance to do something together, something we all enjoy."

He admits a lot of racing people were surprised when Foyt went with him. Gilmore said, "A. J. and I have always gotten along well. We haven't had any problems at all. I hope he respects me. I respect him. He's such a great competitor and driver. We both have automobile agencies and can talk about business. And he respects my interest in racing. I can go down to Houston and spend a day or so at his shop just talking to all the guys and seeing what they've done and I'm happy I've always been intrigued about engines. I've had a lot of fun messing around the engines in my own cars. I think I know enough not to stand around asking dumb questions.

"I go to as many races as I can. Foyt called me a few days before

Trenton and asked me if I was going to be there. I told him he'd told me he wasn't going to run there and I'd made commitments and now I couldn't go. He said I should be there because we were going to win. And darned if he didn't win. I wasn't there, which is nothing new, because I've never been at a race when one of my cars won."

Gilmore admitted he was hooked on every aspect of the sport. He said, "Some people are shocked when they come here and stroll around the infield and see some of the things that are going on. But this is it, this is life in the raw maybe, but it's the way life is." Some day he hoped to walk into Victory Lane at Indianapolis. "Let's just say if I were standing in Victory Lane at Indianapolis and had a heart attack and died right there on the spot it would be worth it."

With the backing of such enthusiasts, Foyt may have as much as a million dollars with which to run his racing program annually. And he decides how much he keeps for himself and how much he pours into his program. However, he does not stint on his racing expenses. And he tries to be fair with his sponsors. Once when he was testing tires for Goddyear he rented them the use of the cars, but when the engine failed he refused to accept payment. He bought the rights to the Ford racing engine and develops and builds them himself and races some himself and sells others for around $35,000. Competitors have been hesitant to buy them for fear he will not give them as good as he keeps for himself, but he has been improving them and if they prove themselves to be the best they will be in demand. Goodyear officials reportedly pay him $100,000 a year to test their product and $100,000 for each car he runs on their rubber. Other companies pay him to race their products.

Foyt takes a million dollars' worth of equipment to Indianapolis annually. He estimates he spends $15,000 just for housing his crew during the month of May alone. There is no way racing returns can justify this except in the promotion it provides products. Accordingly, while he had been winning in Mercurys on the stock car circuit, Foyt switched to Chevrolets because he felt if he was associated with them and sold them he should promote them. He has not been winning much with them, but feels it is his job to see that they become winners. At times he has switched equipment from what he was contracted to run because he felt he'd be better able to win with something else, but these were only temporary moves forced by his competitive instincts.

He transferred from Goodyear to Firestone one year when the new Goodyear racing tires weren't ready, but he returned to Goodyear, helped get them ready, and put them in Victory Circle at Indianapolis for the first time in about fifty years. Soon Goodyear was represented by as many racers as Firestone.

When there was some question about the Goodyear tire one year, Foyt refused to release his for tests, saying, "I bought 'em and they're mine and anyone who wants to look at one can just buy their own to look at."

He dropped the Ford turbocharged engine when it wasn't ready, but returned to it, made it ready, and made it a winner, which made it as attractive to the competitors as the Offy.

He builds his own Coyotes, races some and sells some. It is an extremely competitive business and builders guard their secrets and latest developments as closely as do Detroit auto manufacturers. Once when he spotted a mechanic from the McLaren team who, he figured, was "sneaking around" to steal a look at a new stabilizer wing he was installing on a car in an Indianapolis garage, he stalked over to the McLaren garage and looked their new creations over.

"And I didn't sneak around, either. I told them not to come sneaking around trying to check out my cars," he said.

He builds his cars in his Houston shop with the help of his father—whom he considers his chief mechanic—and the mechanics on his crew. One of them, Jack Starnes, has been with him long enough and done well enough to be trusted a great deal by a man who seldom trusts others to do what he feels he can best do for himself. Herb Porter and Harold Gilbert help with the engines.

A prominent and knowing man long involved in racing and product development says, "If Foyt has a failing it's that he is a perfectionist who spreads himself too thin. If hard work will do it, Foyt will get it done, but there are only so many arms on the man and so many hours in a day. He is the only man in racing who is doing it all—designing, building, and preparing his cars and racing them. And he can't stop tinkering with his cars trying to improve them.

"All right, he's no Bignotti, but then neither is any other mechanic. Foyt is one of the best mechanics in the business and if he was just a mechanic he might be another Bignotti, but he's also driving and you can't do everything and do it all perfect. He can't concentrate on chassis work if he also has to develop an engine. And then he has to think about how to drive the car. And wet-nurse the crew.

"He could go over to one of those high-powered teams and drive for Gurney or Parnelli or Penske or McLaren and get the best equipment and help and just have to drive and he'd blow the boys off the track again. Or he could just build cars and get a good driver and start winning again. But he has to have it his way and it's a hard way to go."

Foyt has a cattle ranch outside Houston. Lucy loves it and A. J. likes to spend time there, but he doesn't have a lot of time to spare. He once admitted, "I really shouldn't say this, but racing comes even before my wife and family. It's my job, but it's a job I love and the only way I know how to do it is to concentrate on it completely."

He is closing in on forty now, which is when he has said he might retire, but he is going almost as hard as ever. He stays close to his crew on the road. Rather than run around, he prefers to play cards and cut up with them on such off-hours as he is willing to take. He usually eats dinner with crewmen and refuses to let anyone else pay. He carries around a typical Texas bankroll—a wad of money wrapped in a rubber band—and he is generous. It is said he is not driven by money but respects it and wants his fair share of it. It is said that if he loans anyone anything he expects to get it back, but if he owes anyone anything they can be sure they will get it back.

When he first went into racing it was a sport in which a small man might succeed on a shoestring, but it has become exclusively a sport for big men, for wealthy sportsmen and major companies. He has said, "It costs me $10,000 just to test tires one day. If you're not a millionaire you don't have any business running cars in this sport."

He likes to pose as a country boy, but behind his mask his eyes see everything and his mind understands everything. At Le Mans, he went out to dinner at a fancy place with some of his fellow drivers. They were served trout almandine. Foyt sent it back because he said he never ate anything with the head still on it.

"Everyone around us was saying how good it was," A. J. chuckled later. "But I didn't like the looks of it. It wasn't done and it was kind of raw. So I sent it back. What I like is fried chicken, hamburger, and steaks."

A friend says, "He likes the simple things. He's a plain person at heart. He lays the catsup on an inch thick. He doesn't want anyone to think he's putting on airs. But he's a smart cookie. Let's say someone was hustling a diamond ring supposedly worth ten grand for a lot less. Most racers would buy it fast and give it to their wives or girl friends and brag about what a deal they'd gotten. Maybe they got a deal and maybe they didn't. Foyt would borrow the ring for awhile. Maybe he wanted it for Lucy. But first he'd sneak off and have it appraised. If it was a good buy, he'd bring it back and buy it. *Then* he'd brag about the deal he got. *Then* he'd know it was a good deal."

He has his vanities, but his grasp of reality, his down-home nature tends to overcome them. He remains good-looking but is sensitive to his thinning hair and receding hairline. He spent $650 to have a hairpiece woven out of his own hair, wore it awhile, then took it off and discarded it. It was too hot, for one thing. It wasn't A. J. Foyt, for another.

"I can't help being completely honest," he says. "I can't be a phony. I can't stand myself when I am. The hairpiece was real expensive. You couldn't tell the difference. It just stayed in place all the time. Made me look real young, too. But I realized after about two weeks that I was only trying to fool people and wasn't being myself."

Others wear them. Parnelli does, for example. And Jerry Grant. But Foyt couldn't.

He is conscious of his image. Gwilym Brown quoted him in *Sports Illustrated* as saying after he had beaten the southerners in a stock car race he was ready to beat the sports car crowd. He was quoted as making a statement about long-haired European drivers which he regarded as defamatory to him. Foyt subsequently filed a $1 million damage suit against Time, Inc., and the magazine and testified he never made the remarks. Brown said he got the remarks second-hand from Jackie Stewart. Stewart testified he simply heard about it, but hadn't told the writer. The federal jury in Houston awarded Foyt $75,000, which the publisher appealed and later settled. But those close to Foyt felt it was not so much the money as the vindication that made him happy.

He always has spoken with respect of his southern rivals in stock cars and the Grand Prix group he has opposed. He admires good drivers. He likes to beat good drivers because that means something to him. He has some regrets that he never has taken opportunities offered him to try the Grand Prix circuit. Mario Andretti and Peter Revson have taken time to race on this circuit and have won some races there and, of course, Dan Gurney won some before he turned to the championship trail. Presumably if Foyt had spent a season or two on the Grand National or Grand Prix circuits, he could have won those championships.

A Grand Prix victory is the only major triumph he has missed. But as much as he has been tempted at times, he has never given in to it.

"I can make more money in one race in one day on my circuit

than I can in a month of races overseas," he says. "I'm away from home enough without going across the ocean. And I wouldn't want to do it unless I could concentrate on it and give it the effort it would take to do well at it and I've always been too tied up with commitments on my own circuit to leave it long enough."

Foyt refused an invitation to be one of 12 top drivers from various circuits to compete at Riverside and Daytona in 1973 and 1974 in a four-race series in identical cars for $150,000. This shocked his fans and followers of the sport who always felt that, all other things being equal, Foyt would prove he was the best and so they wanted to see him in this "race of champions." But Foyt felt the money wasn't sufficient for the time, trouble, and risks, especially when only $5,000 was guaranteed each driver. He resented the fact that all the races would be in sports cars and on road courses, which would be an enormous disadvantage to him and others from the championship circuit, since they are primarily used to smaller open-cockpit cars and oval courses on which you turn only left and do not have to shift much. He believed he could beat the best at high-speed oval racing and stated that at least half the races should be that way. He asked for more money than the sponsors were willing to give him. Eventually, when Jackie Stewart withdrew, Foyt gave in.

"If it's a 'race of champions,' I guess I should be in it," he shrugged.

Though he did not win any of the first three races at Riverside, he drove well enough with half the field to qualify for the final race, won by Mark Donohue early in 1974 at Daytona. The others were closer to their peak and had more time to practice.

At his peak, Foyt would have been favored. He no longer is driving 50 races a year. The fact is he has driven various kinds of cars on various kinds of courses with stunning success. Also when this car is as good as the best, and when the race is meaningful, Foyt still seems to be the best.

Scene: Nassau, Bahamas, December 1963: They were saying young A. J. Foyt was outclassed in sports car competition because he was not familiar with it. Now he had to shift gears a hundred times a lap and turn right as well as left as he steered his strange car around a winding up-and-down road course. But the crewcut Texan fit fine in a Scarab Chevrolet sponsored by John Mecom, a fellow Texan. Foyt poured it on in practice and paced the field. On Friday he led from start to finish to win the preliminary 25-lap race over the four-and-a-half-mile run. On Saturday he led from start to finish to triumph in the four-lap sprint Nassau Classic. On Sunday, at the start of the featured 56-lap 250-mile Nassau Trophy Race, his engine would not turn over. Thirty second after the rest of the field had got under way, Foyt made his start.

He caught Roger Penske in a Zerek Chevy on the 27th lap and wound up winning by more than a lap over Pedro Rodriquez in a Ferrari. Foyt's average speed was a record of more than 95 miles per hour and he won more than $5,000 for Mecom, who didn't need the money.

Scene: Daytona, Florida, February 1964: Foyt said, "I've got what it takes." He had an old rear-engine Scarab, formerly owned by millionaire playboy Lance Reventlow and outfitted with a 430-horsepower Chevrolet power-plant to take on the sports car crowd in the 250-mile America Challenge Cup over the 3.81-mile road course. Dan Gurney had a smaller but nimbler Colin Chapman Lotus.

When Foyt turned 113 miles per hour in practice, Gurney ripped off a 113 mph lap. But when the racing began, Foyt got by Gurney. Gurney shot through the corners quicker, but Foyt blasted down the straights stronger. Foyt hit 185 mph in some stretches that were long enough for it. They exchanged the lead sixteen times in the first twenty laps. By then they were a lap ahead of the rest of the field. And they kept lapping the others.

But Gurney's Lotus had a smaller fuel tank than Foyt's Scarab and on the 38th lap he had to pit for fuel. Foyt flew a lap in front. Gurney drove so hard trying to catch up that his gearbox gave out. Foyt went on to win easily and he said in Victory Lane, laughing, "It got pretty lonely out there after Gurney left. But I would have won anyway."

Some people complained that his big car had been beefed up beyond reason. Picking up his $5,500 check, Foyt laughed, shrugged, and said, "Heck, we're all in this for the money. They can buy the same stuff for their cars that I buy for mine. These sports car boys figure that a little bitty car with a little bitty engine can win the big ones. Not me. I'll take horsepower."

Scene: Le Mans, France, June 1967: Foyt had just won his third Indianapolis classic. Now, within a week, he was driving for an awesome double, a victory in the 24 Hours of Le Mans, the classic of sports car competition, with Dan Gurney as his co-driver in the grueling day-night-and-day grind over an 8.3-mile highway course that winds savagely through the countryside. Foyt hadn't wanted to run this race, but he was working for Ford and Ford was anxious to win it. Ford had spent a fortune in a long-range effort to beat the Ferraris and other foreign cars that had dominated this event, and had turned to Foyt to popularize the Mark IV sports car.

A tire executive said, "Some thought it craziness to team Foyt with Gurney. They were too competitive of each other. Foyt wasn't at home here as Gurney was. Some thought Foyt couldn't stand the strain of shifting gears and jumping in and out of a car monotonously around the clock and Gurney would have to go most of the way. But Gurney had never won this race and he was eager to have another crack at it. And he knew Foyt could help him win it. Dan didn't try to show A. J. up in practice. He didn't try to break any records in qualifying. He helped A. J. wherever he could. And right away Foyt didn't need any help. He appeared to be right at home. He wound up sharing the work load equally."

Some 54 cars started at 4 P.M. on Saturday. Thirty-eight did not finish. Gurney started for his side. The drivers ran to their cars and took off. After awhile, Gurney came in and Foyt took over the wheel. He didn't know how to take it easy, but his rugged red car could take it. He stormed the 1,800-pound car around, taking some laps at 144, speeding through some straights at 215, but shifting down almost to zero in some tight corners. Cars began to come apart or break down. Denis Hulme and Mark Donohue stopped during the first hours. Hulme resumed, but his windshield was broken by flying rocks and he went off the road and had to return to the pits for new rear wheels.

After three hours, Mike Salmon's car caught fire and he was burned before he got it off the road. Then Chris Amon blew a tire and his car crashed and burned. It turned dark but the big cars behind bright headlights continued to careen around the black course.

Mario Andretti in a Ford swerved into a wall. Roger McCluskey in another Ford swerved and crashed to avoid him. Then Jo Schlesser in a third Ford ploughed into both of them. All the cars were wrecked, though the drivers emerged without serious injury. However, in one chain-reaction accident three of the four Fords had been wiped out. Only the Foyt-Gurney Ford remained in contention.

With a huge crowd peering through the darkness, the survivors continued to pick their way through the littered course, pitting frequently, changing drivers regularly.

Coming in, Foyt was advised to take a nap. He negated the idea. "I was all worked up," he laughed. "And it really wasn't hard." A short time later he jumped back into his Ford to relieve

Gurney. By morning they had pulled far in front of the field. Three Ferraris chased them at dawn, waiting for them to break down or slow down, but they would not. The sun rose to noon. The day grew warm. The weary drivers pressed on.

At 4:00 P.M. Foyt was at the wheel when he drove home past a row of Ford pits piled deep with Henry Ford II and assorted vice presidents and engineers from the firm. Foyt and Gurney had covered 3,220.5 miles at a record averaged speed of 135 mph, ten miles faster than the previous record, and their nearest rival, a Ferrari co-piloted by Ludovica Scarfiotti of Italy and Mike Parks of England, was more than 30 miles behind. Only 16 cars still were running. But Foyt still was running and Gurney hopped on the hot hood for a free ride to the winner's stand where Foyt jumped out and he and Gurney popped champagne corks and sprayed the bubbly all over themselves and their wealthy sponsors, who didn't mind a bit.

"Shucks, this wasn't so tough. Indy is harder," Foyt laughed. Someone pointed out that he was the first man ever to win Indy and Le Mans. "Well, I guess that ain't bad," he said and banged Gurney on the back.

Scene: Daytona, Florida, February 1972: Foyt had won here on the NASCAR Grand National circuit twice before. On the Fourth of July, 1964, starting 19th, he fought through the field, careening his new Dodge around the high banks at an average speed of better than 151 miles per hour and on the last turn of the last lap he bolted by Bobby Isaac to stream through the homestretch a winner over his stunned southern stock car rivals.

Exactly one year later Foyt took a new Ford prepared by master stock car creators John Holman and Ralph Moody and streaked through a series of accidents that removed Ned Jarrett, Cale Yarborough, and other rivals; survived extreme heat and a blazing pace, removed Junior Johnson, Fred Lorenzen, Lee Roy Yarbrough, and others; and beat Buddy Baker's Plymouth home by almost a full lap to take his second straight Firecracker 400.

But he had never won the big one here. He had relieved Marvin Panch to win the Atlanta 500 in 1965 shortly after returning to racing from his severe Riverside wreck. And he returned to Georgia to win all alone in a Wood Brothers Mercury in the Atlanta 500 in 1971. It was a hard-fought triumph. He led most of the way but he had to make ten pit stops while Petty made only eight and Petty caught him with 25 miles left and led near the finish. Foyt had to get by him again and resolutely hung to Petty's tail through the last lap, caught him right at the end, outbraved him down the straight, and squeezed past a car careening out of control to win by two slim seconds.

But it was the big one at Daytona, the big one on this circuit, the Daytona 500, that he wanted most.

The Wood Brothers were the best at their business. They prepared the fastest, strongest cars on the southern stock car circuit. They provided the smoothest, surest, swiftest pit service. They wanted the best driver to drive for them, and if they couldn't have Foyt all the time they would keep a car aside for him and take him whenever he was available and let such driver as David Pearson, who won Grand National driving titles, run it when Foyt couldn't.

Richard Petty, the A. J. Foyt of the southern stock car racers, said, "We don't much like carpetbaggers coming in and making off with our money, but if they're good enough to get it they can have it and Foyt is good enough. I like to see him in the field because I like to beat the best. But ol' A. J., he takes some beatin'."

In the warm winter weather in Florida early in 1971 Foyt took a lot of beatin'. He captured the pole position at a speed of close to 183 miles per hour. He ran so hard in the first half of the race, leading six times in a savage, see-saw struggle, that he ran out of fuel. He came back out of the pits a lap back in eighth place, shot to third within 20 laps, then ran out of time and settled for third behind Petty and Baker.

In 1972 Foyt would not be beat at Daytona. He swapped the lead with Petty 12 times in the first 200 miles of the most spectacular racing possible by the best of two circuits. And then Petty's Plymouth, put together by the Granatelli team, expired and Foyt was all by himself. He wound up leading for 167 laps and as he took the checker on the 200th lap he was a lap in front of his nearest follower. The thirty-seven-year-old veteran picked up $38,000 for his triumph, saying, "I especially like to beat the best in the big ones. When you beat Petty and the rest of the NASCAR racers, you know you're beating the best."

Scene: Ontario, California, March 1972: When the southern stockers went west, Foyt usually found time to greet them. In 1970 he chauffeured a Ford to victory in the Riverside 500, a rough road race for the big stock cars, outlasting Parnelli Jones, Petty, Gurney, McCluskey, and Lee Roy Yarbrough through a grueling run around the 2.6-mile course that covered five hours, 18 minutes, and eight seconds at an average speed of close to 100 miles per hour to win nearly $20,000.

In 1971, in the Ontario 500 he took a Wood Brothers Merc

to the pole at better than 153 miles per hour and triumphed by eight seconds over Baker and 11 seconds over Petty to pocket a $50,000 prize. In 1972 he returned for the renewal of the race, won the pole at better than 153 miles per hour, and sped to victory after four hours by a few seconds over Bobby Allison, Baker, and Petty, for another $50,000 payoff.

The 1972 Ontario race showed how tough he remained. Foyt fought his heavy car around the big track in a bitter battle with brilliant rivals for four hours. During the race, he dueled especially daringly with Richard Petty, the king of the southern stockers, who is in his prime.

Petty got so close behind Foyt at one point that he banged his car from behind. When he passed Foyt, A. J. passed him back, squeezing through an opening on the inside so small that he banged Petty's car. You can sometimes bump these big stockers and stay in shape. They did. They were good enough to get away with it. And when it was all over, on this day at least, Foyt was the best.

Later, weary and sweat-streaked in his soiled white coveralls, he stood in the press box and a writer suggested it was a harder victory than his one the year before. Foyt looked at the writer and said flatly, "They're all hard."

The writer said, "But last year's was easy."

Foyt fixed the writer with a chill look, shook his head, and said with a suggestion of anger, "None of them are easy. They may look easy sitting up here, but they are not easy sitting down there. Hell, these things don't drive themselves. You've got to get them out in front and keep them there and keep them in one piece and keep them on the track. If you think the easiest of them is easy, well you don't know what the hell you're talking about."

Later, after he had moved away, he stopped a second and he said, "These damn writers write that I haven't been winning and they don't know what the hell they're writing. I won this one here today, didn't I? Doesn't it count? Four blanking hours. Five hundred damn miles. Some of the best drivers in the business. Fifty grand for winning. You can get hurt out there. What are we doing if it doesn't count? I won it last year. I won Daytona this year. I won here and I won there.

"All they think about is the championship trail. Sure, I want to win there. All they think about is Indianapolis. Sure I want to win there. More than anywhere. But you take your wins where you can get them. Sometimes your luck runs bad one place and good another place. As long as you're still winning some anywhere, you're all right, you've still got a chance."

After twenty years as a race driver Foyt had won almost everywhere throughout his career. He had won sports car classics, had won a record of almost $3 million in purses. He had won seven NASCAR classics, far more than any other individual who was not a regular on the southern stock car circuit, and more than most of the regulars. And he had made more starts (around 500) and won more races (120) than any driver in the history of USAC competition. He was the only driver to have won 20 or more races in each of the four club classes—20 in midget cars, 26 in sprint cars, 27 in stock cars, and 43 in championship cars. The closest to him in championship cars was Andretti, and he was a long way back with 31. Andretti, Bryan, and a few others have won three national titles. Foyt has won five.

But he had not been winning national titles nor many championship trail races for some years now and some experts were saying as he went into 1973 that he was on his way out. Even if you are Foyt, you do not win the Indianapolis 500 every year. During one period he took top honors there every third year—1961, 1964, and 1967. Some superstitiously predicted his turn would come up again in 1970. But it did not. And that unprecedented fourth Indianapolis triumph eluded him in 1971, 1972, and again in 1973.

He thought he had it hooked in 1973. He created a Coyote IV that was swift, steady, and seemed strong. It was the widest and lowest championship car he or anyone else had ever constructed. It was 15 feet long, almost the maximum 80 inches wide, and only 32 inches high. He felt he had solved his engine problems and had built reliability into the power-plant. The car weighed 1,500 pounds and the turbocharged Ford eight-cylinder engine could produce more than 900 horsepower. Foyt figured it would do 300 miles an hour on a long, straight stretch, 220 on a big, banked track, and 200 on the old Indy oval.

He figured that was too fast for safety but knew it was the sort of speed he needed to win. His car wore wings he didn't like but had to have to be competitive. He tested secretly and turned in some terrific laps and confided to friends that he was ready to roll. Rumors spread around the circuit that Foyt had come up with the hot car.

They held twin 150-milers at Trenton in April before the racers turned to Indianapolis. Foyt's Coyote flew in the first race to bring him his first title trail triumph since November 1971 and an $8,800 payoff. But before the second race Foyt felt he would go faster if he lowered his wing. He did and he went so slowly in the race he had to stop in the pits to raise it again. By the time he got back in the race, he was out of contention. Andretti won it—his first victory since 1970.

"That's Foyt's fault," an official said. "Good enough isn't good enough. It has to be better. Even winning isn't enough. He has to win better. He can't stop tinkering."

"We shouldn't have re-engineered the car between races," Foyt admitted. "I made a mistake. But it looks like I've got me a car that can go."

Still, he worried that it was too hot to handle. "Race cars are going too fast," he told Shav Glick of the *Los Angeles Times*. "They are definitely unsafe. The wings slow you a little in the straights but speed you up a lot through the turns. They push the car down so it grips the track real good and you can run the turns almost as fast as you can the straights. But since you don't slow down much for the corners, the engine doesn't get much breathing room; it runs hot and always is about to break. Also, running behind a winged car you can't see the track ahead of you. The wings create a turbulence which tosses you around if you get too close to them. And if you get out of shape they throw you into a spin.

"A wing is a crutch. It takes away a driver's ability to overcome problems with his own talent. It gives young drivers a false sense of security. It's like learning to drive with an automatic transmission —you never learn to shift. There's no sense to trying to lie to ourselves. We're not racers now. We're just sitting in a projectile. Something must be done before someone gets killed."

The entries at Indianapolis were impressive. There were 83 cars entered for 47 drivers. Of the cars, 29 were Eagles and 15 McLarens. All were powered by turbocharged engines. There were 59 Offys and 20 Foyts, which the Fords were now called. Bignotti had taken over a share of the Offenhausen engine operation as part of a deal to depart Parnelli and join Pat Patrick for 50 percent of the profits and a free hand in the operation. So now it was Bignotti's Offys against Foyt's "Ford" engines. Bignotti had Gordon Johncock and Swede Savage as his drivers. And Andy Granatelli bought in as backer of the whole team for his STP promotions for one last year before Granatelli and STP parted company.

Foyt said, "I'm not bitter about Bignotti. We won a lot when we were together, you know. And he's won a lot with other drivers. Hey, his cars are almost always the ones to beat. He's brilliant. But he's always got to be boss. Which is why we parted company. And why he and Parnelli have parted company."

Bignotti said, "I enjoyed great success with Parnelli's teams but it was getting to the point where there was a lot of competition for credit and a lot of interference from a lot of people as to how things should be done, so when the opportunity came to run my own show I grabbed it."

He was asked about Foyt. He said, "A. J. was getting to the point where he wanted to run the show instead of me. I thought that I'd gone about as far as I could with him. We're still friends. If we'd stayed together, we'd have won a lot of races. He'd have won a lot more races if he'd just stick to the driving instead of trying to engineer the car. No one has done all of it and it's getting more and more complicated every year.

"Does he still have what he used to? Oh, sure. If he's competitive, he likes to race. But if he's not competitive, he'd just as soon park the car. He's past the stage where he'd just keep going and run the risk of getting banged up when he's running out of competition. He's a multimillionaire, so why should he?"

Bignotti said he thought he could win with Johncock or Savage with the Eagles he bought from Gurney. "Gurney took pictures of my Parnelli car for two years. He finally got it. He did a fantastic job of working it up. He's got a production line that stamps out the Eagle cars perfectly. He keeps some and sells some. And he's got parts readily available. So why should I build my own cars when I can buy these Eagles and fix them to my own satisfaction?"

Johncock said, "He fixes them up fantastic. He does it his way. I can see why he and Foyt had such personality problems. They both have big egos. Of course they're both brilliant. But they both have to have their own way. I've found out how to get along with Bignotti. I can take his car out and practice it and come back and tell him what I think is wrong with it, but I don't dare tell him how to fix it. It's his car, not the driver's, and he fixes it the way he wants it."

The racing life had been rough for the talented little Johncock, who had not been winning a lot. He had divorced his first wife and the mother of his five children and was separated from his second wife many months. He was lonely and considering marriage again. But his business investments had gone bad and he'd declared bankruptcy. He said, "Right now all I want to do is race. And win for a change. I need it."

Teammate Savage said, "I had a good chance with Gurney but I wasn't ready. I was almost killed in my sports car wreck. When I came out of my coma I didn't even know what a race car was for. But I found I still wanted to race. It set me back but now I feel I'm ready. I have my best ride. My wife is pregnant. I'm ready to make some money."

Gurney had returned with new Eagles with Bobby Unser and Jerry Grant to drive them for his team. Parnelli was back with Andretti, Leonard, and Al Unser as drivers, a new mechanical team, and revised cars. Team McLaren was back with Peter Revson and

Johnny Rutherford as drivers. Roger Penske entered with Mark Donohue and Gary Bettenhausen in McLarens. Lindsey Hopkins hooked up with Roger McCluskey in a McLaren. Lloyd Ruby was back with an Eagle, J. C. Agajanian entered the fold with Mike Mosley as his driver in an Eagle and A. J. Watson as his mechanic. Clint Brawner was back with Art Pollard and Jim Caruthers in Eagles.

Pollard, at forty-six, was the oldest entry. Divorced and remarried, and a grandfather as well, he said, "It's not an easy life. I should quit, but I can't. I still have hopes of winning here."

The youngest entry was Salt Walther, who was twenty-five. He wore lace shirts and expensive sports clothes, drove around town in a Caddy, danced until dawn at discothèques, and went home to a $100,000 pad he built himself with a swimming pool that had his name at the bottom.

"A couple of the drivers are a little old and kinda conservative," Walther stated. "I think it's tremendous for racing to have a little flamboyance. I probably spend $6,000 a year on clothes. Billy Vukovich calls me 'Pretty Boy.' Some of the drivers call me 'Cassius.' I get tired of being called a poor little rich kid. I work hard at what I'm doing."

His sponsor, his father, said, "I worry about him as any father would. But if he wants to drive I want him to drive for me. I realize that an accident is the chance you take in this sport. The day Salt says he wants to walk away, then I'm ready."

In practice on the opening day of qualification runs, old Art Pollard lost control of his car at better than 190 miles per hour —faster than he had driven in previous years—cracked a wall, hurtled fifty feet into the air, flipped twice, and crashed in flames. He was rushed to the hospital where he died of massive head injuries. He was the first driver ever killed in a Clint Brawner car. Brawner broke down and wept when he got the word.

The fastest qualifier was Johnny Rutherford with one lap at 199 mph and four at 198. Bobby Unser was just a few ticks behind him. Donohue rolled in at 197. Savage clocked in at 196. Bettenhausen and Andretti tallied 195. McCluskey, Walther, Ruby, Grant, Vukovich, and Mosley got in farther back. In all, 23 cars qualified.

Incredibly, the slowest was Foyt. He'd blown five engines and still couldn't get one to work. He aborted one run after three laps, finally took a full run at 188.927, which some experts regarded as a mistake because it was so slow that it seemed in danger of being bumped by faster cars that qualified on later days.

He could not qualify his backup car unless and until he was

bumped. And even if he remained in the field, there was no way he could start closer than the eighth row, which was the farthest back he'd ever been. He had said he would never again start in the rear of the field. The fact was that almost all the winners came from the first three rows. The rest spotted the field too much of a headstart.

Bitterly disappointed, Foyt talked of quitting the race. "I don't know if I can get the engine running right. Even if I can, I don't think I want to start that far back. It's too dangerous to be in the back at the start. And if you can't giddy-up-and-go with the rest of them, I would rather just sit in my suite and watch it."

However, Foyt flew home to Houston to work on his engines in his shop. He wouldn't let his second driver, George Snider, try to qualify his second car until Foyt found out if he needed it for himself. He worked twenty hours a day for five days and flew back Friday. By then, six more cars had qualified faster on Sunday, shoving him within five places of being bumped.

He finally put his car with a reworked engine on the track and turned in 194, his fastest speed of the month, but not as fast as the front-runners had established. With the help of Herb Porter he seemed to have solved some of his problems, though perhaps not all.

"I feel better, but I don't feel good about things," he said. "I don't think I'll be bumped, but I'll have engines ready for my other car and if I have to qualify it, I will. I still don't know if I'll run. I'll make a last-minute decision."

Saturday's third day of time trials was rained out. This was a break for him, giving his rivals only one remaining day to bump him from the field. Although he wouldn't admit it for fear Foyt would be upset, Gurney conferred with Foyt and offered him a ride in one of his Eagles if he was bumped, figuring if Foyt had to start at the back of the field he at least could do so in a fast enough car to catch up to the leaders. Provided it lasted, Foyt probably could have won in an Eagle, or in a McLaren for that matter, possibly even from the rear, but he stubbornly refused to switch from his own Coyote car, which was working fine, even though his own engine was not.

On Sunday the field was filled as bumping began. Late in the day only one car in the field had a slower time than Foyt. Foyt put not only his second car with Snider but his third car with Johnny Parsons in the cockpit in line. If the slowest driver got bumped near the day's end, Foyt planned to put his own cars out there one at a time, taking up time, running them slowly, preventing others from getting out there to run faster.

As cars went out and ran too slow, Foyt kept shuffling his cars back in line. The last hour passed slowly. Just before the 6:00 P.M. gun, when there was time for only one more car to take the track, Foyt pulled Parsons from one car and shoved Snider in the other car out on the track. Snider ran fast enough to bump one car out and make the field.

After the gun had sounded, Foyt smiled and said, "I knew I had a damn good poker hand. It was just a case of how to play it."

He had decided to race. It was his 16th consecutive start. This was a record for consecutive starts and tied the record for total starts in this classic event.

The race was scheduled eight days later, on Monday. The huge crowd of more than 300,000 gathered. The ceremonies were conducted. And it rained. Everyone waited four hours for the race to start. When it stopped raining and the race started, it lasted less than 300 feet.

As the front row charged across the starting line, Foyt was flying. He appeared to pass all three cars in the row ahead of him before he even reached the starting line. It made the sixth row four cars wide. Ahead of him, Steve Krisiloff slowed suddenly, causing the racers to bunch up. Peter Revson darted past him. Salt Walther, who later said another car (possibly Jerry Grant's) hit him, suddenly veered right and sailed over Jerry Grant's car and onto a steel mesh fence atop the mainstretch wall. His right side fuel tank split and exploded, spraying flaming fuel over the spectators behind the screen at that point. The car came down and cartwheeled along the track, coming to a rest upside down with Salt's feet dangling out of it. Behind him ten cars tangled in a splintering, thunderous crash as the drivers maneuvered desperately to avoid the accident.

Other cars got through. Foyt got through. He said later, "I just dove under Salt and peeled off. I turned left and stood on it."

Wally Dallenbach skidded his car to a stop and ran to help pry Walther from his wrecked vehicle. He was rushed to a hospital, still conscious. A number of spectators were injured by the flying debris or flaming fuel, including two teen-aged girls. All the injured were carried out through a hole in the fence ripped by Walther's racer to an ambulance on the track. A few drivers suffered minor injuries. Walther was grievously hurt, but he and all the others recovered—though he spent ten agonizing weeks in the hospital and had to learn to walk all over again. But after he recovered he announced he would drive again. In February he was practicing and in March he was racing at Ontario.

Foyt, Revson, and Krisiloff were fined $100 each for what officials termed failure to follow instruction to maintain proper intervals between rows at the start. Foyt shrugged and said he'd pay, but protested any suggestion that he was in any way responsible for the mishap. Walther backed him up, too.

The race had been red-flagged to a halt. Twenty minutes later, even as cleanup crews were clearing the track, the heavens opened up again. As the rain poured down in the late afternoon, the race was postponed one day. It rained sporadically all the next day. They started up the engines and took a couple of preliminary laps at one point when it was dry, but then it began to rain again. After six hours the race was postponed until Wednesday.

It is very hard for the enormous crowd of spectators to get to the track and into the stands, but they do it good-naturedly once a year. They were willing to wait good-naturedly through one long, rainy day. And most of them were willing to do it a second time on Tuesday. But many could not stay or had no accommodations in town, and it was almost beyond reason for them to return for a third day. Still, half the original crowd, around 150,000 people, returned for the third day even though it rained all morning. Many waited for the rain to stop before leaving for the track. They missed the start and the first part of the race. For as soon as the rain stopped and the track dried, the race started.

Within an hour Swede Savage lost control coming out of the fourth turn. His car veered sharply left and shot directly across the track and hit a cement wall near the entrance to the pit row and exploded like a bomb. Remains of the car hurtled hundreds of feet down the mainstretch. The blazing chassis containing Savage came to rest 600 feet away, the engine another 300 feet away.

A member of the STP pit crew, Armando Teran, turned from the pit wall and began running toward the accident. Cars are supposed to go in only one direction, north, through the pits, but a safety truck speeding in the wrong direction—south—struck the pitman and hurled him 60 feet in the air.

Teran died that afternoon. Savage died five days later. His wife gave birth to their second daughter six months later.

When Savage was nine years old his father had bought him a miniature racer. He later said that from that day his ambition was to be a race driver. He admitted before the race that he knew it was dangerous but he felt safe because he was in a safe car and Bignotti built safe cars. Bignotti said later he considered retiring from racing until he studied films of the race and decided Savage's car slid on an oil slick, which was something he could not control.

Savage was the 36th driver to die in an accident on this track. Teran was the 25th mechanic, truck worker, or spectator to die.

Yet the incidence of fires from crashes, of death or serious injuries, had been dramatically decreased by safety regulations during the preceding ten years. And right after the race parts of the track were rebuilt for safety. No one was able to explain why there was such a series of accidents and sudden return of fire from crashes in 1973, except to speculate that the wings and increased speed must have contributed to it.

The attrition rate was high from the very beginning. All but Walther's car were able to restart. But Bobby Allison's car broke down in the first lap. Revson's car crashed in the third. Andretti's broke down in the fourth. Ruby's in the 21st. And Foyt's chassis caved in when a connecting rod bolt broke on the 37th lap. He was severely disappointed. Although he had once stated that he would not in such a situation replace another driver in a team car, he did call in Snider in the team car and took his place. The maneuver brought boos and catcalls from the fans and in the end it was futile because the second car's gearbox gave way and he was sidelined a second time just past the halfway point.

By that time, both Unsers, as well as the Leonard, Grant, and Donohue cars had caved in, too. Shortly afterward Mosley's car gave way. At this point many seemed simply to want this disastrous race ended. On the nationwide radio broadcast, Sid Collins kept pointing to the halfway point as a time when at least the race would be official and finished, whatever happened afterward. By then Gordon Johncock was ahead. Bobby Unser had led. Brother Al had led. Even Savage had led. But Johncock led from the 80th lap on. When it started to rain again he was the leader, and when the race was stopped at 133 laps, he was the winner, Bignotti's sixth winner at Indianapolis.

Although the leader at this point seldom holds the lead, he was not going to lose because officials were not going to wait for the rains to stop and call for a restart. Swiftly, they called it a race.

Johncock had gone 332.5 miles, for which he collectd $236,000 for his team. Granatelli seemed subdued in Victory Lane. So did Bignotti with his sixth Indianapolis winner and first with the turbo-Offy he had reworked. Vukovich collected just under $100,000 for finishing second. McCluskey picked up $60,000 for third place.

The terrible toll of the race brought a storm of adverse reaction from the press and public, which usually followed fatalities and thus was expected. USAC has always pressed for safety rules that either anticipated problems or followed problems that hadn't been anticipated. However, the organization may have been stirred to act too hastily this time.

The drivers were divided as to what was needed. Foyt wanted the wings on race cars reduced drastically or eliminated completely. He also wanted a reduction in the fuel that could be carried and called for enclosed cockpits. Bettenhausen asked for at least roll bars over the cages. Andretti wanted impact-resistant fuel tanks. Johncock wanted horsepower cut back sharply to slow the cars and increase competitive racing. Some wanted two-abreast starts. Others felt little could be done. Both Unsers suggested they'd simply had a freak series of accidents in a sport that was bound to be dangerous. And both felt USAC overreacted when it ruled the width of the wings had to be reduced from 64 to 55 inches, the right side fuel tanks had to be removed, and the fuel that could be carried in the car had to be reduced from 75 to 40 gallons and in the pits from 375 to 340 gallons, effective with the forthcoming 500 at Pocono. Later the wings were further cut to 43 inches and fuel in the pits to 280 gallons.

Racing men feel they must buy any rules put forth in the name of safety. But without engine restrictions to reduce speed and increase fuel consumption to more than two miles per gallon, these rules threatened to remove the racing from racing. And to increase the risks at the most critical point—the fuel-laden pits where there would now be increased traffic because of the new gasoline-carrying limitations. The cars were certain to go from two or three meaningful pit stops with most of the action occurring on the track to ten or 12 stops with most of the action in the pits and a series of short sprints on the track. The cars might run out of fuel at any time and the usually confused scoring would be made totally chaotic. And that's precisely what happened at Pocono. They had taken the racing out of racing.

Peter Revson captured the pole at 190 miles per hour. Foyt was far back in 14th spot below 185. But Revson broke down early while Foyt ran strong all day. Al Unser crashed at 20 miles. Johncock crashed at 200 miles. By then Dallenbach and Donohue had broken down. Bobby Unser, Andretti, Johncock, McCluskey, and Foyt took turns leading the field. Then Johncock crashed and Bobby Unser's engine went sour. Cars had been in and out of the pits all day. The lead changed hands in the pits, not on the track. There was little time for passing on the track.

At 172 laps, with only 62 miles to go, McCluskey led Foyt by 12 seconds and was speeding toward triumph when he ran out of fuel, slowed, and coasted toward the pits as Foyt sped happily past him. Foyt made 11 pit stops. McCluskey made 10 and he should have made one more. Of course, if he had he would have been behind. He wound up behind Foyt anyway. Foyt charged under the checker and then suddenly there was ol' A. J. back in Victory Lane with the 45th triumph of his championship car career, the fourth 500-mile triumph of his USAC career, and his ninth 500-mile race victory anywhere, though not the one he wanted most.

But there he was, grease-smeared, sweaty, and smiling, saying he was happy to win but sorry for ol' Roger McCluskey. And he picked up almost $95,000 while McCluskey garnered a lot of points he needed en route to the first national title of his long career and settled for almost $50,000 in consolation cash. Foyt ducked out quickly, apologizing to his fans for not sticking around to sign autographs because he had a plane to catch. After all, he had a race to run down south. Had he changed so much after all?

The race down south was the Firecracker 400, which he had won twice. He never was in contention in this event because his car broke down early. Back on the title trail he led a 200-miler in Michigan after shooting up from the second row to make it four cars abreast in the front row at the start, but he broke down and lost to McCluskey. However, he came back to beat McCluskey in a companion 200-miler in stock cars for the 120th victory of his USAC career.

The fine Ontario facility was in trouble in its fourth year. It was a splendid all-purpose racetrack at which spectators could see every part of the track from every seat in the house. It was situated in a strong racing sector, but it had cost so much to build and promote that its owners had been unable to meet their taxes, bond payments, and other financial obligations.

It had run through a series of bosses and had at least temporarily been taken over by a group headed by Parnelli Jones, Vel Miletich, and Tony Hulman and operated by Parnelli's associate, Jim Cook. And there in Gasoline Alley was Foyt telling the press that they never should have built this track in such a windy, dusty part of California and never should have run this race in such a hot month as September. Anything to help old pal Parnelli, of course, who was set to shift the race to March, who was running qualifying races in conjunction with the time trials and who was ready to do anything to rescue this splendid place for racing.

Before practice began, Foyt declared that he felt fine. He'd had his eyes tested and they were as good as ever. And the eyes mattered more than anything else in driving for the eyes ruled the reflexes, he said. If he'd lost anything—and he hadn't noticed that he'd lost anything—he probably made up for it in experience.

And he'd certainly had his share of experiences. So many had died driving in his races: Bettenhausen, Bryan, Sachs, and Clark. Too many had gone, even this year. But that was racing. He didn't want to talk about it. He didn't want to think about it. What he constantly reminded himself was that it was a matter of percentages. When your number turned up, that was it.

He wouldn't stop racing because of it. You didn't stop driving the highways to work when you passed a fatal accident, did you? It shook you, but you went on doing what you had to do. Oh, he no longer pretended he was unafraid. "I'll never say I'm fearless," he said. People who say they have no fear are crazy. But he would go on with it. As he had said, "If I die in a race car tomorrow, I'll be doing what I want to do."

Down the line, a retired Parnelli was running one team, a retired Gurney another. Down the line was Donohue, who would retire at season's end. Ward and Rathmann had retired. But Foyt was still running. He didn't even walk well anymore. He limped around. His ankle still hurt a year and a half after his accident in the dirt at DuQuoin. He had to have an operation on it when he had time. But he couldn't seem to find time.

Brawner was struggling now, seldom with a contender. Watson was struggling. The cars had changed completely. Speeds had increased tremendously.

Down the line Johncock was telling a writer he'd won $150 at blackjack in the Foyt garage the morning of the abbreviated 500 at Indianapolis, which he considered a good-luck charm for his victory. Oh no, Foyt hadn't been in the game himself, he said. He'd never get in a card game with Foyt. He'd never beat Foyt at cards.

This was a tough business, but no one slickered ol' A. J. Guys loaned other guys equipment with one hand and cheated with the other. Someone changed the numbers on a car at Indianapolis so the same car could be qualified twice. They were caught, but guys got away with a lot of tricks. No one gave him any breaks, Foyt said, so he didn't give anyone any. If they thought they had him down, they'd jump on him. No one wept when he lost.

A young photographer wearing a Gurney team shirt stepped over the pit wall to snap a picture of Foyt's car and Foyt's father charged at him in a fury and told him to get the hell out of there. The fellow fled back over the wall and stood there twitching nervously while old Tony Foyt glared at him, and his son turned and saw what it was and fixed the kid with a cold stare.

The kid said, "I just wanted a picture. I thought the old man was going to tear my head off." He was shaking a little. Someone smiled and said, "You're lucky it was the father and not the son."

Foyt practiced the car and it performed poorly. From one race to the next, you never knew what a car would do. He limped around it, poking it here and there, talking to his father and the rest of the crew. He was still a big, good-looking guy, but he had thickened with the years and his hair had thinned out and now he kept his head covered. He spoke softly, but often profanely. He wanted them to get this damn thing working.

On the morning of the first qualifying day, he stood in his garage telling his crew a story and they were laughing with him. When he laughed, he showed even white teeth and his eyes sparkled. After awhile they pushed the car out and were ready to run. He had drawn the 13th qualifying spot, which was unlucky. He watched others run while he waited. He wore a white driver's suit with a blue cap bearing a Goodyear emblem. He was letting his hair grow longer now, like those Grand Prix guys, and it poked from behind his cap. He walked around in his heavy way. After awhile he stood by his car, his hands wrestling nervously behind his back.

When it was time, he spit on his hands, wiped off his visor, pulled his cap off fast and his helmet on fast, buttoned up, covering a scar that showed on his neck, and climbed into the cramped cockpit. He went out and ran. He settled for 191. Coming back to the pits, he muttered, "It's not fast enough. It's about nine miles short."

He was right. Peter Revson took the pole at 200. The next day Foyt didn't even bother to run the qualifying races. He was in the race far back no matter what he did in these races. He settled for the 26th starting spot. That left him in the ninth row. Johnny Rutherford and Wally Dallenbach won the qualifying races, which placed them in the second row.

The morning of the race, while the big crowd gathered, Foyt stood off by himself in his garage, hands behind his back, whistling an old song. When they pushed his car to the track, he followed it, chewing gum. He was restless, waiting with his car on line while they made their music. He nervously slapped his hands in front of him. It was time to race.

Tony Hulman said, "Gentlemen, start your engines."

Cars kept crashing, but no one was seriously hurt. Grant, Rutherford, and Ruby crashed. Johncock and Donohue suffered blown engines. Five of the first six qualifiers were finished in the first 75 miles. Before the halfway point, Revson, Leonard, and Bettenhausen had engines blow on them and less than half the starters were left. The survivors kept scrambling in and out of the pits. The lead kept changing, but never on the track. The lead was swapped 31 different times among 13 drivers on pit stops. It was a confusing scramble.

Bobby Unser led the field for a long time, but then his wing tore loose and by the time they fixed it for him in the pits he was far back. Dallenbach, Al Unser, and Andretti were the front-runners in the late stages. Foyt, who had led twice, was within reach of the lead when his engine started to go sour and he lost a lot of power. He kept going, but very slow, a forlorn figure in his crippled car.

After Unser slowed, too, Dallenbach forged ahead to lead Andretti by five seconds and he held that lead to the finish. His winning margin really was three pit stops. He'd made nine, but that was three less than Andretti made. Dallenbach had been driving seven years and he'd won his first race this season when he replaced Savage on the Bignotti-Granatelli team. He pulled into Victory Lane in his blood-red STP machine and Andy hugged him and Bignotti smiled benevolently down on him. He represented Bignotti's 64th championship trail triumph, and Bignotti's drivers would win two more before season's end. And it was Bignotti's ninth triumph in a 500-miler.

Foyt paid them no mind. Limping in tenth he didn't go to Victory Circle. He passed right by it and went back to his garage to pack up and move on. He was thinking about the next race at Indianapolis. He had said, "The Indy 500 is the .World Series, the Masters, and the Kentucky Derby all wrapped up in one. Elsewhere you run for a hundred thousand. At Indy you run for a million." He wanted that fourth victory there.

Leaving Ontario, he said, "I think everyone lives to go to Indy. I'm thinking about next year's race right now. I already know what type of car I'm going to take back there."

It was going to be a good car. What almost worked in 1973 was made to work early in 1974. The 1973 car was improved to the point Foyt felt sure it would not disappoint him in 1974 as it had in 1973 and the improvements were incorporated into a new 1974 car and his tests were so outstanding that Foyt walked around grinning like the cat who had the mouse cornered. The hepatitis he'd suffered in November hadn't slowed him much. He seemed to feel he was going to get that fourth Indianapolis 500 in 1974 and so might just go out while he was back on top.

Cornered on his thirty-ninth birthday in January, A. J. was in a mellow mood. Asked when he would walk away from racing, he said he might do just that this year. He said, "Last year was a pretty good year, but I really can't holler about none of my years. I've had a pretty good life. This year could be a good year. It would be nice to win Indianapolis one more time. Then, maybe I'll feel like quitting. Maybe I will, anyway.

"My desire to win is as strong as it ever was, but I probably won't do some of the stupid things out there that I did when I was younger. If I have the car, you can bet your butt, I'll try to be there. If I don't, I won't take stupid chances. People who know me know I'm out to win. If you run second, you're not worth a damn.

"I enjoy the challenge as much as I ever did or I still wouldn't be at it, but my family and friends have been on me the last five years to quit. And, really, there's not much left. I'm very serious about it. I won't run much longer, and this could be my last year."

He spent the next couple of months denying he'd said he was on the way out. It was as if he had been caught in a moment of weakness and hated to admit it. He went to Daytona resolved to prove he was as determined as ever and did so in a daring display of his toughness. He led the classic at the midway point. His Chevvy was in contention most of the way. Late in the race, Donnie Allison's car blew a tire in Foyt's face. A chunk of rubber flew up and knocked out the right side of Foyt's windshield and shattered the left side. What was left was loose. Foyt drove the final laps with his left hand, holding the cracked glass in place with his right hand. Richard Petty won. Foyt finished fifth. But less than three months after his hepatitis, Super Tex provided a powerful testimony to his unique physical and mental capabilities.

Early in March it rained a lot in Ontario, but it was not as hot as when the California 500 was held here in September, and when the cars got on the track Foyt was by far the fastest. The horrors of the year before and the gasoline crisis had provoked restrictions on the Indianapolis cars which slowed them sharply and threatened to turn the championship trail's 500-miles events into economy runs rather than races. More than ever, it had become a question not of which cars were fast but which would last. However, Foyt seemed able to get more from a gallon of alcohol than his rivals. He captured the pole position in time trials with an average speed of 190.617 miles per hour, which was around five miles an hour faster than his nearest rivals. And he won his half of the Twin 100 Qualifying Races easily. It was his forty-sixth national championship triumph.

No one ever had seen old A. J. walking around with a grin pasted on his mug the way he was that week. Bobby Unser said, "Foyt's back and happy as hell about it. He's so happy it scares us. He's got us by the tails and he knows it. I don't know how he's doing it, but if his car holds up, ain't none of us gonna' be able to keep up with him this race or any other race this year." A. J. grinned and said, "I ain't never been away. But I ain't been winnin', and I guess that's what it's all about. I guess it's time to get back to winning. You know this is a very competitive business and it's hard for one guy to stay ahead of the next guy. Every year someone gets onto something that works better than the next guy's and then it's his year. I've been tryin' things that haven't been working as well as the next guy's, but maybe this is my year."

As always, when he was on top, he was spreading around the credit. He had changed the shape of his car up front with the help of his father and his crew, he said, and he now had the lowest profile on the track and was superior aerodynamically to his rivals. While the others were altering the angle of their rear wings drastically to compensate for their reduced size, A. J. regarded this as a drag and was tempted to take the damn thing off entirely, he said. With his car now he could run the corners flat out without a wing, he said. With the help of Harold Gilbert, the Foyt engine had come into its own, A. J. said. Of course you never know what will happen in racing, but he was ready, A. J. said, grinning broadly.

He, more than anyone else, brought out a big crowd of around 100,000 fans on a chill, overcast race day, which may have saved this race for another day. Waiting for the race, he was grinning when a pretty blonde with freckles pushed to the front of the crowd around his car and wished him well. "Want to go with me?" Foyt asked, grinning. She wanted to, but they wouldn't let her. They cleared her and the rest away and started the race. Bobby Unser jumped Foyt at the first, but on the second lap A. J. sped past him and started to pull away from the field. He led for 22 laps, running easily, and was far in front when a fiberglass pannel tore off Salt Walther's car and spun down the track and was sucked up into the underbelly of Foyt's car, severing an oil line.

He was whipped and he knew it at once. He came into the stretch off the fourth corner and angled along pit row and turned left into the garage area without even stopping in his pits. He got out of his car and stood there looking at it, the grin now gone. A member of his crew picked the small hunk of panelling out of the car's rear axle housing and handed it to the boss. Foyt held it and looked at it. "A million to one," he said without expression. Well, that's racing.

He put on his jacket and went out to help out in the pits of George Snider, driving a team car. When Snider ran out of fuel coming into the homestretch, Foyt joined the others in running a mile down the track to him to push the car back to the pits for fuel. The car was still running at the finish, but eight laps back of Bobby Unser, who beat out brother Al by less than six-tenths of one second. Well, it was a great race. But it wasn't Foyt's race. What would he do now? "Go home," he said, "and get ready for Indy."

Someone had asked him about his having announced his retirement. He had drawn erect in annoyance. "That was a bunch of malarkey," he snapped. "When I decide to retire, I'll just pull into the pits, jerk off my helmet, and tell you guys and everybody else to go to hell," he said.

INDEX